Intersecting Voices

Intersecting Voices

DILEMMAS OF GENDER, POLITICAL PHILOSOPHY, AND POLICY

Iris Marion Young

PRINCETON UNIVERSITY PRESS

PRINCETON, NEW JERSEY

Copyright © 1997 by Princeton University Press
Published by Princeton University Press, 41 William Street,
Princeton, New Jersey 08540
In the United Kingdom: Princeton University Press, Chichester, West Sussex

Library of Congress Cataloging-in-Publication Data

All Rights Reserved

Young, Iris Marion, 1949–
Intersecting voices : dilemmas of gender, political
philosophy, and policy /Iris M. Young.
p.   cm.
Includes bibliographical references and index.
ISBN 0-691-01201-6 (cl : alk. paper).
ISBN 0-691-01200-8 (pb : alk. paper)
1. Feminist theory.   2. United States—Social
policy—1993–   3. Sex role.   I. Title.
HQ1190.Y678   1997
305.42′01—dc21   97-2102
                                                              CIP

This book has been composed in Baskerville

Princeton University Press books are printed on acid-free paper and meet the
guidelines for permanence and durability of the Committee on Production
Guidelines for Book Longevity of the Council on Library Resources

Printed in the United States of America
by Princeton Academic Press

1 3 5 7 9 10 8 6 4 2
1 3 5 7 9 10 8 6 4 2
(Pbk.)

In memory of my mother,
Marion Cook Young

and for
Sandra Lee Bartky

———————————————

CONTENTS

ACKNOWLEDGMENTS

MOST OF THESE ESSAYS have been previously published. I am grateful to the following journals and publishers for permission to reprint them here: University of Chicago Press, for "Gender as Seriality: Thinking about Women as a Social Collective," which originally appeared in *Signs: A Journal of Women in Culture and Society*, vol. 19, no. 3 (1994); and for "Mothers, Citizenship and Independence: A Critique of Pure Family Values," which originally appeared in *Ethics: A Journal of Political, Legal and Moral Philosophy*, vol. 105, no. 3 (1995); *Feminist Studies*, vol. 20, no. 1 (Spring 1994), where first appeared "Punishment, Treatment, Empowerment: Three Approaches to Policy for Pregnant Addicts"; *Constellations: An International Journal of Critical and Democratic Theory*, for "Asymmetrical Reciprocity: On Moral Respect, Wonder, and Enlarged Thought," first published in vol. 3 no. 3 (January 1997); Bridget Williams Publisher, for "Communication and the Other: Beyond Deliberative Democracy," first published in Anna Yeatman and Margaret Wilson, *Justice and Identity: Antipodean Practices* (1995); and Westview Press, for "Reflections on Families in the Age of Murphy Brown: On Justice, Gender and Sexuality," first published in Christine DiStefano and Nancy Hirschmann, *Revisioning the Political* (1996).

I am lucky to have a wide community of friends and colleagues with whom I have discussed the ideas in most of these essays at seminars and conferences. In each essay I acknowledge those people who helped me improve it through critical readings. Here I thank a few people for their ongoing intellectual support over the years those essays were written: Linda Alcoff, Robert Beauregard, Seyla Benhabib, Joe Carens, Frank Cunningham, David Ingram, Jenny Nedelsky, Molly Shanley, Bill Scheuermann, and Joan Tronto.

For a quarter century David Alexander has given unflinching criticism and unflagging support to my work, for which I remain ever grateful. Finally, I dedicate this book to Sandra Lee Bartky, the first philosopher who made me believe that I had something to say to the world.

Intersecting Voices

INTRODUCTION

THESE SEVEN ESSAYS share a project of feminist critical theory. With the term "feminist" I refer to no particular doctrine or concrete political program. Rather, the term refers to a mode of questioning, an orientation and set of commitments, with two aspects. First, feminism here means attention to the effects of institutions, policies, and ideas on women's well-being and opportunities, especially insofar as these wrongly constrain, harm, or disadvantage many if not all women. Entailed by such attention is a commitment to ameliorating such harms and disadvantages. Second, some of the work in these essays is feminist in the sense that it draws on women's experiences, or on social and philosophical reflection that takes itself to be from women's perspectives, as resources for developing social descriptions and normative arguments. Neither of these meanings of feminism entails a claim to common attributes, circumstances, or harms that all women share.

Some people think that questions and commitments like these are out of date. Unfortunately, fashion seems to guide contemporary intellectual and political life as much as it rules hairstyles or shoe heels. Too many people think that ideas should be rejected on the grounds that they were first espoused more than five years ago, rather than asking whether they have intellectual substance. Others think that political claims to justice should be rejected because people are tired of hearing about the same old grievances, rather than asking whether the social conditions that seemed to validate the grievances uttered twenty years ago have changed.

There is no doubt that feminist ideas and movements have brought about major changes in attitudes and institutions all over the world in the last thirty years. These changes have improved the lives of many women, and I would hazard to say many men as well. But the basic social conditions to which feminists called attention twenty years ago for the most part have not improved, and in some areas of the world they have deteriorated.

I will give just two examples. First, many countries today attempt to collect data on rates of rape and battery of women, and in many countries women appear to have become more willing to report their victimization. Both official data and victimization surveys show shockingly high—and increasing—rates of violence against women in many parts of the world.

Second, while the operations of global capitalism have significantly increased women's labor force participation rates compared with men's, there has been virtually no change in the burden of unpaid household work that the vast majority of women also carry, often without much help from or even the household presence of men. Indeed, it can be argued that in the last twenty years women's domestic work has increased in many places, at least partly because governments have reduced the social service provision that often eases these burdens.

Thus continues a need to pay specific attention to the situation of women, in particular their social, cultural, and economic circumstances, and to have normative criteria for evaluating whether society specially constrains or oppresses women. Women's movements in the Northern Hemisphere have been more quiescent in the past ten years than before, but feminist organizing persists in those societies. In the meantime, women's movements in many parts of the Southern Hemisphere have caught up with and perhaps even surpassed the strength and creativity of the Northern movements. Anyone who doubts the contemporary appeal and capacity for mobilization of issues of women's freedom and opportunity for the 1990s need only consider the amazing diversity of women and issues that converged on Beijing in conjunction with the fourth U.N. conference on women in September 1995. That gathering expressed no unity of women or feminism, but it did manifest a determination to keep women's specific well-being on the policy agenda of governments and international organizations.

These essays, all written since 1990, combine several projects under critical theory: developing concepts for describing social relations and processes; accounts of subjectivity and communicative interaction; and normative moral and political theory. Each of these kinds of theorizing aids the others. Moral and political theory assumes both accounts of agents and their interaction and descriptions of the social relations they constitute and which condition their actions. Such ontology and social theory, however, themselves presuppose normative commitments—to freedom, equal moral worth, welfare, and human flourishing. Not only does critical theory take social and normative theory to be mutually conditioning in this way, it is also guided by practical commitment to emancipation in posing questions and evaluating answers. Consistency, coherence, empirical support, and like criteria remain standards of knowledge, but critical theory in addition specifically asks questions the answers to which, it argues, enable liberatory action and institutions. Some of the essays in this volume are more generally theoretical, while others reflect on the concrete context of lifeworld experience of moving through rooms or public debate about drug or welfare policy. I reject a distinction between "pure" and "applied" philosophy, however. The most policy-oriented essays in this volume claim to make original theoretical contributions, and the primary value of the more generally theoretical essays, I believe, is their illumination of action and policy.

My aim in theorizing with such a practical intent is not to develop systematic theories that can account for everything in a particular field of questioning, but rather to follow a line of reasoning in order to solve a conceptual or normative problem that arises from a practical context. The first essay in the volume, "Gender as Seriality," theorizes, for example, social collectivity in general but makes no claim to offer a complete social ontology.

Nor do I align my theorizing with one systematic school of thought. Among other frameworks, these essays both draw on and criticize contemporary liberal political philosophy, feminist psychoanalysis, existential phenomenology, deconstruction, and communicative ethics. I treat the conceptual frameworks and ideas of others as tools for building an account or solving a problem, and I do not defend the shape or material of one of them against another. In some essays the theoretical voices I call upon to help me intervene in practical concerns play off one another, often in order to show one conceptual or normative position as better than another. In each case, however, I hope that the ultimate criterion of "better" is to what extent an account allows practice to get beyond a dilemma, paradox, or inconsistency.

Each chapter is a self-contained essay written from a particular context of discussion. A number of themes cross two or more essays, however, and in the rest of this introduction I will signal some of these themes.

CRITIQUES OF IDENTITY

In recent years many theorists of postcolonialism, multiculturalism, or the politics of race and gender have questioned the "identity politics" they associate with some academic and political writing. Social movements responding to sexist and racist structures or minority exclusion have tried to express a positive group identity to foster solidarity and resistance. Any such rhetoric of group identity, however, founders on the shoals of essentialism and normalization. Defining a group identity tends to normalize the experience of some group members and marginalize others. Both the first and last essays of this book build on these critiques of identity politics but also argue against the conclusions that some draw from these critiques.

"Gender as Seriality" proposes that the critique of essentialism poses a dilemma for feminism. On the one hand, if "women" is not the name of a specific social collective, then there seems to be no basis for a specifically feminist politics. On the other hand, any attempt to define women as a group with common attributes either is absurdly reductionist or normalizes some of those meant to be included in the definition while marginalizing or excluding others. "Gender as Seriality" offers a way out of this dilemma by showing how Sartre's concept of "series" helps to theorize a social collective that neither has specific boundaries nor defines identity.

Among the several projects of "House and Home" is to reflect on the meaning of home for personal identity. In that essay I agree with those feminist theorists who argue that appeals to "home" as a value are dangerous because they often express a yearning for fixed identity. I argue, however, that the concept of home can and should be reconstructed to construe home as a material anchor for fluid and shifting identity. In both these essays, moreover, I reject a concept of *group* identity and argue that identity making is a project that individuals take up in relation to the collective social structures and histories in which they are situated.

COMMUNICATION ACROSS DIFFERENCE

Both chapters 2 and 3 reflect on the differentiation of moral and political agents. They argue that theories of communication and democracy tend to assume an unrealistic identification among dialogue participants in ways that can have oppressive or excluding consequences. "Asymmetrical Reciprocity" stands at a higher level of abstraction in moral theory and ontology. I argue there that the injunction to adopt the standpoint of other people in making moral judgments asks something impossible, and that trying to do so can have undesirable political consequences. The argument follows Irigaray's critique of a logic of identity that tends to treat the relation between self and other as mirroring or complementary. This stance of symmetry appears in everyday life as a will to sympathize with others only insofar as one can see them as like oneself. Since I am most interested in the implications of this ontological and moral theoretical position for political theory, the argument emphasizes that the structural differentiation of social groups makes problematic the idea of such identification and reversibility. But the argument of "Asymmetrical Reciprocity" also calls attention to the irreversibility and asymmetry of relations between any persons, even intimates.

Some people reason that if individuals and groups cannot reverse perspectives then we cannot understand each other. This is too strong a conclusion to draw, however; irreversibility implies only that respect and effective communication cannot assume that we understand one another. Communicative ethics must be more open to listening and questioning than are stances that presume shared understandings of a common good.

While "Asymmetrical Reciprocity" theorizes difference between both individuals and groups, "Communication and the Other" focuses more on relations among groups in a large-scale polity. Both these essays assume, however, a nonessentialist concept of social collective such as that articulated in chapter 1. "Gender as Seriality" theorizes a concept of structured social position. Individuals are positioned in structures of class, sexuality, gender, race, age, ethnicity, and so on, which give those similarly positioned experiences that have affinity with one another and similar perspective of other social positions and events. Being positioned in a similar serialized structure, however, neither determines people's identities nor produces a common identity among them. Both "Asymmetrical Reciprocity" and "Communication and the Other" suggest that people bring specific and differing perspectives to public life and communication because of these serialized structural positionings.

COMMUNICATIVE ETHICS

These two latter essays align themselves with the theory of communicative ethics developed by Jürgen Habermas and refined by, among others, Seyla Benhabib; both also criticize that theoretical approach. I endorse the project of theorizing moral knowledge by making explicit the normative presuppositions of communication that aims at understanding. With theorists of communicative ethics I believe this implies that impulses for democracy and justice are already presupposed by contexts of communicative action. I find Habermas's theory, however, and to a lesser extent Benhabib's, too rationalist and unifying. To infuse communicative ethics with more desire and difference, I bring its discourse and problematic into dialogue with certain so-called postmodern theorists of communication and ethics, especially Irigaray, Levinas, and Derrida. The result, I hope, is a more nuanced approach to communicative ethics, one more mindful of the fragility and always provisional nature of understanding, and one that puts more emphasis on modes of questioning and listening.

In chapter 4, "Punishment, Treatment, Empowerment," I apply communicative ethics to the concrete situation of service provision in drug treatment programs. I construct a distinction between talk-based therapy that is monological and forms that are dialogical. Drawing on Foucault's analysis of the confessional norms of modern therapeutic practice, I argue that models of group therapy in services like drug treatment programs tend to be monological. Even where they involve people interacting through talk, the form of discourse is advice, lecture, or bearing witness. A dialogical therapeutic method invites participants to reflect together upon their situation and action in the context of more general social and political conditions; the consciousness of the general social conditions as well as the capacity to take reflective distance from one's own situation are created by group discussion and exchange. The latter forms of therapy are more empowering, I suggest, while the former are more individualizing.

SOCIAL POLICY

Chapter 4 is the most policy-oriented paper, but the next two chapters aim to intervene in policy discussion as well, specifically that which appeals to "family values." "Reflections on Families in the Age of Murphy Brown" criticizes marriage as ideological and recommends legal thinking about family relationships that will not discriminate against same-sex couples or household partnerships not bound by sexual relations. Both "Punishment, Treatment, Empowerment" and "Mothers, Citizenship, and Independence" respond to a rhetoric and practice that demonizes single or otherwise deviant mothers. Those bitten by the "postfeminist" bug seem to believe that misogynist attitudes no longer inform public and private life, that respect and equality for women as full citizens have been achieved. The viciousness of the condemnation of large groups of women in the American "welfare reform" and drug policy discourses should disabuse us of any delusion that women enjoy general respect. Perhaps in the United States white middle-class women have equality and respect, but even they only as long as they are married. The popular press has decried "walkaway moms," and lawmakers have moved to restrict divorce. In "House and Home" I relate the story of my own mother's punishment at the hands of state agencies partly to make the point that being a white suburbanite may offer little protection for a substance-using single mother.

Normative reflection on issues of public policy is best done within a specific social and political context. The three policy essays in this volume thus respond to specific political discourses in the United States. I nevertheless believe that the ideas in these essays can be useful to readers elsewhere, for several reasons. Unfortunately, prejudice against single mothers exists in many societies besides the United States, even as the proportion of families headed by women worldwide increases. It is also common in many parts of the world for political rhetoric to appeal to a mythic idea of family as a symbol of security and legitimacy in order to displace the causes of economic insecurity. For these reasons, as well as because gay men and lesbians suffer stigma and discrimination nearly everywhere, questions about what families are and how publicly to recognize the diversity of actual family forms are relevant to many social contexts today.

Furthermore, I believe that the theoretical frameworks in these essays can be used for normative reflection on policy issues in other contexts. "Punishment, Treatment, Empowerment," for example, both criticizes the framework of care ethics and applies it to social policy. When I wrote that essay such application of the ethics of care was nearly nonexistent. While more policy work now appeals to an ethics of care, as well as other feminist ethical approaches, much insight would be gained from analyzing many policy issues within this framework.

When preparing the essay I was also surprised to find very little use of Foucault's ideas about disciplinary and confessional practices to analyze and criticize public policy and social services. Especially since Foucault's writing reflects on historical texts of academics and bureaucrats developing state services, it would seem natural to apply his insights to contemporary social policies, programs, and services. The gap between theory and applied research remains wide in academic life, however, and thus the mountains of academic writing about Foucault remain mostly abstractly theoretical. Here again much work could fruitfully be done to close the gap and use Foucauldian insights to interpret and criticize policies and programs in specific social contexts.

"Reflections on Families in the Age of Murphy Brown" appeals to strictly liberal principles of freedom of choice, formal equality, and non-discrimination to argue for quite radical changes in the principles of family law. These appeals may surprise some readers familiar with those of my writings that take a more critical stance toward liberal principles. None of those writings reject liberal principles, however, but rather aim to show their limits for addressing many problems of social justice. Where family and sexuality are concerned, the simple liberal principle that people should be able to live their lives as they choose without interference from others so long as they are not preventing others from doing the same remains a radical and unfulfilled ideal almost everywhere. Legal recognition and protection certainly would not bring complete freedom and equality to people who trangress heterosexual norms, but such limited goals are nevertheless worth arguing and fighting for.

"Mothers, Citizenship, and Independence," however, questions a contemporary liberalism that makes respect for the autonomy of individuals contingent on the ability to be self-sufficient. The rhetoric of "personal responsibility" and independence promotes the image of free-standing households, each of which ought to be able to take care of itself. The global net of interdependence becomes denser every day, tying the fate of poor and working people in one place to boardroom decisions and markets in other, far-off places. Such global economic realities make an anachronism of the idea of independence as self-sufficiency. In this essay I confront the unquestioned yet absurd expectation that all able-bodied people ought to have jobs, in particular private-sector jobs. Unemployed people are scapegoats for a world economy less and less able to use them. While this essay concentrates on criticizing U.S. "welfare reform" discourse, the issues it addresses apply globally. There is plenty of socially useful work to be done to meet people's needs, clean the environment, build and rebuild infrastructure. Private capital investment, however, does not generate nearly enough jobs for those willing and able to work, and what jobs it does create often contribute little to such basic social usefulness. If we want people to make useful contributions to the work of knitting the social fabric, vehicles additional to markets must be found to bring them to the work and support them in it. The work of mothering, I remind us, itself constitutes such socially useful work.

PHENOMENOLOGY AND FEMALE EXPERIENCE

I consider "House and Home" continuous with those of my earlier essays that use the tools of phenomenology and other frameworks of continental philosophy to reflect on the female body experience. While not about women's bodies as such, the concept of "home" I develop here refers partly to the way body habits and activities arrange things in living spaces, and how that meaningful arrangement of things in space supports a sense of self and agency. I quarrel with Simone de Beauvoir's negative description of housework as immanence and argue that positive aspects of housework involve establishing and preserving the meanings of individual and collective history.

"House and Home" also extends some of my earlier work on female body experience in its attempt to construct suppressed positive values from activities and experience culturally marked as feminine, in this case from the activities of homemaking. As in some of my earlier essays, I criticize those aspects of traditionally female activities and male-centered descriptions of them that contribute to male privilege and women's subordination. But rather than simply turn my back on the feminine, as is one feminist impulse, I dig into typically womanly activities for raw materials to construct alternative accounts of human, and not only womanly, values. In this project I continue to be inspired by the methods and analyses of Luce Irigaray. As I read her, she aims to use ideas and symbols that have been culturally coded feminine in the West as bases both for criticizing male-dominant institutions and for expressing some alternative values.

In each of these essays I aim to offer both social critique and some vision of alternatives. I hope that they will spark in readers questions and arguments for further critical examination of contemporary social and political practice and discourse. Just as much, I hope that they might inspire readers' imagination to envision and enact better institutions and practices.

Chapter I

GENDER AS SERIALITY: THINKING ABOUT WOMEN AS A SOCIAL COLLECTIVE

If feminism is set forth as a demystifying force,
then it will have to question thoroughly the belief
in its own identity.
　　　　　—Trinh Minh-ha.

IN THE SUMMER OF 1989 I worked in Shirley Wright's campaign for a seat on the Worcester School Committee. Shirley is black, in a city where about 5–7 percent of the population is black, and 7–10 percent is Hispanic. As in many other cities, however, more than 35 percent of the children in the public schools are black, Hispanic, or Asian, and the proportion of children of color is growing rapidly. For more than ten years all six of the school committee seats have been held by white people, and only one woman has served, for about two years. In her announcement speech Shirley Wright pledged to represent all the people of Worcester. But she noted the particular need to represent minorities, and she also emphasized the importance of representing a woman's voice on the committee.

A few weeks later a friend and I distributed Shirley Wright flyers outside a grocery store. The flyers displayed a photo of Shirley and some basics about her qualifications and issues. In the course of the morning at least two women, both white, exclaimed to me, "I'm so glad to see a woman running for school committee!" This black woman claimed to speak for women in Worcester, and some white women noticed and felt affinity with her as a woman.

This seemed to me an unremarkable, easily understandable affinity. Recent discussions among feminists about the difficulties and dangers of talking about women as a single group, however, make such incidents puzzling at least. In this essay I explore some of this discussion, which has cast doubt on the project of conceptualizing women as a group. I will agree with those critiques that show how the search for the common characteristics of women or women's oppression leads to normalizations and exclusions. I will also agree with those who argue that there are pragmatic political reasons for insisting on the possibility of thinking about women as some kind of group.

These two positions pose a dilemma for feminist theory. On the one hand, without some sense in which "woman" is the name of a social collective, there is nothing specific to feminist politics. On the other hand, any effort to identify the attributes of that collective appears to undermine feminist politics by leaving out some whom feminists ought to include. To solve this dilemma I argue for reconceptualizing social collectivity or the meaning of social groups as what Sartre describes as a phenomenon of serial collectivity in his *Critique of Dialectical Reason*. Such a way of thinking about women, I will argue, allows us to see them as a collective without identifying common attributes that all women have or implying that all women have a common identity.

I

Doubts about the possibility of saying that women can be thought of as one social collective arose from challenges to a generalized conception of gender and women's oppression by women of color, in both the Northern and Southern Hemispheres, and by lesbians. Black, Latina, Asian, and indigenous women demonstrated that white feminist theory and rhetoric tended to be ethnocentric in its analysis of gender experience and oppression. Lesbians, furthermore, persistently argued that much of this analysis relied on the experience of heterosexual women. The influence of philosophical deconstruction completed the suspension of the category of "women" begun by this process of political differentiation. Exciting theorizing has shown (not for the first time) the logical problems in efforts to define clear essential categories of being. Let me review some of the most articulate recent statements of the claim that feminists should abandon or be very suspicious of a general category of woman or female gender.

Elizabeth Spelman shows definitively the mistake in any attempt to isolate gender from identities of race, class, age, sexuality, ethnicity, etc., to uncover the attributes, experience, or oppressions that women have in common.[1] To be sure, we have no trouble identifying ourselves as women, white, middle class, Jewish, American, and so on. But knowing the "right" labels to call ourselves and others does not imply the existence of any checklist of attributes that all those with the same label have in common. The absurdity of trying to isolate gender identity from race or class identity becomes apparent if you ask of any individual woman whether she can distinguish the "woman part" of herself from the "white part" or the "Jewish part." Feminist theorists nevertheless have often assumed that the distinctive and specific attributes of gender can be identified by holding race and class constant, or by examining the lives of women who suffer only sexist oppression and not also oppressions of race, or class, or age, or sexuality.

The categories according to which people are identified as the same or different, Spelman suggests, are social constructs that reflect no natures or essences. They carry and express relations of privilege and subordination, the power of some to determine for others how they will be named, what differences are important for what purposes. Because it has assumed that women form a single group with common experiences, attributes, or oppression, much feminist theorizing has exhibited such privileged points of view by unwittingly taking the experience of white, middle-class, heterosexual women as representative for all women. Even when feminists attempt to take account of differences among women, moreover, they often manifest these biases because they fail to notice the race or class specificity of white, middle-class women and how these also modify our gender. Much feminist talk about paying attention to differences among women, Spelman points out, tends to label only women of color or old women or disabled women as "different."

Chandra Mohanty believes that feminism has assumed women "as an already constituted, coherent group with identical interests and desires, regardless of class, ethnic or racial location, or contradictions."[2] Feminism has assumed "a notion of gender or sexual difference or even patriarchy which can be applied universally or even cross-culturally" (p. 55). She believes that this category of "woman" as designating a single, coherent, already constituted group influences feminists to regard all women as equally powerless and oppressed victims. Rather than developing questions about how and whether women in a particular time and place suffer discrimination and limitation on their action and desires, which can then be empirically investigated, the assumption of universal gender categories bypasses such empirical investigation by finding oppression a priori. This tendency is especially damaging in the way European and American feminists think and write about women in the Southern and Eastern Hemispheres. Assumptions about a homogeneous category, "women," help create a homogeneous category of Third World Women who stand as the Other to Western feminists, who define Third World Women as powerless victims of patriarchy.

Judith Butler draws more explicitly on postmodern theories to argue against the viability of the category of "woman" and gender.[3] In a Foucaultian mode, Butler argues that the idea of gender identity and the attempt to describe it have a normalizing power. The very act of defining a gender identity excludes or devalues some bodies, practices, and discourses, at the same time that it obscures the constructed, and thus contestable, character of that gender identity.

Feminism has assumed that it can be neither theoretical nor political without a subject. Female gender identity and experience delineates that subject. Feminist politics, it is assumed, speaks for or in the name of someone, the group women, who are defined by this female gender identity.

The category of gender was promoted by feminism precisely to criticize and reject traditional efforts to define women's nature through biological sex. In its own way, however, gender discourse tends to reify the fluid and shifting social processes in which people relate, communicate, play, work, and struggle with one another over the means of production and interpretation. The insistence on a subject for feminism obscures the social and discursive production of identities.

In one of her most important arguments of the book, Butler shows that the feminist effort to distinguish sex and gender itself contributes to such obscuring by ignoring the centrality of enforced heterosexuality in the social construction of gender. However variable its content is understood to be, the form of gender differentiation is always a binary opposition between the masculine and the feminine. Inasmuch as sexual difference is classified only as man and woman, then, gender always mirrors sex. The binary complementarity of this sex/gender system is required and makes sense, however, only with the assumption of the heterosexual complementarity. Gender identification thus turns out not to be a culturally variable overlay on a pregiven biological sex; rather, the categories of gender construct sexual difference itself.

> Gender can delineate a *unity* of experience, of sex, gender and desire, only when sex can be understood in some sense to necessitate gender. The internal coherence or unity of either gender, man or woman, thereby requires both a stable and oppositional heterosexuality. Thus we see the political reasons for substantializing gender. (p. 23)

This mutual reinforcement and reification of (hetero)sex and gender suppresses any ambiguities and incoherences among heterosexual, homosexual, and bisexual practices. This unity of sex and gender organizes the variability of desiring practices along a single scale of normal and deviant behavior. Butler concludes that feminism's attempt to construct or speak for a subject, to forge the unity of coalition from the diversities of history and practice, will always lead to such ossifications. The primary task for feminist theory and politics is critical: to formulate genealogies that show how a given category of practice is socially constructed. Feminist discourse and practice should become and remain open, its totality permanently deferred, accepting and affirming the flows and shifts in the contingent relations of social practices and institutions.

These analyses are powerful and accurate. They identify ways that essentializing assumptions and the point of view of privileged women dominate much feminist discourse, even when it tries to avoid such hegemonic moves. They draw important lessons for any future feminist theorizing that wishes to avoid excluding some women from its theories or freezing contingent social relations into a false necessity. But I find the exclusively critical orientation of such arguments rather paralyzing. Do these arguments imply that it makes no sense and is morally wrong ever to talk about women as a group, or in fact to talk about social groups at all? It is not clear that these writers claim this. If not, then what can it mean to use the term "woman"? More importantly, in the light of these critiques, what sort of positive claims can feminists make about the way social life is and ought to be? I find such questions unasked and unaddressed by these critiques of feminist essentialism.

II

What is the genealogy of the essentializing discourse that established a normative feminist subject, woman, which excluded, devalued, or found deviant the lives and practices of many women? Like most discursive constructs, this is overdetermined. But I suggest that one important source of the oppressive and paradoxical consequences of conceptualizing women as a group is the adoption of a *theoretical* stance. In large part feminist discourse about gender was motivated by the desire to establish a countertheory to Marxism, to develop a feminist theory that would conceive sex or gender as a category with as much theoretical weight as class. This desire employs a totalizing impulse. What *is* a woman? What *is* woman's social position such that it is not reducible to class? Are all societies structured by male domination, and of the same form, or variable forms? What are the origins and causes of this male domination?

These are all general and rather abstract theoretical questions. By "theory" I mean a kind of discourse that aims to be comprehensive, to give systematic account and explanation of social relations as a whole. A theory tells the way things are in some universal sense. From it one can derive particular instances, or at least one can apply the theoretical propositions to particular facts, which the theory's generalities are supposed to "cover." A social theory is self-enclosed, in the sense that it offers no particular purpose other than to understand, to reveal the way things are.

Despite much work in the last twenty years to make theories along these lines, feminists do not need and should not want theory in this sense. Instead, we should take a more *pragmatic* orientation to our intellectual discourse. By being "pragmatic" I mean categorizing, explaining, developing accounts and arguments that are tied to specific practical and political problems, where the purpose of this theoretical activity is clearly related to those problems.[4] Pragmatic theorizing in this sense is not necessarily any less complex or sophisticated than totalizing theory, but rather it is driven by some problem that has ultimate practical important and is not concerned to give an account of a whole. In this essay I take the pragmatic problem to be a political dilemma generated by feminist critiques of the concept "woman," and I aim to solve it by articulating some concepts without claiming to provide an entire social theory.

From this pragmatic point of view, I wish to ask, why does it matter whether we even consider conceptualizing women as a group? One reason to conceptualize women as a collective, I think, is to maintain a point of view outside of liberal individualism. The discourse of liberal individualism denies the reality of groups. According to liberal individualism, categorizing people in groups by race, gender, religion, and sexuality, and acting as though these ascriptions say something significant about the person and his or her experience, capacities, and possibilities, is invidious and oppressive. The only liberatory approach is to think of people and treat them as individuals, variable and unique. This individualist ideology, however, in fact obscures oppression. Without conceptualizing women as a group in some sense, it is not possible to conceptualize oppression as a systematic, structured, institutional process. If we obey the injunction to think of people only as individuals, then the disadvantages and exclusions we call oppressions reduce to individuals in one of two ways. Either we blame the victims and say that the disadvantaged person's individual life-styles and capacities render them less competitive; or we attribute their disadvantage to the attitudes of other individuals, who for whatever reason don't "like" the disadvantaged ones. In either case structural and political ways to address and rectify the disadvantage are written out of the discourse, leaving individuals to wrestle with their bootstraps. The importance of being able to talk about disadvantage and oppression in terms of groups exists just as much for those oppressed through race, class, sexuality, ethnicity, and so on, as through gender.[5]

The naming of women as a specific and distinct social collective, moreover, is a difficult achievement, and one that gives feminism its specificity as a political movement. The possibility of conceptualizing ethnic, religious, cultural, or national groups, for example, rarely comes into question because their social existence itself usually involves some common traditions—language, rituals, songs and stories, or dwelling place. Women, however, are dispersed among all these groups. The operation of most marriage and kinship forms brings women under the identity of men in each and all of these groups, in the privacy of household and bed. The exclusions, oppressions, and disadvantages that women often suffer can hardly be thought at all without a structural conception of women as a collective social position. The first step in feminist resistance to such oppressions is the affirmation of women as a group, so that women can cease to be divided and believe that their sufferings are natural or merely personal. Denial of the reality of a social collective *women* reinforces the privilege of those who benefit from keeping women divided.[6]

Feminist politics evaporates, that is, without some conception of women as a social collective. Radical politics may remain, as a commitment to social justice for all people, among them those called women. But the claim that feminism expresses a distinct politics allied with anti-imperialism, anti-racism, gay liberation, and so on, but asking a unique set of enlightening questions about a distinct axis of social oppression, cannot be sustained without some means of conceptualizing women and gender as social structures.

The logical and political difficulties inherent in the attempt to conceptualize women as a single group with a set of common attributes and shared identity appear to be insurmountable. Yet if we cannot conceptualize women as a group, feminist politics appears to lose any meaning. Is there a way out of this dilemma? In my reading of recent feminist discussions of this problem I have found two strategies for solving it: the attempt to theorize gender identity as multiple rather than binary, and the argument that women constitute a group only in the politicized context of feminist struggle. I shall argue now that both of these strategies fail.

Spelman herself explores the strategy of multiple genders. She does not dispense with the category of gender, but instead suggests that a woman's gender identity and gender attributes are different according to what race, class, religion, etc., she belongs to. Gender is a relational concept, not the naming of an essence. One finds the specific characteristics and attributes of the gender identity of women by comparing their situation with that of men. But if one wishes to locate the gender-based oppression of women, it is wrong to compare all women with all men. For some women are definitely privileged when compared to some men. To find the gender-specific attributes of a woman's experience, Spelman suggests, one must restrict the comparison to men and women of the same race or class or nationality. Women of different races or classes, moreover, often have opposing gender attributes. On this reasoning women as such cannot be said to be a group. Properly designated groups are "white women," "black women," "Jewish women," "working-class women," "Brazilian women," each with specific gender characteristics.[7]

In a recent paper Ann Ferguson proposes a similar solution to the contradictions and quandaries that arise when feminists assume that all women share a common identity and set of gendered attributes.

> Instead of a concept of sisterhood based on a shared gender identity, it may be more helpful to posit different racial gender positions, and possibly different class gender positions. Processes of racialization in U.S. history have created at least ten gender identities informed with racial difference if we consider the various subordinate races: black, Latino, Native American, and Asian, as well as the dominant white race.[8]

There is much to recommend this concept of multiple genders as a way of describing the differentiations and contradictions in the social experience of gender. The idea of multiple genders highlights the fact that not all men are equally privileged by gender. It also makes clear that some women are privileged in relation to some men, a privilege that derives partly from their gender. It allows the theorist to look for race- or class-specific gender interactions and expectations, without essentializing them. Multiple-gender conceptualization may also address the problems of binarism and heterosexism that Butler finds with gender theory. According to a concept of multiple genders, the gender identity of lesbians, for example, can be conceptualized as different from that of straight women.

Despite its promising virtues, the strategy of multiplying gender also has some dangers. First, it is just not true, as Spelman suggests, that gender relations are structured primarily within a class, race, nationality, and so on. A working-class woman's gendered experience and oppression is not properly identified only by comparing her situation to that of working-class men. Much of her gendered experience is conditioned by her relation to middle-class or ruling-class men. If she experiences sexual harrassment at work, for example, her harrasser is at least as likely to be a middle-class professional man as a working-class assembler or deliveryman. Examples of such cross-class or cross-race relations between men and women can be multiplied. In such relations it would be false to say that the class or race difference is not as important as the gender difference, but it would be equally false to say that the cross-class or cross-race relations between men and women are not gendered relations. But if we conceive African American feminine gender, for example, as having one set of attributes in relation to African American men and another in relation to white men, one of two things results: either we need to multiply genders further, or we need to draw back and ask what makes both of these genders womanly.

Second, the idea of multiple genders presumes a stability and unity to the categories of race, class, religion, ethnicity, etc. that divide women. To conceptualize "American Indian woman" as a single identity different from "white woman," we must implicitly assume "American Indian" or "white" as stable categories. As Susan Bordo points out, feminist arguments against conceptualizing women as a single group often privilege categories of race or class, failing to challenge the appropriateness of these group categories.[9] But the same arguments against considering these categories as unities can be used as the arguments against thinking about women as a unity. American Indians are divided by class, region, religion, and ethnicity, as well as by gender. Working-class people are divided by race, ethnicity, region, religion, and sexuality, as well as by gender. The idea of multiple genders can solve the problems and paradoxes involved in conceptualizing women as a group only by presuming categorical unities to class and race.

This last point leads to the final objection to the idea of multiple genders. This strategy can generate an infinite regress that dissolves groups into individuals. Any category can be considered an arbitrary unity. Why claim that black women, for example, have a distinct and unified gender identity? Black women are American, Haitian, Jamaican, African, Northern, Southern, poor, working class, lesbian, or old. Each of these divisions may be important to a particular woman's gender identity. But then we are back to the question of what it means to call her a woman. The strategy of multiple genders, then, while useful in directing attention to the social specificities of gender differentiation and gender interaction, does not resolve the dilemma I have posed. Instead, it seems to swing back and forth between the two poles of that dilemma.

Some feminist theorists propose "identity politics" as a different answer to the criticism of essentializing gender while retaining a conception of women as a group. An identity "woman" that unites subjects into a group is not a natural or social given, but rather the fluid construct of a political movement, feminism. Thus Diana Fuss agrees that the concept "woman" cannot name a set of attributes that a group of individuals has in common, a substantial subject, nor is there a female gender identity that defines the social experience of womanhood. Instead, feminist politics itself creates an identity "woman" out of a coalition of diverse female persons dispersed across the world.

Coalition politics precedes class and determines its limits and boundaries; we cannot identify a group of women until various social, historical, political conditions construct the conditions and possibilities for membership. Many anti-essentialists fear that positing a political coalition of *women* risks presuming that there must first be a natural class of women; but this belief only makes the fact that it is coalition politics which constructs the category of women (and men) in the first place.[10]

Interpreting the theoretical writings of several black feminist writers, Nancie Caraway proposes a similar understanding of women as a group. Unity and solidarity among women is a product of political discussion and struggle among people of diverse backgrounds, experiences, and interests who are differently situated in matrices of power and privilege. The process of discussion and disagreement among feminists forges a common commitment to a politics against oppression that produces the identity "woman" as a coalition.

> Identity politics advances a space for political action, praxis, justified by the critical *positioning* of the marginalized subjects against hierarchies of power—the Enlightenment promise of transcendence. . . . These emerging theories are codes about the fluid construction of identity. They are not racially specific; they speak to both white and black feminists about the shared and differentiated faces of female oppression.[11]

The identity politics position has some important virtues. It rightly recognizes that the perception of a common identity among persons must be the product of social or political process that brings them together around a purpose. It retains a conception of women as a group that it believes feminist politics needs, at the same time clearly rejecting an essentialist or substantive conception of gender identity. There are, however, at least two problems with identity politics as a way to get out of the dilemma I have articulated.

Judith Butler points out the first. Even though identity politics' coalition politics and deconstructive discourse avoids substantializing gender, the dangers of normalization are not thereby also avoided. The feminist politics that produces a coalition of mutually identifying women nevertheless privileges some norms or experiences over others. Thus Butler suggests that feminist politics should be suspicious of settling into a unified coalition. The question of solidarity should never be settled, and identities should shift and be deconstructed in a play of possibilities that exclude no one.

My second objection to the idea that women are a group only as the construction of feminist politics is that it seems to make feminist politics arbitrary. Some women just choose to come together in a political movement and form themselves as a group of mutually identifying agents. But on the basis of what do they come together? What are the social conditions that have motivated the politics? Perhaps even more important, do feminist politics not refer to women who do not identify as feminists?

These questions all point to the need for some conception of women as a group prior to the formation of self-conscious feminist politics, as designating a certain set of relations or positions that motivate the particular politics of feminism.

III

Stories like Shirley Wright's race for school committee remind us that everday language seems to be able to talk about women as a collective in some sense, even though women's experiences vary considerably by class, race, sexuality, age, or society. But Spelman, Mohanty, Butler, and others are right to criticize the exclusionary and normalizing implications of most attempts to theorize this everyday experience. Feminist theory today lives in a dilemma. We want and need to describe women as a group, yet it appears that we cannot do so without being normalizing and essentialist.

I propose a way out of this dilemma through a use of the concept of seriality that Sartre develops in the *Critique of Dialectical Reason*. I propose that we understand gender as referring to a social series, a specific kind of social collectivity that Sartre distinguishes from groups. Understanding gender as seriality, I suggest, has several virtues. It provides a way of thinking about women as a social collective without requiring that all women have common attributes or a common situation. Gender as seriality, moreover, does not rely on identity or self-identity for understanding the social production and meaning of membership in collectives.

One might well question any project that appropriates Sartrian philosophy positively for feminist theory.[12] Much of Sartre's writing is hopelessly sexist and male biased. This is certainly manifest in his theorization and functionalization of heterosexual relations. Perhaps more fundamentally, Sartre's early existentialist ontology presumes human relations as oppositional, egoistical, and basically violent. While the later philosophy on which I will draw is less individualistic than the early philosophy, the later philosophy retains the assumption of human relations as latently violent. In the later philosophy boxing is a paradigm of the relation of self and other as mediated by a third.

Although Sartre's writing is sexist and his ontological assumptions about human relations tend to derive from masculine experience, I nevertheless have found the idea of seriality in particular, and its distinction from other kinds of social collective, of use in thinking about women as a collective. Linda Singer has talked about the feminist philosopher as a "Bandita," an intellectual outlaw who raids the texts of male philosophers and steals from them what she finds pretty or useful, leaving the rest behind.[13] I aim to approach Sartre's texts with the spirit of this Bandita. From them I take out and rearticulate for my purposes the concepts I think will help resolve the dilemma I have posed. In doing so I need not drag all of Sartre with me, and I may be "disloyal" to him.

In the *Critique of Dialectical Reason,* Sartre distinguishes several levels of social collectivity by their order of internal complexity and reflexivity. For the purposes of addressing the problem of thinking about women as a social collective, the important distinction is between a group and a series. A group is a collection of persons that recognize themselves and one another as in a unified relation with one another. Members of the group mutually acknowledge that together they undertake a common project. Members of the group, that is, are united by *action* that they undertake together. In acknowledging himself or herself as a member of the group, an individual acknowledges himself or herself as oriented toward the same goals as the others; each individual thereby assumes the common project as a project for his or her individual action. What makes the project shared, however, is the mutual acknowledgment among the members of the group that they are engaged in the project together; this acknowledgment usually becomes explicit at some point in a pledge, contract, constitution, set of by-laws, or statement of purpose. The project of the group is a collective project, moreover, insofar as the members of the group mutually acknowledge that it can only be or is best undertaken by a group—storming the Bastille, staging an international women's conference, achieving women's suffrage, building an amphitheater.[14]

So far in this essay I have used the term "group" loosely, as does ordinary language, to designate any collection of people. Since my theorizing about women depends on Sartre's distinction between group and series, however, from now on in this paper I shall reserve the term "group" for the self-consciously mutually acknowledging collective with a self-conscious purpose. Much of an individual's life and action takes place in and is structured by a multitude of groups in this sense. Not all structured social action occurs in groups, however. As Sartre explains it, groups arise from and often fall back into a less organized and un-self-conscious collective unity, which he calls a series.

Within Sartre's conception of human freedom, all social relations must be understood as the production of action. Unlike a group, which forms around actively shared objectives, a series is a social collective whose members are unified passively by the objects their actions are oriented around and/or by the objectified results of the material effects of the actions of the others. In everyday life we often experience ourselves and others impersonally, as participating in amorphous collectives defined by routine practices and habits. The unity of the series derives from the way that individuals pursue their own individual ends in respect to the same objects conditioned by a continuous material environment, in response to structures that have been created by the unintended collective result of past actions.

Sartre describes people waiting for a bus as such a series. They are a collective, insofar as they minimally relate to one another and follow the rules of bus waiting. As a collective they are brought together by their relation to a material object, the bus, and the social practices of public transportation. Their actions and goals may be different; they have nothing necessarily in common in their histories, experiences, or identity. They are united only by their desire to ride on that route. Though they are in this way a social collective, they do not identify with one another, do not affirm themselves as engaged in a shared enterprise or identify themselves with common experiences. The latent potential of this series to organize itself as a group will become manifest, however, if the bus fails to come; they will complain to one another about the lousy bus service, share horror stories of lateness and breakdowns, perhaps assign one of their number to go call the company, or discuss sharing a taxi.

Serial collectivity, according to Sartre, is precisely the obverse of the mutual identification typical of the group. Each goes about his or her own business. But each is also aware of the serialized context of that activity in a social collective whose structure constitutes them within certain limits and constraints. In seriality, a person experiences not only others, but also himself or herself as an Other, that is, as an anonymous someone. "Everyone is the same as the other insofar as he is Other than himself" (p. 260). Individuals in the series are fungible; while not identical, from the point of view of the social practices and objects that generate the series, the individuals could be in one another's place. It is contingent that I am third in line for the bus today. Thus in the series individuals are isolated, but not alone. They understand themselves as constituted as a collective, as serialized, by the objects and practices through which they aim to accomplish their individual purposes. Often their actions take into account their expectations of the behavior of others in the series whom they nevertheless do not encounter. For example, I ask for a later schedule at work so that I will miss the rush hour.

Sartre uses the example of radio listening to illustrate some of the characteristics of seriality. The collective of radio listeners is constituted by their individual orientation toward objects, in this case radios and their material possibilities of sound transmission. As listeners they are isolated, but nevertheless they are aware of being part of a series of radio listeners, of others listening simultaneously linked to them indirectly through broadcasting. One's experience of radio listening is partly conditioned by the awareness of being linked to others from whom one is separated, and that one is other for them. Frequently the radio announcer explicitly refers to the serialized being of the listeners.

Sartre calls the series a practico-inert reality. The series is structured by actions linked to practico-inert objects. Social objects and their effects are the results of human action, they are *practical*. But as material they also constitute constraints on and resistances to action, which make them experienced as *inert*. The built environment is a practical-inert reality. All of the products of human decision and action, daily used by and dwelt in by people, the streets and buildings are inert. Their material qualities enable and constrain many aspects of action.

Sartre calls the system of practico-inert objects and the material results of actions in relation to them that generate and are reproduced by serial collectives the milieu of action. The milieu is the already-there set of material things and collectivized habits against the background of which any particular action occurs. Thus for the series designated "commuters," for example, the milieu is the totality of the structured relations of the physical space of streets and rail lines, together with the predictable traffic patterns that emerge from the confluence of individual actions, together with the rules, habits, and cultural idiosyncracies of driving, riding, and walking.

Serialized action within the milieu results in *counter-finalities*: the confluence of individual intentional actions to produce a result that is counter to some purposes and that no one intended. Within a certain kind of milieu the series "commuters" will produce a gridlock; each individual driver pursues his or her own individual ends under material conditions that eventually make a large cluster of them unable to move.

The collective otherness of serialized existence is thus often experienced as constraint, felt necessities that often are experienced as given or natural. Members of the series experience themselves as powerless to alter this material milieu, and they understand that the others in the series are equally constrained. "A series reveals itself to everyone when they perceive in themselves and Others their common inability to eliminate their material differences" (p. 277). At the same time, the material milieu and objects are conditions of enablement for action. Objectives can be realized only through the mediation of already there things, practices, and structures. A market is paradigmatic of such structured relations of alienation and anonymity that are felt as constraints on everyone. I take my corn to market in hopes of getting a good price, knowing that some people are trading on its price in a futures market, and that other farmers bring their corn as well. We know that by bringing our large quantity of corn we contribute to a fall in its price, and we might each play the futures market ourselves. But we are all equally as individuals unable to alter the collective results of these individual choices, choices which themselves have been made partly because of our expectations of what is happening to market prices.

Membership in serial collectives defines an individual's being, in a sense—one "is" a farmer, or a commuter, or a radio listener, and so on, together in series with others similarly positioned. But the definition is anonymous, and the unity of the series is amorphous, without determinate limits, attributes, or intentions. Sartre calls it a unity "in flight," a collective gathering that slips away at the edges, whose qualities and characteristics are impossible to pin down because they are an inert result of the confluence of actions. There is no *concept* of the series, no specific set of attributes that form the sufficient conditions for membership in it. Who belongs to the series of bus riders? Only those riding today? Those who regularly ride? Occasionally? Those who may ride buses and know the social practices of bus riding? While serial membership delimits and constrains an individual's possible actions, it does not define the person's identity in the sense of forming his or her individual purposes, projects, and sense of self in relation to others.

Thus far the examples of seriality have been rather simple and one-dimensional. Sartre's theoretical purpose in developing the concept, however, is to describe the meaning of social class. Most of the time what it means to be a member of the working class or the capitalist class is to live in series with others in that class through a complex, interlocking set of objects, structures, and practices in relation to work, exchange, and consumption.

Class being does not define a person's identity, because one is a class member in a mode of otherness, otherness to oneself in one's subjectivity. If one says "I am a worker" in naming serialized class being, this does not designate for one a felt and internalized identity, but a social facticity about the material conditions of one's life. (To be sure, one can and many do say "I am a worker" as a badge of pride and identity. But when this happens the class being is not experienced in seriality; rather, one has formed a *group* with other workers with whom one has established self-conscious bonds of solidarity.) As serialized, class lies as a historical and materialized background to individual lives. A person is born into a class in the sense that a history of class relations precedes her, and the characteristics of the work that she will do or not do are already inscribed in machines, the physical structure of factories and offices, the geographic relations of city and suburb. An individual encounters other members of the class as alienated others, separated through the materiality of the things that define and delimit one's class being—the factory with its machines, the physical movements and demands of the production process, the residential districts, buses, and highways that bring the workers into contact. As class members the individuals are relatively interchangeable, and nothing defines them as workers but the practico-inert constraints on their actions that they find themselves powerless to change. "If you want to eat, then you have to get a job" expresses the anonymous constraints on anyone who lacks independent means of support.

Let me now summarize the major elements in the concept of seriality. A series is a collective whose members are unified passively by the relation their actions have to material objects and practico-inert histories. The practico-inert milieu, within which and by means of whose structures individuals realize their aims, is experienced as constraints on the mode and limits of action. To be said to be part of the same series it is not necessary to identify a set of common attributes that every member has, because their membership is defined not by something they are, but rather by the fact that in their diverse existences and actions they are oriented around the same objects or practico-inert structures. Membership in the series does not define one's identity. Each member of the series is isolated, Other to the Others, and as a member of the series Other than themselves. Finally, there is no concept of the series within attributes that clearly demarcate what about individuals makes them belong. The series is a blurry, shifting unity, an amorphous collective.

Seriality designates a level of social life and action, the level of habit and the unreflective reproduction of ongoing historical social structures. Self-conscious groups arise from and on the basis of serialized existence, as a reaction to it and an active reversal of its anonymous and isolating conditions. After I express how gender is seriality, I shall explain the relationship between groups of women and the series women.

IV

Applying the concept of seriality to gender, I suggest, makes theoretical sense out of saying that "women" is a reasonable social category, expressing a certain kind of social unity. At the same time, conceptualizing gender as a serial collectivity avoids the problems I summarized earlier that feminist theorists have argued emerge from saying that women are a single group.

As I explained earlier, seriality designates a certain *level* of social existence and relations with others, the level of routine, habitual action, which is rule-bound and socially structured, but as a prereflective background to action. Seriality is lived as medium, or, as I developed earlier *milieu*, where action is directed at particular ends that presuppose the series without taking them up self-consciously.

Thus, as a series *woman* is the name of a structural relation to material objects as they have been produced and organized by a prior history, which carries the material necessities of past practices congealed
in their matter. But the series *women* is not so simple and one-dimensional as bus riders or radio listeners. Gender, like class, is a vast, multifaceted, layered, complex, and overlapping set of structures and objects. *Women* are the individuals who are positioned as feminine by
these activities.

The loose unity of the series, I have said, derives from the fact that
individuals' actions are oriented toward the same or similarly structured
objects. What are the practico-inert realities that construct gender?
Clearly female bodies have something to do with the constitution of the
series "women," but it is not merely the physical facts of these female
bodies themselves—attributes of breasts, vaginas, clitorises, and so on—
that construct female gender. Social objects are not merely physical but
also inscribed by and the products of past *practices*. The female body as a
practico-inert object toward which action is oriented is a rule-bound body,
a body with understood meanings and possibilities. Menstruation, for
example, is a regular biological event occurring in most female bodies
within a certain age range. It is not this biological process alone, however, that locates individuals in the series "women." Rather, the social
rules of menstruation, along with the material objects associated with
menstrual practices, constitute the activity within which the women live
as serialized. One can say the same about biological events like pregnancy, childbirth, and lactation.

The structure of the social body defining these bodily practices, however, is enforced heterosexuality. The meanings, rules, practices, and
assumptions of institutionalized heterosexuality constitute the series
women as in a relation of potential appropriation by men. Likewise the
series *men* appears in the structures of enforced heterosexuality. The
assumptions and practices of heterosexuality define the meaning of
bodies—vaginas, clitorises, penises—not as mere physical objects but as
practico-inert.

Even one so anti-essentialist as Gayatri Spivak locates heterosexuality
as a set of material-ideological facts that constitute women cross-culturally. The material practices of enforced heterosexuality serialize women
as objects of exchange and appropriation by men, with a consequent
repression of autonomous active female desire.

> In legally defining woman as object of exchange, passage, or possession in
> terms of reproduction, it is not only the womb that is literally "appropri-
> ated"; it is the clitoris and signifier of the sexed object that is effaced. All
> historical the theoretical investigation into the definition of women as legal

object—in or out of marriage; or as politico-economic passageway for property and legitimacy would fall within the investigation of the varieties of the effacement of the clitoris.[15]

Bodies, however, are only one of the practico-inert objects that position individuals in the gender series. A huge complex of other objects and materialized historical products condition women's lives as gendered. Pronouns locate individual people, along with animals and other objects, in a gender system. Verbal and visual representations more generally create and reproduce gender meanings that condition a person's action and her interpretation of the actions of others. A multitude of artifacts and social spaces in which people act are flooded with gender codes. Clothes are the primary example, but there are also cosmetics, tools, even in some cases furniture and spaces that materially inscribe the norms of gender. I may discover myself "as a woman" by being on the "wrong" dorm floor.

What usually structures the gendered relation of these practico-inert objects is a sexual division of labor. Though their content varies with each social system, a division of at least some tasks and activities by sex appears as a felt necessity. The division between caring for babies and bodies and not doing so is the most common sexual division of labor, over which many other labor divisions are layered in socially specific ways. Other sexual divisions of tasks and activities are more arbitrary but in practice are also felt as "natural." Think, for example, about the genderization of football and field hockey in most American colleges. The context of the sexual division of labor varies enormously across history, culture, and institutions. Where the division appears, however, it usually produces a multitude of practico-inert objects that constitute the gendered series. The offices, workstations, locker rooms, uniforms, and instruments of a particular activity presuppose a certain sex. The language, gestures, and rituals of exclusion or inclusion of persons in activities reproduce the divisions by attracting people to or repelling people from those activities.

Bodies and objects constitute the gendered series women through structures like enforced heterosexuality and the sexual division of labor. As I have interpreted Sartre's concept, being positioned by these structures in the series "women" does not itself designate attributes that attach to the person in the series, nor does it define her identity. Individuals move and act in relation to practico-inert objects that position them as "women." The practico-inert structures that generate the milieu of gendered serialized existence both enable and constrain action, but they do not determine or define it. The individuals pursue their own ends; they get a living for themselves in order to have some pleasures of eating and relaxation. The sexual division of labor both enables them to gain that living and constrains their manner of doing so by ruling out or making difficult some possibilities of action. The bathroom enables me to relieve myself, and its gender-marked door constrains the space in which and next to whom I do it.

The practico-inert structures of the gender series are abstract in relation to individuals and to groups of individuals. They are possibilities and orientations for concrete actions that give them content. The gender structures are not defining attributes of individuals, but material social facts that each individual must deal with and relate to. The subjective experiential relation that each person has, and sometimes groups have, to the gender structure are infinitely variable. In a heterosexist society, for example, everyone must deal with and act in relation to structures of enforced heterosexuality. But there are many attitudes a particular individual can take toward that necessity: she can internalize norms of feminine masochism, she can try to avoid sexual interaction, she can affirmatively take up her sexual role as a tool for her own ends, and she can reject heterosexual requirements and love other women, to name just a few.[16]

In seriality, I said above, the individual experiences herself as anonymous, Other to herself, and Other to the others, contingently fungible with them. Sometimes when I become aware of myself "as a woman" I experience this serial anonymous facticity. The serialized experience of being gendered is precisely the obverse of mutual recognition and positive identification of oneself as in a group. "I am a woman" at this level is an anonymous fact that does not define me in my active individuality. It means that I check one box rather than another on my driver's license application, that I use maxipads, wear pumps, and sometimes find myself in situations when I anticipate deprecation or humiliation from a man. As I utter the phrase, I experience a serial interchangeability between myself and others. In the newspaper I read about a woman who was raped, and I empathize with her because I recognize that in my serialized existence I am rapeable, the potential object of male appropriation. But this awareness *depersonalizes* me, constructs me as Other to her and Other to myself in a serial interchangeability, rather than defining my sense of identity. I do not here mean to deny that many women have a sense of identity as women, and I will discuss this issue in the next section. Here I only claim that the level of gender as series is a background to rather than constitutive of personal or group identity.

I have already referred to the fact that Sartre's main purpose in developing the concept of seriality is to describe unorganized class existence, the positioning of individuals in relations of production and consumption. Race or nationality can also be fruitfully conceptualized as seriality.[17] At the level of seriality racial position is constructed by a relation of persons to a materialized racist history that has constructed racially separated spaces, a racial division of labor, racist language and discourse, and so on. A person can and often does construct a positive racial identity along with others from out of this serialized positioning. But such racial identification is an active taking up of a serialized situation. Which, if any, of a person's serial memberships become salient or meaningful at any time is a variable matter.

Like gender structures, class or race structures do not primarily name attributes of individuals or aspects of their identity, but practico-inert necessities that condition their lives and with which they must deal. Individuals may take up varying attitudes toward these structures, including forming a sense of class or racial identity and forming groups with others they identify with.

Thus the concept of seriality provides a useful way of thinking about the relationship of race, class, gender, and other collective structures to the individual person. If these are each forms of seriality, then they do not necessarily define the identity of individuals and do not necessarily name attributes they share with others. They are material structures arising from people's historically congealed, institutionalized actions and expectations that position and limit individuals in determinate ways with which they must deal. An individual's position in each of the series means that they have differing experiences and perceptions from those differently situated. But individuals can relate to these social positionings in different ways; the same person may relate to them in different ways in different social contexts or at different times in their lives.

A person can choose to make none of her serial memberships important for her sense of identity. Or she can find that her family, neighborhood, and church network makes the serial facts of race, for example, important for her identity and development of a group solidarity. Or she can develop a sense of herself and membership in group affiliations that makes different serial structures important to her in different respects, or salient in different kinds of circumstances.

V

The purpose of saying that *women* names a series is to resolve the dilemma that has developed in feminist theory: that we must be able to describe women as a social collective, yet apparently we cannot do so without false essentialism that normalizes and excludes. Thinking about gender as seriality avoids both the problem of essentialism and the problem of identity that have plagued efforts to define what it means to be a woman.

An essentialist approach to conceiving women as a social collective treats women as a substance, a kind of entity in which some specific attributes inhere. One classifies a person as a woman according to whether that person has the essential attributes all women share: something about their bodies, their behavior or dispositions as persons, their experience or oppression. The problem with this approach to conceptualizing women as a collective is that any effort to locate those essential attributes has one of two consequences. Either it empties the category *woman* of social meaning by reducing it to the attributes of biological female, or in the effort to locate essential social attributes it founders on the variability and diversity of women's actual lives. The effort to locate particular social attributes that all women share is likely to leave out some persons called women, or to distort their lives to fit the categories.

Conceptualizing gender as seriality avoids this problem because it does not claim to identify specific attributes that all women have. This is part of what it means to say that the series is not a concept, that its unity is fuzzy, in flight. There is a unity to the series "women," but it is a passive unity, not one that arises from the individuals called women, but rather that positions them through the material organization of social relations as enabled and constrained by the structural relations I have called enforced heterosexuality and the sexual division of labor. These are not attributes that attach to some or all women, but rather the structure of actions and expectations of others along with their material results toward which the actions of particular female persons are oriented. The content of these structures varies enormously from one social context to the next. Saying that a person is a woman may predict something about the general constraints and expectations she must deal with. But it predicts nothing in particular about who she is, what she does, how she takes up her social positioning.

Thinking of gender as seriality also avoids the identity problem. At least since Nancy Chodorow developed her theory of the psychodynamics of mother-infant relations, gender has been understood as a mode of personal identity.[18] By identity, I mean one of two conceptions, which sometimes appear together. First, identity designates something about who persons are in a deep psychological sense. This is the primary meaning of identity in Chodorow's theory of gender identity. She argues that feminine gender identity gives women more permeable ego boundaries than men, thus making relations with other persons important for their self-conception. Many recent moral and epistemological theories have been influenced by this notion of gender identity and suggest that theories, modes of reasoning, ways of acting tend to be structured by those feminine and masculine identities.

Second, identity can mean self-ascription as belonging to a group with others who similarly identify, who affirm together or are committed together to a set of values, practices, meanings, and so on. This is the sense of identity expressed by theorists of identity politics. Identity here means a self-consciously shared set of meanings interpreting conditions and commitments of being a woman.

Criticisms of gender as identity in either of these senses are similar to criticisms of gender essentialism. This approach to thinking about women as a social collective either leaves out some individuals who call themselves or are called women or distorts the experience of some of them. Many women deny that being a woman is an important part of their sense of self, or that they particularly identify with other women. They regard their womanness as an accidental or contingent aspect of their lives, and they conceive other social group relations—ethnic or national relations, for example—as more defining their identity. Many women resist efforts to theorize shared values and experiences specific to a feminine gender identity—in a caring orientation to relationships, for example—claiming that such theories privilege the identities of particular classes of women in particular social contexts. Among women who do take their womanhood as an important aspect of their identity, the meaning of that identity will vary a great deal.[19]

One of the major virtues of thinking about gender as seriality is that it disconnects gender from identity. On the one hand, as Elizabeth Spelman argues, at the level of individual personal identity there is no way to distinguish the "gender part" of the person from her "race part" or "class part." It may be appropriate, as Butler argues, to think of subjects, personal identities, as constituted rather than as some transcendental origin of consciousness or action. Nevertheless, it would be misleading to think of individual persons as "mixtures" of gender, race, class, and national "attributes." Each person's identity is unique, the history and meaning she makes and develops from her dealings with other people, communicative interactions through media, and her manner of taking up the particular serialized structures whose prior history position her. No individual woman's identity, then, will escape the markings of gender, but how gender marks her life is her own.

Conceptions of gender as an identity, however, more often seek to name women as a group—that is, a self-conscious social collective with common experiences, perspectives, or values—than to describe individual identity. Conceiving gender as seriality, distinguishing a series from a group, and showing the relation between the series and the group become especially important for addressing this mistake. In Sartre's conceptualization, which I am appropriating, a group is a collection of persons who do mutually identify; they mutually recognize one another as belonging together to the group with a common project that defines their collective action. A series, on the other hand, is not a mutually acknowledging identity with any common project or shared experience. Women need have nothing in common in their individual lives to be serialized as women.

Sartre articulates a relationship between series and groups. Groups, as self-conscious collectives of persons with a common objective that they pursue together, often, if not always, arise on the basis of and in response to a serialized condition. The group-in-fusion is a spontaneous group formation out of seriality. When those who have waited for the bus too long begin complaining to each other and discussing possible courses of action, they are a group in fusion. Once groups form and take action they either institutionalize themselves by establishing meetings, leaders, decision-making structures, methods of acquiring and expending resources, and so on, or they disperse back into seriality. Social life consists of constant ebbs and flows of groupings out of series; some groups remain and grow into institutions that produce new serialities, others disperse soon after they are born.

At its most unreflective and universal level, being a woman is a serial fact. But women often do form groups, that is, self-conscious collectives that mutually acknowledge one another as having common purposes or shared experiences. Let me give an example of a movement from women as a serial collective to a group of women. In her novel *Rivington Street*, Meredith Tax vividly portrays the lives of Russian Jewish immigrant women on the Lower East Side of Manhattan at the turn of the century. In one episode of the novel some women in the neighborhood discover that a local merchant has manipulated the chicken market in order to get more profits on his sale of chickens in the neighborhood. They talk with one another with anger and then go about their business. One of them, however, thinks a bit more in her anger and decides to act. She calls her three or four women friends together and tells them that they should boycott the butcher. The women organize a boycott by going from apartment to apartment talking to women. Gradually these neighborhood women, formerly serialized only as shoppers, come to understand themselves as a group, with some shared experiences and the power of collective action. When the boycott succeeds they hold a street celebration and honor their leader, but then they quickly disperse back into the passive unity of the series.

The gendered being of women's groups arises from the serial being of women, as taking up actively and reconstituting the gendered structures that have passively unified them. The chicken boycott arises from the serialized condition of these women defined by the sexual division of labor as purchasers and preparers of food. While the gendered series *women* refers to the structured social relations positioning all biologically sexed females, groups of women are always *partial* in relation to the series—they bring together only some women for some purposes involving their gender-serialized experience. Groups of women are usually more socially, historically, and culturally specified than simply women—they are from the same neighborhood or university, they have the same religion or occupation. Groups of women, that is, will likely, though not necessarily, emerge from the serialities of race and class as well as gender. The chicken boycotters live in the same neighborhood, speak the same Russian-Yiddish, are passively united in a marginal working-class series in the class structure of Manhattan. All of these serialized facts are relevant to their story and partially explain their grouping.

The chicken boycott example shows a case of women grouping self-consciously as women and on the basis of their gendered condition, but the boycott is not feminist. There can be many groupings of women as women that are not feminist, and indeed some are explicitly antifeminist. Feminism is a particularly reflexive impulse of women grouping—women grouping as women in order to change or eliminate the structures that serialize them as women.

Let me return to my story of Shirley Wright in order to clarify and elaborate the relation of series and group in understanding women as a collective. In the announcement of her candidacy for school committee, when Shirley Wright says that she intends to "represent" women, she is referring to a gender series defined primarily by the sexual division of labor. *Women* names a position in the division of labor that tends to be specifically related to schools, the primary parent to deal with schools, at the same time that it names a position outside authority structures. In that speech Wright is not claiming a group solidarity among the women of Worcester, either around her candidacy or in any other respect, but she is referring to, gesturing toward, a serial structure that conditions her own position and that she aims to politicize. To the degree that Shirley Wright aims to politicize gender structures in her campaign and on the school committee, she invites or invokes the positive grouping of women out of the gender series, but her candidacy speech neither names a group nor generates it. Her claim to represent "minorities" is also a reference to a serial structure of race and racism that she claims conditions her position and that she aims to politicize.

The women who responded to my handing them a flyer with satisfaction at seeing a woman running are also serialized, as women, as voters. Their identification with Shirley Wright as a woman, however, makes for a proto-group. If some women are motivated to come together to form a "Women for Shirley Wright" committee, they have constituted an active grouping. In relation to the series women, or even to the series "the women of Worcester," the group is necessarily partial—it will probably attract only certain kinds of women, with only some kinds of experiences, and it will focus only on some issues.

In summary, then, this is how I propose that using the concept of seriality and its distinction from the concept of a group can help solve the conundrums about talking about women as a group in which feminist theory has recently found itself. *Woman* is a serial collective defined neither by any common identity nor by a common set of attributes that all the individuals in the series share, but rather names a set of structural constraints and relations to practico-inert objects that condition action and its meaning. I am inclined to say that the series includes all female human beings in the world, and also others of the past, but how and where we draw the historical lines is an open question. We can also claim that there are social and historical subseries. Since the series is not a concept but a more practical-material mode of the social construction of individuals, one need not think of it in terms of "genus" and "species," but as vectors of action and meaning.

Unlike most groups of women, feminist groups take something about women's condition as the explicit aim of their action, and thus feminist groups at least implicitly *refer* to the series women, which lies beyond the group. Feminist politics and theory refers to or gestures toward this serial reality. In that sense it is what feminism is about. Feminist reflection and explicit theorizing draw on the experience of serialized gender, which has multiple layers and aspects. Feminism itself is not a grouping of women; rather, there are many feminisms, many groupings of women whose purpose is to politicize gender and change the power relations between women and men in some respect. When women group, their womanliness will not be the only thing that brings them together; there are other concrete details of their lives that give them affinity—such as their class or race position, their nationality, their neighborhood, their religious affiliation, or the fact that they are teachers of philosophy. For this reason groupings of women will always be partial in relation to the series. Women's groups will be partial in relation to the series also because a group will have particular objectives or purposes that cannot encompass or even refer to the totality of the condition of women as a series. This is why feminist politics must be coalition politics. For the series, as process, as a unity in flight, as a set of structures and practico-inert objects in relation to action, cannot be a totality. Feminism thus will tend to be multiple, and itself cannot be totalized. Feminist organizing and theorizing thus always refers beyond itself to conditions and experiences that have not been reflected on, and to women whose lives are conditioned by enforced heterosexuality and a sexual division of labor who are not feminist and are not part of feminist groups. We should maintain our humility by recognizing that partiality and by remaining open to inquiring about the facts of the series beyond us.

Chapter II

ASYMMETRICAL RECIPROCITY: ON MORAL RESPECT, WONDER, AND ENLARGED THOUGHT

> Perhaps, first of all, however, one must ask oneself,
> in a manner that is in some way absolutely preliminary:
> What is the relation between a language and *giving-taking* in general? The definition of language, of a
> language, as well as of the text in general, cannot
> be formed without a certain relation to the gift, to
> giving-taking and so forth, having been involved
> there in advance.
>
> —Jacques Derrida

IN EVERYDAY moral discourse it is common for people to enjoin one another to think about an issue from the point of view of others before drawing conclusions about what is right or just. Those discussing issues of a just health care policy in the United States, for example, might say that people who now get low-cost health insurance coverage through their place of work should imagine themselves in the situation of those low-wage or part-time workers who receive no health care coverage at all. The injunction to look at an issue from the point of view of others differently situated is often effective in pulling people away from selfishness or parochialism in their reasoning about moral issues. For this reason, the ordinary language appeal "Just look at it from their position" is often an important move in moral discourse where people try to reach conclusions about what is right, good, or just.

When this rough-and-ready appeal to look at issues from the point of view of others is systematized into a moral theory, however, problems may arise. In her elaboration and revision of Habermas's theory of communicative ethics, Seyla Benhabib performs one such systematization. She conceptualizes moral respect as a relation of symmetry between self and other, and she thinks of moral reciprocity as entailing that the perspectives of self and other are reversible. I agree with Benhabib's overall project of elaborating a communicative ethics that recognizes difference and particularity. I argue in this essay, however, that identifying moral respect with a reversibility and symmetry of perspectives impedes that project. It is neither possible nor morally desirable for persons engaged in moral interaction to adopt one another's standpoint.

I develop a concept of *asymmetrical* reciprocity as an alternative to this notion of symmetrical reciprocity developed by Benhabib. A communicative ethics should develop an account of the nonsubstitutable relation of moral subjects. Each participant in a communication situation is distinguished by a particular history and social position that makes their relation asymmetrical. A theory of communication as leading to moral judgment should attend more to the structure of gifts and questions than does Habermas's theory of communication; this structure of gifts and questions expresses the asymmetrical reciprocity between communicating subjects. A communicative theory of moral respect should distinguish between taking the perspective of other people into account, on the one hand, and imaginatively taking their positions, on the other hand. Through dialogue people sometimes understand each other across difference without reversing perspectives or identifying with each other. The distinctive and asymmetrical positioning of people discussing moral or political issues, finally, forms the best basis for understanding why dialogue with others produces what Arendt, following Kant, calls the "enlarged thought" that moves people from their merely subjective understanding of issues to a moral objective judgment.

Moral Respect Conceived as Symmetrical Reciprocity

In her cogent and inspiring book, *Situating the Self*, Seyla Benhabib endorses the basic outlines of Habermas's discourse ethics.[1] She argues with Habermas that modern universalist norms of egalitarian reciprocity make explicit norms embedded in everyday speech. She follows him in seeking to construct an account of relations of moral respect as arising from dialogue in which persons aim to reach understanding.

Benhabib incorporates feminist and postmodern criticisms of Habermas, however, into her formulations of discourse ethics. Habermas believes that universalizable moral norms are generated through a dialogic process in which participants leave behind their particular experiences, perspectives, and feelings. In his version of communicative ethics, the dialogic process leads to the formulation of general principles on which all can agree, whatever their particular experience or point of view. While Benhabib does not reject this standpoint of the "generalized other," she wishes to supplement it with activities of judgment that preserve the "standpoint of the concrete other." She endorses the universality of modern moral theory but insists that it include respect for concrete particular others in their narrative contexts, and not simply adherence to generalized principles that apply to all equally. She invokes Hannah Arendt's notion of enlarged thought, which "enjoins us to view each person as one to whom I owe the moral respect to consider their standpoint" (p. 136).

Habermas shares with Rawls and many other moral theorists the idea that moral dialogue requires people to adopt a standpoint of impartiality toward all particular experiences, and assent to only those principles and judgments that are consistent with that impartial standpoint. Benhabib proposes to arrive at similar results by theorizing that moral subjects reverse their particular standpoints in dialogical moral reasoning. The stance of moral respect, according to Benhabib, arises from putting oneself in the place of others. Equal respect for the situation and point of view of others requires being able to reverse positions with each of them. Benhabib suggests that parents teach children their stance of symmetrical reciprocity whenever they admonish them to imagine how they would feel if another child did that to them.

According to Benhabib, for a person to acknowledge others to be as valuable, morally, as herself means that she understands their positions as symmetrical and reversible.

> Universality enjoins us to reverse perspectives among members of a moral community and judge them from the point of view of the others(s). Such reversibility is essential to the ties of reciprocity that bind communities together. (p. 32)

> All communicative action entails symmetry and reciprocity of normative expectations among group members. (p. 32)

To characterize moral judgment, Benhabib adopts Hannah Arendt's interpretation of Kant's notion of "enlarged thought." Such judgment should not be understood as applying general moral principles to particular cases, she suggests, but more specifically as reflection on the basis of the contextualized narratives of moral subjects. A person is able to make judgments that take the needs and interests of everyone equally into account, according to Benhabib, because she has imaginatively represented to herself the point of view of all those others. The enlarged thought of moral judgment, she says,

> requires for its successful exercise the ability to take the standpoint of the other. . . .The more perspectives we are able to present to ourselves, all the more are we likely to appreciate the possible act-descriptions through which others will identify deeds. Finally, the more we are able to think from the perspective of others, all the more can we make vivid to ourselves the narrative histories of others involved. (p. 137)

With Benhabib, I agree that communicative ethics is a fruitful framework for moral theory, partly because it is so directly linked to the values of democracy. With a communicative ethics I agree that norms of moral respect and egalitarian reciprocity are expressed implicitly in ordinary situations of discussion where people aim to reach understanding. I also endorse the idea that moral and political norms are best tested by actual dialogue in which multiple needs, interests, and perspectives are represented. I agree, moreover, with the direction of Benhabib's critique of Habermas's approach to communicative ethics. With her I wish to develop an account of moral respect and egalitarian reciprocity that depends less than his on unity and consensus and attends more to the specific differences among people. I believe, however, that identifying moral respect and reciprocity with symmetry and reversibility of perspectives tends to close off the differentiation among subjects that Benhabib wants to keep open.

In this essay I criticize the idea that moral respect entails being able to adopt the standpoint of others. Instead of an ideal of symmetrical reciprocity between moral subjects, I offer an ideal of asymmetrical reciprocity. Moral respect between people entails reciprocity between them, in the sense that each acknowledges and takes account of the other. But their relation is asymmetrical in terms of the history each has and the social position they occupy. I offer the practice of giving gifts as an illustration of this asymmetry. From Luce Irigaray I take over the value of wonder in ethical relations, and I suggest that a theory of communicative action should give more attention to questions as a way of expressing moral respect. I argue that the assumption of asymmetrical reciprocity facilitates a better interpretation of Hannah Arendt's notion of "enlarged thought" than an interpretation that assumes the possibility and desirability of taking the standpoint of other people.

THREE STORIES OF IRREVERSIBILITY

Before I develop a conceptual critique of the idea of moral respect as taking the other person's standpoint, I propose to render the idea intuitively problematic through some stories. In each of them some people attempt or claim to take the perspective of others differently situated as an element in their reasoning about a moral issue. As I interpret the stories, in each case the very attempt of some to take the standpoint of others risks not respecting them.

I'd Rather Be Dead Than Crippled

When the state of Oregon first proposed its priorities for state funding of health care services, it denied people with disabilities reimbursement for some treatments or procedures for which it would reimburse able-bodied people. Anita Silvers reports that state officials gave people with disabilities lower priority because they believed the lives of people with disabilities are less important. Officials thought that they had objective grounds for this judgment because they had conducted a telephone survey of Oregon citizens as a means of determining the qualitative grounds for their priorities. Among other things, this survey of able-bodied people asked them to put themselves in the situation of a person in a wheelchair, or a blind or deaf person. The majority of respondents said that they would rather be dead than wheelchair-bound or blind. They said that their lives would not be worth living if they became disabled. This claim was the grounds for a political judgment that health services for people with disabilities would not be subsidized in the same way as those for able-bodied people. Because these regulations were found to violate the Americans with Disabilities Act, eventually they had to be changed.[2]

Silvers points out that the actual statistics of suicide among people with disabilities are rather low. People with disabilities usually think that their lives are quite worth living, and they strongly wish to have discriminatory impediments removed so they can live those lives as well as possible. Generally speaking, able-bodied people simply fail to understand the lives and issues of people with disabilities. When asked to put themselves in the position of a person in a wheelchair, they do not imagine the point of view of others; rather, they project onto those others their own fears and fantasies about themselves. Thus, more often than not, well-meaning, able-bodied people seeking to understand and communicate with a disabled person express the patronizing attitudes of pity that so enrage many people with disabilities.[3] As I will discuss later, with careful listening able-bodied people can learn to understand important aspects of the lives and perspective of people with disabilities. This is a very different matter from imaginatively occupying their standpoint, however, and may require explicit acknowledgment of the impossibility of such a reversal.

"Going Native"

Since the time of their first European contacts, the indigenous peoples of North America have been constructed by whites as romanticized figures. The white imagination of the Indian is of course complex, contradictory, and variable. One rather stable image is of the Indian as a noble authentic relation to nature, with a deep and meaningful social, cultural, and religious life. The Indian is noble, strong, blessed, and whole, in contrast to the fragmentation, mechanism, and commercialism characteristic of life in white society.[4]

Some white people seek to see the world from the perspective of a particular Indian group. Some wish to know their stories, songs, and rituals, and some wish to practice those rituals themselves. According to a report on National Public Radio aired in the fall of 1993, some white Americans are practicing religious rituals derived from the Lakota. The movement has become so popular that when some Lakota recently climbed one of their traditional sacred mountains in the Black Hills to perform a fall ceremony, a large group of white devotees was already encamped there. Some of the Indians interviewed expressed sadness more than anger; they insisted that however sincerely the whites wish to see the world from an Indian perspective and perform rituals properly, they cannot adopt an Indian standpoint because they lack the personal and group history.

More generally, many Indians are suspicious of white efforts to take their standpoint, reverse perspectives with them, because they believe that such a desire is at least partly motivated by a fanciful longing to compensate for a perceived cultural poverty of white society. If whites sometimes wish to enter Indian culture because of their own romanticization of Indians as having a "richer" culture, then white desire to understand an Indian perspective may be a form of cultural imperialism. Many Indians would prefer a stance of respectful distance in which whites acknowledge that they cannot reverse perspectives with Indians today and thus must listen carefully across this distance.

Getting It

When Anita Hill claimed she had been sexually harassed by Clarence Thomas, many men, including several senators questioning her, did not believe her. How could she have experienced the violations and indignities she claims and not have filed any complaint at the time, continued to work with the perpetrator, and even gone with him to another position? Men who put themselves in Hill's alleged position knew that they would never have remained silent and compliant. But many women told these men that they just did not "get it," that their sexual privilege prevents them from understanding the reasoning and motives of an ambitious career woman being sexually harassed by her boss.

Many white feminists claimed that they did "get it," and claimed Anita Hill as a martyr for feminism. They were baffled when some African American women denied the ability of white feminists to take Hill's standpoint; at least on issues of sexual harassment, many white feminists thought, women's interests and experiences are symmetrical. But even many African American women who believed Hill were nevertheless sympathetic to Thomas's claim that he was being subject to a "high-tech lynching." For them, unlike for many white feminists, the case did not concern sexual harassment "pure and simple," but a complex racial drama in which once again white society was acting out its fears and

power struggles through the body of a black man. There are certainly
dynamics of sexual privilege between African American men and
women, but when these come before a white public they are so intertwined with the dynamics of racism that other women simply cannot take
the perspective of African American women.

CRITIQUE OF THE IDEA OF SYMMETRICAL RECIPROCITY

I develop three arguments against the claim that moral respect requires
that each of us should take the perspectives of all the others in making
our moral judgments. First, this idea of a symmetry in our relation obscures the difference and particularity of the other position. Second, it
is ontologically impossible for people in one social position to adopt the
perspective of those in the social positions with which they are related in
social structures and interaction. The idea that moral respect involves
taking the other people's point of view, finally, can have politically undesirable consequences.

Obscures Difference

The ideas of symmetry and reversibility that Benhabib relies on evoke
images of mirror reflection. The images of symmetry and reversibility
suggest that people are able to understand one another's perspectives
because, while not identical, they are similarly shaped, and for that reason replaceable with one another. The mirroring evoked by the ideas of
symmetry and reversibility suggests that we are able to understand one
another because we are able to see ourselves reflected in the other people and find that they see themselves reflected in us. But such images of
reflection and substitutability, I suggest, support a conceptual projection
of sameness among people and perspectives, at the expense of their
differences.

In *Speculum of the Other Woman*, Luce Irigaray warns against what she
calls "the blind spot of an old dream of symmetry." Specifically with reference to sexual difference, she suggests that the desire for a symmetrical relation with another person denies the other's difference. The gender system structuring Western culture and philosophy presents the
feminine others as *complementing* the masculine subject position, creating
for it a wholeness, completeness, and return to origins. Woman functions as a mirror in which the male subject can see himself objectified,
bounded, and determinate. In the specular relation of phallocentric
logic the self puts himself in the place of the other in order to return
reflectively to himself. But this circular relation displaces and silences
the other as she might speak in a different, incommensurate register.[5]

Irigaray's argument refers specifically to sexual difference. It can easily be extended, however, to any structured social difference, whether of sex, class, race, or religion. People who are different in such social positionings are not so totally other that they can see no similarities and overlaps in their lives, and they often stand in multivalent relations with one another. It makes little sense, however, to describe their similarities and relations as symmetrical, as mirroring one another or reversible.

Much of my argument in this essay refers to the difficulties of reversing positions across such socially structured difference, which also usually involves relations of privilege and oppression. A similar logic applies, however, to the differences among individuals in which structured social difference is not so obvious. While individuals may have many things they take to be comparable among them, they could rarely be said to share everything. Even when they find their relations defined by similarly socially structured differences of gender, race, class, nation, or religion, individuals usually also find many ways in which they are strange to one another. Individuals bring different life histories, emotional habits, and life plans to relationships, which make their positions irreversible.[6] It closes off the creative exchange these differences might produce with one another if we consider them symmetrical and suggest that despite serious divergences in their experiences and values, one person can put herself in the place of another.[7]

As Irigaray's analysis suggests, moreover, the result of the effort to see others as symmetrical with myself may sometimes be that I project onto them a perspective that complements my own. The perspective of the other can too easily be represented as the self's other represented to itself—its fantasies, desires, and fears. As Melissa Orlie puts it, "When one presumes to adopt another perspective without reflection on the boundaries of one's own *body* and location, more often than not one simply imposes the view from there upon another. Indeed, this is a principal way of bolstering one's location and demonstrates the effects involved in doing so. In such cases, one's own view arrogates another's and thus threatens to violate or do away with it altogether."[8]

I suggest that such projection happened in each of the cases I narrate above. As Benhabib herself says, the only correction to such misrepresentation of the standpoint of others is their ability to tell me that I am wrong about them.

Neither the concreteness nor the otherness of the "concrete other" can be known in the absence of the *voice* of the other. The viewpoint of the concrete other emerges as distinct only as a result of self-definition. It is the other who makes us aware of both her concreteness and her otherness. Without engagement, confrontation, dialogue and even a "struggle for recognition," in the Hegelian sense, we tend to constitute the otherness of the other by projection and fantasy or ignore it in indifference. (p. 168)

If the best expression of moral respect is willingness to listen to others express their needs and perspectives, however, then why do we need the idea that moral respect requires being able to imagine oneself in the position of others?

Impossibility of Reversing Positions

Benhabib appeals to a Hegelian logic of the relation of self and other to explicate the meaning of reversing perspective. "To know how to sustain an ongoing human relationship," she says,

means to know what it means to be an "I" and a "me," to know that I am an "other" to you and that, likewise, you are an "I" to yourself and an "other" to me. Hegel had named this structure that of "reciprocal recognition." Communicative actions are actions through which we sustain such human relationships. The development of this capacity for reversing perspectives and the development of the capacity to assume the moral point of view are intimately linked. (p. 52)

I believe that this passage, interpreted in light of the earlier cited passage on reversibility, wrongly reduces reciprocal recognition to an ontological concept of a reversibility of standpoints. To recognize the other person is to acknowledge that she is an "I" to herself just as I am an "I" to myself and that I am an "other" to her just as she is an "other" to me. This structure of reciprocal recognition is indeed a condition of communicative action. But this structure neither describes nor presupposes a reversibility of standpoints. In fact, it precludes such reversibility because it describes how each standpoint is constituted by its internal relations to other standpoints.

The theory of subjectivity Benhabib refers to in this passage holds that each person's identity is a product of her interactive relations with others. Through my interaction with others I experience how I am an "other" for them, and I internalize this objectification to myself through others in the formulation of my own self-conception. By this knowledge that they have a perspective on me that is different from my immediate experience of myself, I experience them as subjects, as "I"s. This relation of self and other, however, is specifically *asymmetrical* and *irreversible*, even though it is reciprocal.

The reciprocal recognition by which I know that I am other for you just as you are other for me cannot entail a reversibility of perspectives, precisely because our positions are partly constituted by the perspectives each of us has on the others. Think of the relation of mother and daughter. Mother and daughter usually share social positions of gender, race, class, nation, and so on. They often have much in common in their tastes, experiences, and opinions. The relation of mother and daughter is nevertheless asymmetrical and irreversible, in at least two respects. First, the asymmetry of age and generation give each a different perspective on their common world and their relationship. Second, their relationship is itself internally constituted by the asymmetry of positioning between them and the desires and projections that produces. While they may be very close, mother and daughter are also strange to one another, surprised at how it seems they are for the other.

Who we are is constituted to a considerable extent by the relations in which we stand to others, along with our past experience of our relations with others. Thus the standpoint of each of us in a particular situation is partly a result of our experience of the other people's perspectives on us. It is hard to see how any of us could suspend our perspective mediated by our relations to others, in order to adopt their perspectives mediated by their relation to us. The infinity of the dialectical process of selves in relation to others both makes it impossible to suspend our own positioning and leaves an excess of experiences when I try to put myself in the other person's place.[9]

It is true that one of the important moral lessons I learn from an encounter with other people is how I look to them, and this knowledge can carry me beyond my immediate standpoint. It does not carry me into the standpoint of the other person, however, but only into a mediated relation between us. I do not think that we want to characterize our mediated perspectival encounter as each of us reversing positions with the others, because this neglects to conceptualize the relation between us. In the last section I shall argue that taking account of the relation among perspectives, as well as of the perspectives, yields the best interpretation of the "enlarged thought" that moral judgment involves.

Politically Suspect

My final criticism of the idea that moral respect in dialogical interaction involves taking the other's point of view is a political argument. Many contexts of moral interaction and political conflict involve members of socially and culturally differentiated groups that also stand in specific relations of privilege and oppression with respect to one another. In

these contexts the social position of one group is defined by its differentiation from another or others, and where those are relations of privilege
and oppression, this is also part of the definition. Earlier I argued that
the idea of reversing perspectives is incoherent because each perspective
is partly constituted by the response to the perspectives of other perspectives on it. Where the perspectives are also constituted by relations of
privilege and oppression, it is even more difficult to envision that one of
these perspectives can take the perspective of the other.

In each of the examples I narrated above, those who attempt to adopt
the standpoint of others stand in a relation of social privilege to those
whose perspective they claim to adopt.

As I suggested earlier, when people obey the injunction to put themselves in the position of others, they too often put *themselves*, with their
own particular experiences and privileges, in the positions they see the
others. When privileged people put themselves in the position of those
who are less privileged, the assumptions derived from their privilege often allow them unknowingly to misrepresent the other's situation.

The social fact of structural privilege and oppression, moreover, creates the possibility of falsifying projection. Damaging stereotypes and
ideologies often mediate between relations between men and women,
between Christians and Muslims, between European Americans and African Americans. These ideologies and images often function to legitimate the privileges of the privileged groups and to undermine the self-
respect of those in oppressed groups. When members of privileged
groups imaginatively try to represent to themselves the perspective of
members of oppressed groups, too often those representations carry
projections and fantasies through which the privileged reinforce a complementary image of themselves.

The idea of reversing perspectives assumes that the perspectives
brought to a situation are equally legitimate. Where structured social
injustice exists, this may not be true. The perspective of those who maintain privilege under an unjust status quo does not have legitimacy in the
same way as that of those who suffer the injustices. Even under conditions of injustice, the interests and perspectives of those who belong to
privileged groups should not be disregarded; moral respect does require
that everyone's perspective be taken into account. But asking the oppressed to reverse perspectives with the privileged in adjudicating a
conflict may itself be an injustice and an insult.

The injunction to take the other person's standpoint is supposed to
aid communication. It may in fact impede it, however. If you think you
already know how the other people feel and judge because you have
imaginatively represented their perspective to yourself, then you may

not listen to their expression of their perspective very openly. If you think you can look at things from their point of view, then you may avoid the sometimes arduous and painful process in which they confront you with your prejudices, fantasies, and misunderstandings about them, which you have because of your point of view. If you enter a dialogue with all the best intentions of taking the other people's perspectives, and then in the course of the discussion they express anger and frustration at you for misunderstanding their position, you are likely to become defensive and shut down the dialogue. It is more appropriate to approach a situation of communicative interaction for the purpose of arriving at a moral or political judgment with a stance of moral humility. In moral humility one starts with the assumption that one cannot see things from the other person's perspective and waits to learn by listening to the other person to what extent they have had similar experiences.[10] If I assume that there are aspects of where the other person is coming from that I do not understand, I will be more likely to be open to listening to the specific expression of their experience, interests, and claims. Indeed, one might say that this is what listening to a person means.

ASYMMETRICAL RECIPROCITY

I agree with Benhabib that communicative ethics is a fruitful framework for moral theory, partly because it is so directly linked to the values of democracy. I agree that norms of moral respect and egalitarian reciprocity are expressed implicitly in ordinary situations of discussion where people aim to reach understanding. I also endorse the idea that moral and political norms are best tested by actual dialogue in which multiple needs, interests, and perspectives are best represented. I agree, moreover, with the direction of Benhabib's critique of Habermas's approach to communicative ethics. I wish to develop an account of moral respect and egalitarian reciprocity, however, that uses a language and concepts that more precisely express the specific differences among people than do identifying terms like symmetry, reversibility, and imaginatively occupying the position of others.

Thus I propose to understand communicative action as involving an *asymmetrical reciprocity* among subjects, rather than the symmetrical reciprocity Benhabib theorizes. Moral respect does indeed entail *reciprocity*. Communicating parties mutually recognize one another. In a stance of moral respect, each party must recognize that others have irreducible points of view, and active interests that respectful interaction must consider. Free social cooperation requires that each acknowledge that the others are ends in themselves and not means only. Such mutual acknowledgment is the meaning of moral equality.

This reciprocity of equal respect and acknowledgment of one another, however, entails an acknowledgment of an *asymmetry* between subjects. While there may be many similarities and points of contact between them, each position and perspective transcends the others, goes beyond their possibility to share or imagine. Participants in communicative interaction are in a relation of approach. They meet across distance of time and space and can touch, share, overlap their interests. But each brings to the relationships a history and structured positioning that makes them different from one another, with their own shape, trajectory, and configuration of forces.

I derive the idea of asymmetrical reciprocity from a reading of both Emmanuel Levinas's and Luce Irigaray's understanding of ethical relations between people. Levinas criticizes the philosophical impulse to reduce the communicative relation between ethical subjects to a common measure or comparability. While comparing the situation and desert of agents according to some standard of equality is ultimately necessary for theorizing justice, prior to such comparison there is a moment of respect for the particular embodied sensitivity of the person. In this moment of recognition other people's concrete positions are asymmetrical. While people may be in touch and their communication may construct relationships of similarity or solidarity between them, their positions are nevertheless irreducible and irreversible. The ethical relation is also asymmetrical in the sense that opening onto the other person is always a *gift*; the trust to communicate cannot await the other person's promise to reciprocate, or the conversation will never begin.[11]

In *The Ethics of Sexual Difference*, Irigaray speaks of the need for an *interval* separating self and others in order for them to meet and communicate. I understand the ethic of sexual difference as a paradigm of subject differentiation and specificity of any sort. This ethical relation is structured not by a willingness to reverse positions with others, but by respectful distancing from and approach toward them. Speakers cannot communicate unless there is a space differentiating them and across which they communicate. Nancy Love suggests that we conceptualize reaching understanding as a mode of being with rather than being in one another's place, and that we take seriously metaphors of voice rather than metaphors of sight evoked by symmetry: "Individuals cannot 'stand inside' another's world and adopt their 'worldview,' nor should they try to do so. However, they can communicate across the distance and their differences. Voice crosses, even while it respects, boundaries."[12]

Communication is a creative enterprise that presupposes an irreplace-ability of each person's perspective, so that each learns something new, beyond herself or himself, from interaction with the others. Quoting from Irigaray: "The *interval* would never be *crossed*. . . . One sex is not entirely consumable by the other. There is always a *remainder*."[13] And, "the *locomotion toward* and *reduction in interval* are the moments of desire (even by expansion-interaction). The greater the desire, the greater the tendency to overcome the interval while at the same time retaining it."[14]

Thus I propose at least two important ways that the perspectives of subjects are asymmetrical. First, each has its own *temporality*. Irigaray's description of the interval should be heard as involving time as well as space. Each subject position has its own history, which transcends the copresence of subjects in communication. Each person brings to a communication situation the particular experiences, assumptions, meanings, symbolic associations, and so on, that emerge from a particular history, most of which lies as background to the communicating situation. One person can relate some of his or her history to another, thus bringing the other to understand more of what he or she is assuming and what particular ideas and situations mean in the context of his or her history. But that history is inexhaustible, always subject to possible retelling in new contexts. For this reason and because of its temporal difference, one person cannot adopt another person's perspective because he or she cannot live another person's history. To the extent that groups define an identity through constructing a history, the same is true of relations among groups.

In the context of the story I told above, for example, history is a major source of asymmetry between European Americans and Native Americans. Most Native Americans carry a different cultural and religious history than do European Americans, even though for most there is also considerable overlap with the recent history of European Americans. Many Native Americans have grown up seeing certain rituals and practices performed, and their elders have tied these rituals and practices to a group history tracing these rituals and practices to particular places, and to a group history tracing back many generations. While some Native Americans have less direct connection with traditional rituals and practices, their elders have told them mythical and real stories that connect them with Indian histories. Even if hegemonic culture did not operate to segregate some knowledge of these Native histories from other Americans, European Americans would still be distant from the socializing experience of such personal and group history.

Second, asymmetry refers also to the specificity of *position*. As I discussed earlier with regard to the Hegelian ontology of self and other, each social position is structured by the configuration of relationships among positions. Persons may flow and shift among structured social positions, and the positions themselves may flow and shift, but the positions cannot be plucked from their contextualized relations and substituted for one another. The image of a reversibility of positions may assume an unfortunate binarism: it is either one or the other. If we recognize that subject positions and perspectives are multiply structured in relation to many other positions, however, the specificity and irreversibility of each location is more obvious. Thus the Hill-Thomas example offers the overdetermination of such multiple positions, each of which is defined partly by its relation to the others, and thus none of which is reversible with any of the others: African American man in relation to white ruling-class man, working-class African American woman in relation to professional African American woman, white middle-class woman in relation to African American professional woman, and so on. The Hill-Thomas situation is structured by the relation among all these positions at once. Thus there are many perspectives on its meaning, none of which can be substituted for the others.

UNDERSTANDING ACROSS DIFFERENCE

The purpose of theorizing moral respect as involving people putting themselves in one another's places is to give an account of how we can understand one another, so that we can take one another's perspective into account when making moral judgments. But I have argued that we cannot put ourselves in one another's places, and that trying to do so may sometimes lead to misunderstanding. It would seem to follow from this argument that we cannot understand each other. Thus it would seem that there is no point in trying to take account of the perspective of others in making moral and political judgments. I do not believe, however, that my argument leads to this conclusion.[15] Understanding across difference is both possible and necessary. Recognizing the asymmetry of subjects, however, does imply giving a different account of what understanding is and what makes it possible.

We often think that understanding another person's point of view or situation involves finding things in common between us. I listen to the other person, or observe his or her interactions and environment, and then I compare this with my own experience to find similarity. Sometimes to find the similarity I must take my experience apart and put it together in a different way, or I must draw inferences from my experience. But the way I come to understand the other person is by constructing identification and reversibility between us, which means I am never really transcending my own experience.

But we can interpret understanding others as sometimes getting out of ourselves and learning something new. Communication is sometimes a creative process in which the other person offers a new expression, and I understand it not because I am looking for how it fits with given paradigms, but because I am open and suspend my assumptions in order to listen.[16] Sometimes communication that reaches understanding is like a game in which people make new moves that cannot be anticipated by the rules, but which are understood as part of the game and carry it forward.[17] Other people offer me new variations, new modalities on some practice or action or situation that is related to but beyond my experience. They explain to me their aims and presuppositions and events that have happened to them, and I come to understand their valuation because they have explained to me these aims and presuppositions. In the next section I invoke the idea of wonder to describe being open to something new.

Thus the ethical relation of asymmetrical reciprocity looks like this. We meet and communicate. We mutually recognize one another and aim to understand one another. Each is open to such understanding by recognizing our asymmetry. A condition of our communication is that we acknowledge the difference, interval, that others drag behind them shadows and histories, scars and traces, that do not become present in our communication. Thus we each must be open to learning about the other person's perspective, since we cannot take the other person's standpoint and imagine that perspective as our own. This implies that we have the moral humility to acknowledge that even though there may be much I do understand about the other person's perspective through her communication to me and through the constructions we have made common between us, there is also always a remainder, much that I do not understand about the other person's experience and perspective.

I can listen to a person in a wheelchair explain her feelings about her work, frustrations she has with transportation access. Her descriptions of her life and the relation of her physical situation to the social possibilities available to her will point out aspects of her situation that I would not have thought of without her explanation. In this way I come to an understanding of her point of view. I can even spend a day living in a wheelchair in order better to understand the difficulties and social position of a person in a wheelchair. The more I understand about the multiple aspects of her life, the differences and similarities between her life and mine, however, the more I should also understand that there is a great deal I do not understand, because we are so differently socially positioned. Understanding the other person's perspective as a result of her expression to me and my inferences from that expression thus continue to carry my humble recognition that I cannot put myself in her position.

GIFT-GIVING, COMMUNICATION, AND WONDER

Let me refer to gift-giving to illustrate the meaning of asymmetrical reciprocity. Gift-giving is basic to the generation of normative structures in most societies, precisely because it establishes relations of reciprocity: I give a gift to you, and you give a gift to me, or the opening is made for you to give a gift to me. There is an equality and mutual recognition in the relation of gift-giving, but of a different order from the equality of contracts and exchange. When I give a gift this begins a process, makes an opening, whereby you may give me a gift in return, but if I consider that you "owe" me, the gift relation is effaced and has become a commercial exchange. As Jacques Derrida puts it in his quarrel with Mauss's interpretation of the gift relation as ultimately an exchange relation, "For there to be a gift, there must be no reciprocity, return, exchange, countergift or debt. If the other *gives* me *back* or *owes* me or has to give me back what I give him or her, there will not have been a gift, whether this relation is immediate or whether it is programmed by a complex calculation of a long-term deferral or difference."[18]

The relation of gift-giving is an asymmetrical reciprocity in at least two ways. First, the gifts are not equivalent and cannot be reduced to relations of symmetrical equivalence, in the manner of objects of commodity exchange. If you give me a gift, and I give you back the same gift, you are affronted. If I give you the same kind of thing that you have given me, this is uncreative; it does not take our relation further. If you treat your gift to me as the repayment of a debt owed, then this too is ungenerous and endangers our bond. The gift, is a unique offering. The only proper response is acceptance. The relation of offering and acceptance is asymmetrical; I do not return, I accept. If later I give you a gift, it is a new offering, with its own asymmetry.

Second, the moments of gift-giving are separated by time. This is an important meaning of the *interval* Irigaray refers to in the relation between self and other. Gift-giving sets up a chain where the reciprocal bond endures precisely because of the asymmetry of time between gifts. Each moment of gift-giving opens onto a future of our relationships, precisely because there is not a simultaneity of exchange.

> The difference between a gift and every other operation of pure and simple exchange is that the gift gives time. Where there is the gift, there is time. What it gives, the gift, is time, but this gift of time is also a demand of time. The thing must not be restituted immediately and right away. There must be time, it must last, there must be waiting—without forgetting. It demands time, the thing, but it demands a delimited time, neither an instant nor an

infinite time, but a time determined by a term, in order words, a rhythm, a cadence. The thing is not *in* time; it is or has time, or rather it demands to have, to give, or to take time.[19]

You surprise me with a gift of quince marmalade; we visit for a short while in my kitchen. Several weeks later I drop by your house with a loaf of cranberry bread, and we visit some more. We have "exchanged" gifts, created or reaffirmed a reciprocity between us. But there is no measure of equivalence between the marmalade and the bread; they are qualitatively different. The temporal interval makes each act of giving, moreover, an opening rather than the closing of a deal. The equality that our relation of giving creates between us is produced by this substantive and temporal difference which I here call asymmetry.

This account of everyday gift-giving resonates for a theory of communicative action. According to Habermas, the social bond produced by communication occurs not through the locutionary content of what is said, but through the illocutionary acts that accompany that substance. Every speech act that aims at understanding entails an *offer* by the speaker to make good on its meaning, and the understanding of the speech act entails an *acceptance* of that offer by a listener. These illocutionary gestures of offering and accepting meanings create and sustain the social bond.[20] I suggest that we interpret this structure of reciprocity in communicative action as asymmetrical in the same way as gift-giving. The listener who has understood and accepted the meaning of a speaker responds appropriately. This appropriate response, however, cannot usually be seen as symmetrical with the first speaker's speech. I respond to your statement not by saying the same thing back to you, but by making another, different, move in our language game.

In his theory of communicative action, Habermas gives little attention to the role of questions in fostering bonds of solidarity. His theory focuses on the role of statements in reference to objective, social, and subjective worlds, and the illocutionary force with which those statements are made. By contrast, a theory of communicative action that gave more attention to the asymmetry of speakers, to the ways in which there are always excesses and resistances despite overlaps in the speakers' interests and understandings, would attend more to questions as uniquely important communicative acts. Questions can express a distinctive form of respect for the other, that of showing an interest in their expression and acknowledging that the questioner does not know what the issue looks like for them.

The idea that moral respect entails that I reverse perspectives with the other presumes that I can comprehend and identify with the other person's situation and perspective. It assumes that we can be familiar to one another. Certainly communication and moral respect require some sense of mutual identification and sharing. But without also a moment of *wonder*, of openness to the newness and mystery of the other person, the creative energy of desire dissolves into indifference. Irigaray offers the stance of wonder as an alternative interpretation of the attitude of moral respect.

> Wonder which beholds what it sees always as if for the first time, never taking hold of the other as its object. It does not try to seize, possess, or reduce this object, but leaves it subjective, still free.[21]

> This first passion is indispensable not only to life but also or still to the creation of an ethics. Notably of and through sexual difference. This other, male or female, should *surprise* us again and again, appear to us as *new, very different* from what we know or what we thought he or she should be.
>
> Which means that we would look at the other, stop to look at him or her, ask ourselves, come close to ourselves through questioning. *Who art thou? I am* and *I become* thanks to this question. Wonder goes beyond that which is or is not suitable for us. The other never suits us simply. We would in some way have reduced the other to ourselves if he or she suited us completely. An *excess* resists: the other's existence and becoming as a place that permits union and/through resistance to assimilation or reduction to sameness.[22]

This concept of wonder is dangerous. It would not be difficult to use it to imagine the other person as exotic. One can interpret wonder as a kind of distant awe before the Other that turns their transcendence into an inhuman inscrutability. Or wonder can become a kind of prurient curiosity. I can recognize my ignorance about the other person's experience and perspective and adopt a probing, investigative mode toward her. Both stances convert the openness of wonder into a dominative desire to know and master the other person.

A respectful stance of wonder toward other people is one of openness across, awaiting new insight about their needs, interests, perceptions, or values. Wonder also means being able to see one's own position, assumptions, perspective as strange, because it has been put in relation to others. Since the other person is a subject-in-process, I cannot assume that because last week I understood her standpoint I can do so today. Respectful listening thus involves attentive and interested questioning. But answers are always gifts. The transcendence of the other person always means that she can remain silent, or tell only part of her story, for her own reasons.[23]

ENLARGED THOUGHT

Benhabib adapts Hannah Arendt's version of Kant's notion of "enlarged thought" to characterize moral judgment. A moral point of view requires a person to think about a question or proposed action not only in terms of how an issue or action affects him or her, but also in terms of what others want or need and how they may be affected. Modern moral theory most typically interprets this moral point of view as a "view from nowhere" that transcends all particular points of view. Benhabib rejects this transcendent notion of impartiality, however, in favor of the idea of an enlarged thought in which a person thinks from the particular standpoint of all those involved or affected in a moral judgment: "Judgment involves the capacity to represent to oneself the multiplicity of viewpoints, the variety of perspectives, the layers of meaning which constitute a situation. . . .This 'enlarged mentality' can be described precisely as exercising the reversibility of perspectives which discourse ethics enjoins."[24]

In a recent interpretation of Arendt's notion of publicity, Lisa Disch also understands the idea of enlarged thought as constituting a process in which the person judging imagines what the world looks like from other perspectives.[25] Kant's original use of the concept of enlarged thought, on which Arendt relies, explicitly invokes the image of taking the point of view of everyone.[26] Passages in Arendt certainly cohere with this interpretation of the meaning of enlarged thought. But I suggest that there are two problems with this interpretation of the idea of enlarged thought, and that another interpretation is more consistent with at least some of Arendt's ideas.

The concept of enlarged thought is supposed to explain how a person moves from a narrowly subjective, self-regarding perspective on action to a more objective and socially inclusive view. Interpreting enlarged thought as occupying the standpoints of each of the others affected, however, does not yet move from a subjective point of view to a more objective one. When we try to represent a multiplicity of viewpoints to ourselves, we have merely aggregated a series of subjective and self-regarding perspectives, rather than adopting a new, more objective thinking derived from them all. If we represent to ourselves all the perspectives, we still have not represented that upon which these are perspectives.

Second, the idea of taking the standpoint of all the others presumes the possibility of an identification among us all, that we can represent others to ourselves in the sense that we can be substitutable for one another. As I discussed in criticizing the claim that moral respect involves

symmetry, this assumption of reversibility tends to collapse the difference between subjects. As an interpretation of enlarged thought, it thus
fails to emphasize the *plurality* of perspectives that Arendt found constitutive of publicity.

Publicity in Arendt's sense is maintained only if the plurality of perspectives that constitutes it is preserved. The people who appear to one
another in a public situation of communication each have a perspective
on the world that lies between them, as well as on one another. The
public world that lies between us is a creative product of the dialogue
among our multiple perspectives, but distinct from them because it is an
objective relation between us. Arendt puts it this way:

> To live together in the world means essentially that a world of things is
> between those who have it in common, as a table is located between those
> who sit around it. The world, like every in-between, relates and separates
> men at the same time.

> For though the common world is the common meeting ground for all,
> those who are present have different positions on it, and the location of one
> can no more coincide with the location of another than the location of the
> two objects.[27]

Dialogue with one another not only teaches us about the narrative
histories and interests of each of the others. Through it we also construct
an account of the web of social relations that surrounds us and within
which we act. This collective social reality cannot be known or understood from the particular point of view of any one of us alone. Nor can
it be constructed simply by adding the perspectives of each of us together, and having each of us think from the perspectives of all the others, whatever that might mean. In addition to the experiences and interests of each of us, this social reality includes the worldly consequences of
our acting on the basis of our experiences and interests as they affect the
physical processes of the world and also condition one another's perceptions and possibilities. Understanding what Arendt calls the "'web' of
human relations," (p. 183) which both relates and separates us, then,
means reasoning about the connected implications of the actions and
effects on one another that multiple narratives and critical questioning
reveal to us. Melissa Orlie recommends an interpretation of Arendt's
notion of publicity along these lines:

> According to Arendt, contact between human beings facilitates the appear-
> ance of both commonality and plurality. Where people speak and act to-
> gether politically, such spaces engender and sustain whatever perception of
> commonality we achieve. This in turn facilitates recognition of our distinct-
> ness from other persons and the revelation of individual uniqueness or

"natality." Paradoxically, the perception of commonality creates boundaries, or at least a capacity to recognize boundaries as well as connections between oneself and others. If political community is absent or unimaginable, then not only what we potentially share with others but also what distinguishes us from them (our distinct perspectives upon and locations within the world) become precarious.[28]

We make our moral and political judgments, then, not only by taking account of one another's interests and perspectives, but also by considering the collective social processes and relationships that lie between us and which we have come to know together by discussing the world. I suggest that this is a better interpretation of the idea of enlarged thought. [29]

Just because social life consists of plural experiences and perspectives, a theory of communicative ethics must endorse a radically democratic conception of moral and political judgment. Normative judgment is best understood as the product of dialogue under conditions of equality and mutual respect. Ideally, the outcome of such dialogue and judgment is just and legitimate only if all the affected perspectives have a voice. If it were possible for agents to reverse perspective with one another in making moral judgments, this condition that all voices and perspectives should be represented might not be necessary.

I have suggested that in order to attend to particularity in this way, it is necessary to distinguish between taking the perspective of others into account in making moral judgments, on the one hand, and reversing positions with them, on the other. Dialogue participants are able to take account of the perspective of others because they have heard those perspectives expressed. They have had to listen to those expressions with a moral humility that recognizes that they stand in relations of asymmetry and irreversibility with others. By means of openness and questioning, as well as efforts to express experience and values from different perspectives, people sometimes understand one another across difference, even when they do not identify with each other. Through such dialogue that recognizes the asymmetry of others, moreover, people can enlarge their thinking in at least two ways. Their own assumptions and point of view become relativized for them as they are set in relation to those of others. By learning from others how the world and the collective relations they have forged through interaction look to them, moreover, everyone can develop an enlarged understanding of that world and those relations that is unavailable to any of them from their own perspective alone.

Chapter III

COMMUNICATION AND THE OTHER: BEYOND DELIBERATIVE DEMOCRACY

A NUMBER of political and legal theorists in recent years have promoted a concept of deliberative democracy as an alternative to an interest-based theory of democracy. In this essay I endorse such a discussion-based ideal of democracy. I find two problems, however, with the way this ideal is usually articulated. First, by restricting their concept of democratic discussion narrowly to critical argument, most theorists of deliberative democracy assume a culturally biased conception of discussion that tends to silence or devalue some people or groups. Deliberative theorists, moreover, tend inappropriately to assume that processes of discussion that aim to reach understanding must either begin with shared understandings or take a common good as their goal.

After exploring these shortcomings of the ideal of deliberative democracy as usually formulated, I propose some revisions to this approach to democratic theory, which I call communicative democracy.[1] First, I propose that we understand differences of culture, social perspective, or particularist commitment as resources to draw on for reaching understanding in democratic discussion rather than as divisions that must be overcome. Second, I propose an expanded conception of democratic communication. Greeting, rhetoric, and storytelling are forms of communication that in addition to argument contribute to political discussion.

THE MODEL OF DELIBERATIVE DEMOCRACY

Theorists of deliberative democracy usually contrast their view with what I shall call the interest-based model of democracy.[2] Interest-based conceptions of democracy consider democracy primarily as a process of expressing one's preferences and demands, and registering them in a vote. The goal of democratic decision-making is to decide what leaders, rules, and policies will best serve the greatest number of people, where each person defines his or her own interests. In the process of democratic decision-making, individuals and interest groups determine and vote for policies that will best serve their own perceived interests, including in their calculations the knowledge that the others in the polity do the same. Democratic decisions are the outcome of successful completion of ideas and coalitions for self-interested votes.

Deliberative critics of the interest-based model of democracy object to what they perceive as its irrationality and its privatized understanding of the political process. In this model, citizens never need to leave their own private and parochial pursuits and recognize their fellows in a public setting to address one another about their collective, as distinct from individual, needs and goals. Each citizen may reason about the best means for achieving his or her own privately defined ends, but the aggregate outcome has no necessary rationality and itself has not been arrived at by a process of reasoning.[3] People need not leave their own subjective point of view to take a more objective or general view of political issues. Thus the interest-based model of democracy also presumes that people cannot make claims on others about justice or the public good and defend those claims with reasons.[4]

By contrast, the model of deliberative democracy conceives of democracy as a process that creates a public, citizens coming together to talk about collective problems, goals, ideals, and actions. Democratic processes are oriented around discussing this common good rather than competing for the promotion of the private good of each. Instead of reasoning from the point of view of the private utility maximizer, through public deliberation citizens transform their preferences according to public-minded ends, and reason together about the nature of those ends and the best means to realize them. In free and open dialogue others test and challenge these assertions and reasons. Participants are careful to sort out good reasons from bad reasons, valid arguments from invalid. The interlocutors properly discount bad reasons and speeches that are not well argued, and they ignore or discount rhetorical flourishes and emotional outbursts. Putting forward and criticizing claims and arguments, participants in deliberation do not rest until the "force of the better argument" compels them all to accept a conclusion.

I agree with these critics of an interest-based model of democracy that it is better to have a conception of democracy that understands politics as the meeting of people to decide public ends and policies in a rational way. Though the interest-based model of democracy corresponds most to current practice and attitudes in contemporary Western democracies, norms of public reason sometimes do appear in the actual processes of liberal democracies as we know them. Such deliberative democracy appears most often in our current experience in the decision-making structures of voluntary associations outside the state. But processes of state policy formation in legislatures or public hearings sometimes exhibit features of the deliberative model. To the degree that contemporary democracies discourage deliberation and encourage a privatized consumer orientation toward politics on the part of citizens, they ought to be reformed to create more opportunities for deliberation. In what follows, however, I raise two criticisms of the model of deliberative democracy as usually articulated. Its tendency to restrict democratic discussion to argument carries implicit cultural biases that can lead to exclusions in practice. Its assumption that unity is either a starting point or goal of democratic discussion, moreover, may also have exclusionary consequences.

EXCLUSIONARY IMPLICATIONS OF THE
DELIBERATIVE MODEL

A primary virtue of a deliberative model of democracy, I have argued thus far, is that it promotes a conception of reason over power in politics. Policies ought to be adopted not because the most powerful interests win but because the citizens or their representatives together determine their rightness after hearing and criticizing reasons. While there are some elitist tendencies in traditional republicanism, most contemporary deliberative theorists believe that a deliberative democracy is potentially more inclusive and egalitarian than an interest-based democracy.[5] Whereas an interest-based democracy does not preclude money and numbers from influencing decisions, for example, deliberative theorists usually assert that democracy requires an equal voice for all citizens to press their claims, regardless of social position or power.

Joshua Cohen gives a clear picture of the conditions of an ideal of deliberative democracy.[6] His formulation is close to Habermas's ideal of discourse that aims to reach understanding, which John Dryzek relies on as a basis for his conception of discursive democracy.[7] In the ideal of deliberative democracy, participants come to a political problem with an open mind about its solution; they are not bound by the authority of prior norms or requirements. The process of political discussion consists in reasoned argument. Participants put forward proposals and criticize them, and each assents to a conclusion only because of the "force of the better argument." For such assent to be rational, participants must be free and equal. Each must have the equal opportunity to make proposals and criticize, and their speaking situation must be free from domination. No one can be in a position to threaten or coerce others to accept or reject certain proposals. The goal of deliberation is to arrive at consensus; even when this is not possible and participants resort to voting, their result is a collective judgment rather than the aggregate of private preferences.

Deliberative theorists tend to assume that bracketing political and economic power is sufficient to make speakers equal. This assumption fails to notice that the social power that can prevent people from being equal speakers derives not only from economic dependence or political domination but also from an internalized sense of the right one has to speak or not to speak, and from the devaluation of some people's style of speech and the elevation of others. The deliberative ideal tends to assume that when we eliminate the influence of economic and political power, people's ways of speaking and understanding will be the same; but this will be true only if we also eliminate their cultural differences and different social positions. The model of deliberative democracy, that is, tends to assume that deliberation is both culturally neutral and universal. A theory of communicative democracy that attends to social difference, to the way that power sometimes enters speech itself, recognizes the cultural specificity of deliberative practices and proposes a more inclusive model of communication.

The deliberative model of communication derives from specific institutional contexts of the modern West—scientific debate, modern parliaments, and courts (each with progenitors in ancient Greek and Roman philosophy and politics, and in the medieval academy). These were some of the aspiring institutions of the bourgeois revolution that succeeded in becoming ruling institutions. Their institutional forms, rules, and rhetorical and cultural styles have defined the meaning of reason itself in the modern world. As ruling institutions, however, they have been elitist and exclusive, and these exclusions mark their very conceptions of reason and deliberation, both in the institutions and in the rhetorical styles they represent. Since their Enlightenment beginnings they have been male-dominated institutions, and in class- and race-differentiated societies they have been white- and upper class–dominated. Despite the claim of deliberative forms of orderly meetings to express pure universal reason, the norms of deliberation are culturally specific and often operate as forms of power that silence or devalue the speech of some people.

Parliamentary debates or arguments in court are not simply free and open public forums in which all people actually have the right to express claims and give reasons according to their own understanding. Instead of defining discussion as the open reciprocal recognition of the point of view of everyone, these institutions style deliberation as agonistic. Deliberation is competition. Parties to dispute aim to win the argument, not to achieve mutual understanding. Consenting because of the "force of the better argument" means being unable to think of further counterargument, that is, to concede defeat.[8] The agonistic norms of deliberation reveal ways that power reenters this arena, even though deliberative theorists may claim to have bracketed it.

Restricting practices of democratic discussion to moves in a contest where some win and others lose privileges those who like contests and know the rules of the game. Speech that is assertive and confrontational is here more valued than speech that is tentative, exploratory, or conciliatory. In most actual situations of discussion, this privileges male speaking styles over female. A growing literature claims to show that girls and women tend to speak less than boys and men in speaking situations that value assertiveness and argument competition. When women do speak in such situations, moreover, they tend to give information and ask questions rather than state opinions or initiate controversy.[9]

In many formal situations the better-educated white middle-class people, moreover, often act as though they have a right to speak and that their words carry authority, whereas those of other groups often feel intimidated by the argument requirements and the formality and rules of parliamentary procedure, so they do not speak, or speak only in a way that those in charge find "disruptive." Norms of assertiveness, combativeness, and speaking by the contest rules are powerful silencers or evaluators of speech in many actual speaking situations where culturally differentiated and socially unequal groups live together. The dominant groups, moreover, often fail entirely to notice this devaluation and silencing, while the less privileged often feel put down or frustrated, either losing confidence in themselves or becoming angry.

The norms of deliberation also privilege speech that is formal and general. Speech that proceeds from premise to conclusion in an orderly fashion that clearly lays out its inference structure is better than other speech. It is also better to assert one's position in terms of generalities and principles that apply to particular instances. These norms of "articulateness," however, must be learned; they are culturally specific, and in actual speaking situations in our society exhibiting such speaking styles is a sign of social privilege. Deliberation thus does not open itself equally to all ways of making claims and giving reasons. In formal situations of discussion and debate, such as classrooms, courtrooms, and city council chambers, many people feel they must apologize for their halting and circuitous speech.

The norms of deliberation, finally, privilege speech that is dispassionate and disembodied. They tend to presuppose an opposition between mind and body, reason and emotion. They tend falsely to identify objectivity with calm and absence of emotional expression. Thus expressions of anger, hurt, and passionate concern discount the claims and reasons they accompany. Similarly, the entrance of the body into speech—in wide gestures, movements of nervousness, or body expressions of emotion—are signs of weakness that cancel out one's assertions or reveal one's lack of objectivity and control. Deliberative norms tend to privilege "literal" language over figurative language such as hyperbole, metaphor, and so on.

Once again, in our society these differences of speech privilege correlate with other differences of social privilege. The speech culture of white middle-class men tends to be more controlled, without significant gesture and expression of emotion. The speech culture of women and racial minorities, on the other, tends to be more excited and embodied, more valuing the expression of emotion, the use of figurative language, modulation in tone of voice, and wide gesture.[10]

I conclude from these considerations that this discussion-based theory of democracy must have a broader idea of the forms and styles of speaking that political discussion involves than deliberative theorists usually imagine. I prefer to call such a broadened theory communicative, rather than deliberative, democracy, to indicate an equal privileging of any forms of communicative interaction where people aim to reach understanding. While argument is a necessary element in such effort to discuss with and persuade one another about political issues, argument is not the only mode of political communication, and argument can be expressed in a plurality of ways, interspersed with or alongside other communicative forms.

DELIBERATIVE MODEL ASSUMES UNITY

Unlike the interest-based conception of democracy, communicative democracy emphasizes that people's ideas about political questions often change when they interact with other people's ideas and experiences. If in a public discussion about collective action or public policy people simply say what they want, without any claims of justice or rightness, they will not be taken seriously. Instead, they must appeal to others by presenting proposals they claim are just or good and that others ought to accept. In this process people's own initial preferences are transformed from subjective desires to objective claims, and the content of these preferences must also often change to make them publicly speakable, as claims of entitlement or what is right. People's ideas about the solution to collective problems are also sometimes transformed by listening to and learning about the point of view of others.

Deliberative theorists commonly write about this process of moving from subjective self-regarding preferences to more objective or general opinions about the solution to collective problems as a process of discovering or constructing unity among them. I see two approaches that deliberative theorists take in discussing such unity. Some take unity to be a prior condition of deliberation. Michael Walzer, for example, argues that effective social criticism locates and appeals to a community's prior "shared understandings."[11] Sometimes Jürgen Habermas writes as though reaching understanding through discourse about norms depends on restoring a disrupted consensus.[12]

There are at least two problems with this way of constructing the process of discussion. First, in contemporary pluralist societies we cannot assume that there are sufficient shared understandings to appeal to in many situations of conflict and solving collective problems. Second, the assumption of prior unity obviates the need for the self-transcendence, which I cited earlier as an important component of a communicative model of democracy. If discussion succeeds primarily when it appeals to what the discussants all share, then none need revise their opinions or viewpoints in order to take account of perspectives and experiences beyond them. Even if they need the others to see what they all share, each finds in the other only a mirror for him- or herself.

Recognizing such problems, some theorists of discussion-based democracy conceptualize unity not as a starting point but as a goal of political dialogue. In this view, participants transcend their subjective, self-regarding perspective on political issues by putting aside their particular interests and seeking the good of the whole. Participants in a communicative democratic interchange often begin with differences of culture, perspective, interest, but the goal of discussion is to locate or create common interests that all can share. To arrive at the common good it may be necessary to work through differences, but difference itself is something to be transcended, because it is partial and divisive.[13]

The problem with this conception of the unity of democratic discussion is that it may harbor another mechanism of exclusion. Assuming a discussion situation in which participants are differentiated by group-based culture and social position, and where some groups have greater symbolic or material privilege than others, appeals to a "common good" are likely to perpetuate such privilege. As I argued in the previous section, even communication situations that bracket the direct influence of economic or political inequality nevertheless can privilege certain cultural styles and values. When discussion participants aim at unity, the appeal to a common good in which they are all supposed to leave behind their particular experience and interests, the perspectives of the privileged are likely to dominate the definition of that common good. The less privileged are asked to put aside the expression of their experience, which may require a different idiom, or their claims of entitlement or interest must be put aside for the sake of a common good whose definition is biased against them.[14]

Considering Difference a Resource

There is no reason or structure for differently situated groups to engage in democratic discussion if they do not live together in a polity. In this sense some unity is of course a condition of democratic communication. But the unity of a single polity is a much weaker unity, I suggest, than deliberative theorists usually assume. The unity that motivates politics is the facticity of people being thrown together, finding themselves in geographical proximity and economic interdependence such that activities and pursuits of some affect the ability of others to conduct their activities. A polity consists of people who live together, who are stuck with one another.

If a polity is to be a communicative democracy, even more unity is necessary. Its members must have a commitment to equal respect for one another, in the simple formal sense of willingness to say that all have a right to express their opinions and points of view, and all ought to listen. The members of the polity, furthermore, must agree on procedural rules of fair discussion and decision-making. These three conditions—significant interdependence, formally equal respect, and agreed-on procedures—are all the unity necessary for communicative democracy. They are much thinner conditions than those of shared understandings or the goals of finding common goods. Within the context of this minimal unity that characterizes communicative democracy, a richer understanding of processes of democratic discussion results if we assume that differences of social position and identity perspective function as a resource for public reason rather than as divisions that public reason transcends.

I have already argued that one of the problems with assuming unity as a starting point or goal of deliberative democracy is that such a conception cannot account well for the transformation the communicative process should often produce in the opinions of the participants. If we are all really looking for what we have in common—whether as a prior condition or as a result—then we are not transforming our point of view. We only come to see ourselves mirrored in others. If we assume, on the other hand, that communicative interaction means encountering differences of meaning, social position, or need that I do not share and identify with, then we can better describe how that interaction transforms my preferences. Different social positions encounter one another with the awareness of their difference. This does not mean that we believe we have no similarities; difference is not total otherness. But it means that each position is aware that it does not comprehend the perspective of the others differently located, in the sense that it cannot be assimilated into one's own. There is thus something to be learned from the other perspectives as they communicate their meanings and perspectives, precisely because the perspectives are beyond one another and not reducible to a common good. This process of mutual expression of experience and points of view that transcend the initial understanding of each accounts for a transformation in their opinions.

Communication among perspectives that transcend one another preserves the plurality that Hannah Arendt understood as a condition of publicity. The plural standpoints in the public enable each participant to understand more of what the society means or what the possible consequences of a policy will be by each situating his or her own experience and interest in a wider context of understanding something in other social locations. By "understand" I mean something somewhat different from what some deliberative theorists mean. Frequently in communicative contexts when people say they have come to an understanding or they understand one another, they think that this implies a mutual identification. People have reached understanding, in this conception, when they have transcended what differentiates and divides them and now have the same meaning or beliefs or principles.

If communicative democracy is better conceived as speaking across differences of culture, social position, and need, which are preserved in the process, however, then understanding one another and reaching understanding does not imply this identification. Understanding another social location can here mean that there has been successful expression of experience and perspective, so that other social positions learn, and part of what they understand is that there remains more behind that experience and perspective that transcends their own subjectivity.[15]

Preserving and listening across such differences of position and perspective causes the transformation in preference that deliberative theorists recommend. This transformation occurs in three ways. 1) Confrontation with different perspectives, interests, and cultural meanings teaches me the partiality of my own, reveals to me my own experience as perspectival. 2) Knowledge that I am in a situation of collective problem solving with others who have different perspectives on the problems and different cultures and values from my own, and that they have the right to challenge my claims and arguments, forces me to transform my expressions of self-interest and desire into appeals to justice. Proposals for collective policies need not be expressed as general interest, an interest all can share; they may be claims about an obligation on the part of the public to recognize and provide for some unique needs of uniquely situated persons. Nevertheless the plural public perspectives require such expressed claims to appeal across difference, to presume a lack of understanding to be bridged, thus transforming the experience itself. 3) Expressing, questioning, and challenging differently situated knowledge, finally, adds to the social knowledge of all the participants. While not abandoning their own perspective, through listening across difference each position can come to understand something about the ways proposals and claims affect others differently situated. By internalizing this mediated understanding of plural positions to some extent, participants gain a wider picture of the social processes in which their own partial experience is embedded. This greater social objectivity increases their wisdom for arriving at just solutions to collective problems.

THE BREADTH OF COMMUNICATIVE DEMOCRACY

In Plato's *Gorgias*, Socrates discusses the virtues and vices of rhetoric with students of the famous rhetorician, and with Gorgias himself. Socrates pushes his interlocutors to seek a distinction between the art of argument that reveals truth, on the one hand, and mere knack of persuasion that only produces appearances, on the other. Rhetoric is a mere knack of knowing how to please and flatter an audience, the dialogue suggests, in contrast to the critical thinking of philosophy, which sometimes displeases and discomforts the audience in order to lead them to shed comfortable falsehoods. As the dialogue proceeds it becomes clear, however, that Socrates and his interlocutors cannot sustain such a distinction between truth and rhetoric; argument also persuades, and the best one can say is that there is a difference between good rhetoric and bad rhetoric. Through the events of the dialogue Plato also illustrates the untenability of the distinction. Socrates engages in flattery in order to motivate his interlocutors to continue the discussion. He uses countless rhetorical tricks, from humor to irony to ridicule to self-effacement. Here as in nearly every other of Plato's dialogues, Socrates recites a myth, a poetic story that passes over argument to pull on intuition.

Following recent feminist accounts of dialogical reason,[16] as well as male African American and Latino articulations of cultural biases in dominant conceptions of deliberation,[17] I propose three elements that a broader conception of communicative democracy requires in addition to critical argument: greeting, rhetoric, and storytelling. Because they recognize the embodiment and particularity of interlocutors, these three modes of communication help establish and maintain the plurality that I have argued, following Arendt, is necessary to the meaning and existence of publicity. Where such a public contains group-based cultural, social perspectival, and valuative differences, moreover, these communicative forms supplement argument by providing ways of speaking across difference in the absence of significant shared understandings.

Greeting

With the term "greeting" I wish to present the virtuous form of the communication mode that the *Gorgias* presents as the vice of flattery. A logical and motivational condition for dialogue that aims to reach understanding is that the parties in the dialogue recognize one another in their particularity. I call this moment of communication "greeting" to evoke the everyday pragmatic mode in which we experience such acknowledgment. Here is speech necessary to communication that does not *say* anything—it makes no assertion and has no specific content:[18] "Good morning," "How are you," "Welcome," "See you later," "Take care." In the category of greeting I also include such expressions of leave taking, as well as the forms of speech that often lubricate ongoing discussion with mild forms of flattery, stroking of egos, and deference.

Especially when parties to dialogue differ in many ways, either in their culture and values or in the interests and aims they bring to discussion, their effort to resolve conflict or come to agreement on a course of action cannot begin without preliminaries in which the parties establish trust or respect. These preliminaries often consist in various forms of flattery; introductory speeches that name the others with honorific titles, acknowledge the greatness of their achievements and ideals, and so on.[19]

Communicative interaction in which participants aim at reaching understanding is often peppered with gestures of politeness and deference, the absence of which is felt as coldness, indifference, insult. Discussion is also wrapped in nonlinguistic gestures that bring people together warmly, seeing conditions for amicability: smiles, handshakes, hugs, the giving and taking of food and drink.[20] In this respect bodies, and care for bodies, must enter an ideal of communicative democracy. Theorists of deliberative democracy, however, seem to have no place for care-taking, deferential, polite acknowledgment of the Otherness of others. Since much democratic discussion will be fraught with disagreement, anger, conflict, counterargument, and criticism, intermittent gestures of flattery, greeting, deference, and conciliatory caring keep commitment to the discussion at times of anger and disagreement.

Rhetoric

Deliberative theorists typically aim to fulfill the Platonic attempt to distinguish rational speech from mere rhetoric, and in so doing they usually denigrate emotion and figurative language. Rational speech, in this view, the speech to which deliberative democracy should be confined, consists in making assertions and giving sober reasons for them, with the logical connections among them clearly spelled out. Thus Thomas

Spragens, for example, invokes Hitler's disdain for the rationality of the masses as a warning against rhetorical speech that aims to move the masses with hot passion. A rational democracy, he claims, will engage the mind rather than ignite the passions.[21] As James Bohman points out, Habermas also tries to distinguish rational speech from rhetoric by distinguishing between illocutionary and perlocutionary speech acts.[22] But the opposition between rational discourse and rhetoric, in my view, denigrates both the situatedness of communication and its necessary link to desire.

In a discussion situation in which different people with different aims, values, and interests seek to solve collective problems justly, it is not enough to make assertions and give reasons. One must also be heard. As Benjamin Barber points out, democratic theorists value speaking, but they less often discuss listening.[23] Rhetoric names the forms and styles of speaking that reflexively attend to the audience in speech. While there are many aspects to this styling of speech for its listeners, I will focus on the two I mentioned earlier: situatedness and the link to desire.

Rhetoric announces the situatedness of communication. With rhetorical figures a speech constructs the speaker's position in relation to those of the audience. Through rhetoric the speaker appeals to the particular attributes or experience of the audience, and his or her own particular location in relation to them. Rhetoric also constructs the occasion of the speech—today we commemorate, or we have just had an urgent phone call, or there is an ongoing policy discussion we are having. Rhetoric constructs speaker, audience, and occasion by invoking or creating specific meanings, connotations, and symbols, and it serves this connecting function whether the speaker and audience share meanings or not.

Socrates faults the rhetorician for aiming to please the audience rather than telling them hard truths. But Plato shows in Socrates' person that there is an important erotic dimension in communication that aims to reach understanding, that persuasion is partly seduction. One function of rhetoric is to get and keep attention. The most elegant and truthful arguments may fail to evoke assent if they are boring. Humor, wordplay, images, and figures of speech embody and color the arguments, making the discussion pull on thought through desire.

Storytelling

In a communicative democracy participants in discussion aim at reaching understandings about solutions to their collective problems. Although there is hardly a speaking situation in which participants have no shared meanings, disagreements, divergent understandings, and varying perspectives are also usually present. In situations of conflict that discussion aims to address, groups often begin with misunderstandings or a sense of complete lack of understanding of who their interlocutors are, and a sense that their own needs, desires, and motives are not understood. This is especially so where class or culture separates the parties. Doing justice under such circumstances of differences requires recognizing the particularity of individuals and groups as much as seeking general interests. Narrative fosters understanding across such difference without making those who are different symmetrical, in at least three ways.

First, narrative reveals the particular experiences of those in social locations, experiences that cannot be shared by those situated differently but that they must understand in order to do justice to the others. Imagine that wheelchair-bound people at a university make claims upon university resources to remove what they see as impediments to their full participation, and to give them positive aid in ways they claim will equalize their ability to compete with able-bodied students for academic status. A primary way they make their case will be through telling stories of their physical, temporal, social, and emotional obstacles. It would be a mistake to say that once they hear these stories the others understand the situation of the wheelchair-bound to the extent that they can adopt their point of view. On the contrary, the storytelling provides enough understanding of the situation of the wheelchair-bound by those who can walk for them to understand that they cannot share the experience.

Narrative exhibits subjective experience to other subjects. The narrative can evoke sympathy while maintaining distance because the narrative also carries an inexhaustible latent shadow, the transcendence of the Other, that there is always more to be told.

Second, narrative reveals a source of values, culture, and meaning. When an argument proceeds from premise to conclusion, it is only as persuasive as the acceptance of its premises among deliberators. Few institutions bring people together to face collective problems, moreover, where the people affected, however divided and diverse, can share no premises. Pluralist polities, however, often face serious divergences in value premises, cultural practices, and meanings, and these disparities bring conflict, insensitivity, insult, and misunderstanding. Under these circumstances, narrative can serve to explain to outsiders what practices, places, or symbols mean to the people who hold them. Values, unlike norms, often cannot be justified through argument. But neither are they arbitrary. Their basis often emerges from the situated history of a people. Through narrative the outsiders may come to understand why the insiders value what they value and why they have the priorities they have.

How do the Lakota convey to others in South Dakota why the Black Hills mean so much to them, and why they believe they have special moral warrant to demand a stop to forestry in the Black Hills? Through stories—myths in which the Black Hills figure as primary characters, stories of Lakota individuals and groups in relation to those mountains. Values appear as a result of a history, by which a group relate "where they are coming from."

Finally, narrative not only exhibits experience and values from the point of view of the subjects that have and hold them. It also reveals a total social knowledge from the point of view of that social position. Each social perspective has an account not only of its own life and history but of every other position that affects its experience. Thus listeners can learn about how their own position, actions, and values appear to others from the stories they tell. Narrative thus exhibits the situated knowledge available of the collective from each perspective, and the combination of narratives from different perspectives produces the collective social wisdom not available from any one position.

There are two general conclusions to draw from this account of the role of narrative communication in which people aim to solve collective problems through discussion. First, narrative can often play an important role in argument in democratic discussion. Where arguments about policy or action depend on appeals to need or entitlement, narrative provides an important way to demonstrate need or entitlement. Narrative also contributes to political argument by the social knowledge it offers of how social segments view one another's actions and what are the likely effects of policies and actions on people in different social locations.[24]

As Lynn Sanders argues, storytelling complements arguments in a communicative democracy because it tends to be more egalitarian than typical deliberative processes.[25] I discussed earlier how deliberation can privilege the dispassionate, the educated, or those who feel they have a right to assert. Because everyone has stories to tell, with different styles and meanings, and because each can tell her story with equal authority, the stories have equal value in the communicative situation.[26]

I thus propose in this essay an ideal of communicative rather than deliberative democracy. The ideal of communicative democracy includes more than deliberative democracy, because it recognizes that when political dialogue aims at solving collective problems, it justly requires a plurality of perspectives, speaking styles, and ways of expressing the particularity of social situation as well as the general applicability of principles. A theory of democratic discussion useful to the contemporary

world must explain the possibility of communication across wide differences of culture and social position. Such a theory of democracy needs
a broad and plural conception of communication that includes both the
expression and the extension of shared understandings, where they exist, and the offering and acknowledgment of unshared meanings.

Chapter IV

PUNISHMENT, TREATMENT, EMPOWERMENT:
THREE APPROACHES TO POLICY FOR
PREGNANT ADDICTS

IN THIS PAPER I bring some issues and concepts of feminist ethics, post-modernism, and critical theory to reflect on an important women's issue—policy approaches to pregnant women who are habitual drug users. Many people, including many law enforcement officials, child protection agents, and legislators, think that women who use drugs during pregnancy should be punished for the harm or risks of harm they bring to their babies. I analyze this punishment approach and argue that the situation of pregnant addicts does not satisfy the conditions usually articulated by philosophers to justify punishment. A punishment approach, moreover, may have sexist and racist implications and ultimately operates more to maintain a social distinction between insiders and deviants than to protect children.

Most of those who criticize a punishment approach to policy for pregnant addicts call for meaningful treatments as an alternative. I interpret this treatment approach as a version of a feminist ethic of care. For the most part, theorizing about the ethics of care has remained at the level of ontology and epistemology, with little discussion of how the ethics of care interprets concrete moral issues differently from more traditional approaches to ethics. By conceptualizing a treatment approach to pregnant addicts as justified by an ethics of care, I propose to understand this ethics of care as a moral framework for social policy.

Although I agree with a treatment approach to policy for pregnant addicts, from a feminist point of view there are reasons to be suspicious of many aspects of typical drug treatment. Relying on Michel Foucault's notions of disciplinary power and the operation of "confessional" discourse in therapy, I argue that treatment often operates to adjust women to dominant gender, race, and class structures and depoliticizes and individualizes their situations. Thus, I conclude by offering a distinction between two meanings of empowerment in service provision, one that remains individualizing, and one that develops social solidarity through consciousness raising and the possibility of collective action.

PUNISHMENT

According to some estimates, as many as 375,000 babies born every year in the United States are affected by their mothers' drug use during pregnancy, although others think the numbers are lower.[1] Some of these babies suffer some disorders and problems at birth; however, it is difficult to isolate the mothers' drug use from other possible causes, such as poverty, poor prenatal care, or depression.[2] The degree of harm to babies is also quite variable. Some children are permanently retarded or physically impaired but others are normal and healthy, especially as they grow older.[3] For the purposes of this discussion, however, I will assume that a mother's frequent drug use during pregnancy usually brings some kind of harm, whether short term or long term, to the baby she bears.

Punitive responses to the problem of drug-exposed infants have significant support among policy makers, law enforcement officials, and the general public.[4] Many prosecutors, judges, and legislatures in the United States have acted on these sentiments. Some judges have sentenced pregnant addicts convicted of crimes like theft or shoplifting to much heavier sentences than they would have otherwise.[5]

Punitive legislation regarding pregnant addicts has been considered in more than thirty states and by the U.S. Congress.[6] Although the testimony of legal and medical experts appears to have succeeded in preventing the passage of congressional legislation, at least eight states now include drug exposure in utero in their definition of child abuse and neglect.[7] In several states without such laws, prosecutors have used existing drug-trafficking laws to file criminal charges against women who use cocaine or other controlled substances during pregnancy. By July 1992 at least 167 women in twenty-six states had been arrested and charged criminally because of their use of drugs during pregnancy or because of some other prenatal risk.[8] A number of these women have been found guilty and sentenced to as many as ten years in prison.[9] The majority of these cases have involved women of color, even though white women also use illegal drugs.[10] The controversy that has been boiling about this punishment approach to policy for pregnant addicts appears in some of the appeals of these convictions. As of November 1992, twenty-one cases had been challenged or appealed, and all of these were dismissed or overturned.[11]

Even more common than criminal prosecution is court-ordered removal of the baby at birth, without trial or hearing, solely on the ground that the mother or infant has a positive drug test at the time of birth. Child removal on this ground appears to be increasing, even though there is a severe shortage of foster homes in many areas of the United

States.[12] Despite the complaints of many lawyers and medical professionals that such procedures violate privacy rights and proper medical use of the tests, a number of states require healthcare professionals to report to the local welfare agency women who have or are believed to have used a controlled substance during pregnancy.[13]

As a result of increasing controversy over such punitive policies, some state and local governments have encouraged treatment as a complement or alternative to criminal punishment or child removal. Thus, California has enacted a law that requires drug treatment programs to give priority to pregnant women.[14] The state of Connecticut has mandated that outreach workers seek out addicted mothers and mothers-to-be to encourage them to get treatment.[15] In the fall of 1991, the city of New York instituted a program that allows addicted women to take their babies home after birth, provided that they enter treatment and agree to weekly visits from a social worker.[16] This program and many others that emphasize treatment over punishment nevertheless retain a punitive tendency to the degree that they are coercing women to have treatment.

The targeting of women drug users, especially poor women and women of color, for particular surveillance and policies in the "war on drugs" raises questions about sexism and racism implicit in such policies. Most of the municipalities and states that have prosecuted women who gave birth to drug-affected babies do not prosecute other women or men for drug use. There is a particular rage often being directed at *mothers* in this differential application of punishment, which I suggest reflects an identification with the infant.[17] Dorothy Dinnerstein argues that in a society characterized by mother-dominated infant care both adult women and men often carry an unconscious resentment of their mothers which is displaced on to women in general. The pre-ego infant is needy and desiring, and the mother can never be completely and fully there for the child. The lack of the mother, the permanent disappointment that the mother is not always there for me, is the permanent existential trauma of mortality. The social fact of the relative absence of men from infant care allows the unconscious to scapegoat women for this existential trauma that is an element in the human condition as such.[18]

The level of passion directed against pregnant addicts often seems higher than that felt for most ordinary criminals. It is not just anyone who has harmed her baby, as, for example, by shooting it up with cocaine. It's the child's *mother*. The mother is supposed to be the one who sacrifices herself, who will do anything for her child, who will preserve and nurture it. That's what mothering *means*. The rage directed at pregnant addicts unconsciously recalls the feeling that we all had as children of rage toward our mothers who were not always there for us, did not always respond to our needs and desires, and sometimes pursued their own purposes and desires. The mother who harms her child is not merely a criminal; she is a monster.[19]

As Dorothy E. Roberts argues, moreover, the fact that black women are particular targets for the punitive reach of the state against drug-using mothers suggests that we find racism here inextricably tied to sexism. Since the days of slavery, American society has systematically devalued black motherhood. In the tradition of American racial attitudes, all black women are by definition not "good" mothers, and it would be best if they did not bear children at all. The racism black women suffer, combined with the fact that their economic status more often brings them into contact with state institutions, makes them more likely to be punished than white women. Their failure to fit society's image of the "good" mother makes their punishment more acceptable.[20]

Most prosecutors and policymakers who have pursued a punishment approach to pregnant addicts would deny that racist and sexist biases inform their practices. They claim instead that they are exercising their obligations as state agents to protect infants from harm and to hold accountable those responsible for such harms when they occur. Women who take cocaine or heroin while pregnant are wantonly and knowingly risking the lives or health of future persons and deserve to pay for such immoral harm. Punishing women who give birth to drug-affected babies serves notice to others that the state considers this a grave wrong and will thus deter such behavior. As with most punishments, the primary justifications for punitive policies toward pregnant addicts are deterrence and retribution. Neither justification, however, is well grounded.

A deterrence theory of punishment relies on an assumption that people engage in some kind of cost-benefit calculation before taking the actions the policies are aimed at. In some contexts this makes sense. If a city wishes to discourage illegal parking, it raises the fines and threatens to tow, and these policies usually do work to reduce infractions. The idea that a pregnant addict weighs the benefits of taking drugs against the costs of possible punishments, however, is implausible, because it assumes that it is within her power to refrain from taking drugs if she judges that the costs are too high.

Many health professionals argue that punitive policies toward pregnant addicts do deter them from seeking prenatal care.[21] Women are likely to avoid contact with healthcare providers if they believe that their drug use will be reported to state authorities who will punish them. Because drug-using pregnant women's fetuses and babies are often at particularly high risk, they need prenatal attention even more than most. Experts claim that the harmful effects of drug use on infants can be offset, at least in part, by good prenatal care, when health professionals are aware of a woman's drug use in a supportive, nonpunitive atmosphere.[22]

I think that retribution is most often implicitly or explicitly the operative justification for punitive approaches to pregnant addicts. These women ought to be punished and threatened with punishment because their wrongful actions *deserve* sanction. Such a retributive justification for a punitive approach to pregnant addicts must assume that these women are responsible both for their drug use and for their pregnancies; if freedom is a condition for assigning responsibility, however, these are problematic assumptions.

Anyone who starts using drugs is responsible for that use. But the concept of addiction implies a limitation on the free agency, and thus responsibility, of the addicted person. There are paternalistic dangers in promoting a model of addiction that depicts the habitual drug user as completely irrational, unaware, out of control. But there are equal dangers in denying the reality of a substance dependence so ingrained in a person's habits, way of life, and desire that she is not responsible for her continuing use. Virtually no one uses drugs with the aim of becoming dependent. Indeed, affirming the norm of self-control, people deceive themselves into thinking that they can avoid addiction and too often refuse to admit to a dependence. Most experts agree that once a person has become dependent on a substance, stopping her usage is very difficult and cannot be accomplished by a mere act of will. Begun by a series of acts, her drug dependence has become a condition, which she is in rather than something she does. Criminal law should punish people for acts, not conditions. In recognition of this distinction, legal precedent has found that criminalizing drug addition violates a prohibition against cruel and unusual punishment.[23]

Most states where punitive policies toward pregnant addicts have been pursued do not prosecute people for drug use alone. Especially where this is so, women are essentially being punished for carrying a pregnancy to term.[24] Such punishment must presuppose that women are responsible for being pregnant, but there are several social conditions that limit women's choice to be or not be pregnant. Ours is still a society where women often are not really free in their sexual relations with men. Access to contraception, moreover, is not easy for many women, especially poor or young women. And, of course, even when they have it, the contraception sometimes does not work. With rapidly decreasing access to abortion for all women in the United States, but especially for young or poor women, finally, fewer and fewer women have a choice about whether to carry a pregnancy to term.[25]

Some prosecutors and policies claim to use a punishment approach primarily as a means of encouraging or forcing women into drug treatment. In line with the above arguments, one might say that a pregnant addict is morally blameworthy for harming her child only if she does not seek help in dealing with her drug use. In recent years some small steps have been taken to increase the availability of drug treatment for pregnant women, and to design programs specifically for their needs; for the most part, however, access to more than perfunctory drug treatment is limited. Most programs either do not accept pregnant women or have waiting lists that extend long beyond their due dates. Most private health insurance programs offer only partial reimbursement for treatment, and in many states Medicaid will reimburse only a portion of the cost of drug treatment. Most treatment programs are designed with men's lives in mind, and very few have childcare options.[26] Mandatory reporting laws or other procedures that force women into treatment, moreover, create an adversary and policing relation between healthcare providers and the women they are supposed to serve, thereby precluding the trust relationship most providers believe is necessary for effective drug therapy.[27]

These arguments against application of a punishment approach to policy for pregnant addicts should not be understood to imply that pregnant addicts have no obligations regarding the fetuses they carry. There are many matters about which people think that there are obligations and responsibilities, for which people are not held criminally liable.[28] The above arguments show that women's freedom in respect to these responsibilities is often quite circumscribed, although not absent.

Philosophers typically describe the retributive theory of punishment as based on a social contract theory of the relation of the individual to the state. Laws express a compact among citizens, their commitment to limit their personal desires and interests to create a mutually respecting community of citizens. Social membership consists in and depends on such regulation and mutual respect. One who claims social membership and benefits from it implicitly promises to obey the rules. The lawbreaker violates this implied promise. She or he therefore has forfeited her or his membership in society and deserves to be punished as a way of paying a debt for a broken promise.

Jeffrey Murphy argues that this retributive theory of punishment implies a conception of society as a relationship among equals with shared values and ways of looking at the world. A retributive justification only works morally to legitimate punishment if those subject to punishment are indeed equal citizens who receive the social benefits which oblige them to obey the rules in return. Murphy points out, however, that most of those people capitalist societies define as criminals and punish are not in fact equal citizens. They are poor and working-class people, who do not participate in the power to set the rules or derive the benefits from social participation that the theory supposes.[29]

Murphy argues that where punishment is applied to those excluded from the full benefits of social membership, the actual function of punishment is to reinforce that exclusion. Either you obey the rules or you are marked as deviant and punished. The proper law-abiding citizen is not needy, works hard and is independent, has relations with others through contracts of mutual exchange, and exhibits temperance and self-control. Those who do not conform to this model—who are needy, irrational, dependent, unwilling or unable to work, who do not exercise self-control, or for whom there are no benefits in the legitimate market exchange game—are deviant and deserve punishment. As Foucault theorizes, the system of modern law itself creates the category of "delinquents," whose actions its punishments are designed to curtail, and recreates them in subjecting them to the "carceral" system.[30] Because punishing the pregnant addict does next to nothing to prevent the birth of babies harmed by the chronic drug use of their mothers, punishment seems only to have the function of marking the women as deviant, publicly reaffirming their exclusion from the class of upstanding citizens.

ETHICS OF CARE AND TREATMENT

Critics of a punishment approach to addicts in general, and pregnant addicts in particular, argue that addiction is a health problem rather than a problem of criminal justice. The problem of substance-using mothers should be the province of healthcare and social service agencies, not the law and the courts. Like any other needy people, pregnant addicts should be cared for, nurtured, and helped to be made well and independent. The American Medical Association, along with many other organizations that represent service providers, has taken the position that punitive policies toward pregnant addicts, including coerced treatment, interfere with the professional-client relationship to inhibit the provision and acceptance of effective rehabilitative treatment services.[31]

Arguments for an approach to policy for pregnant addicts that emphasizes supportive treatment appeal to values much like those conceptualized by feminist moral theorists as an ethics of care.[32] The ethics of care emphasizes contextualized issues of harm and suffering rather than a morality of abstract principle. This ethic of care directly criticizes at least three aspects of the model of the relation of individual and society that I have argued underlies the punishment approach—its assumption of the moral self as independent, its assumption of social relations as exchanges among equals, and the correlative assumption that these relations are voluntary.

The usual arguments justifying punishment as retribution, I suggested above, presume a contractual model of society where individuals are autonomous and independent. The manual of social obligation in this conception consists of little more than traffic rules to ensure that each person pursuing her or his own distinct interests will not crash into the others. This picture of atomized selves ignores or devalues the facts of interdependence and multivariant relationships that structure human cultures and practices. As Annette Baier argues, reliance on the formalistic ethic of rights that this atomistic contractual picture generates does little "to ensure that the people who have and mutually respect such rights will have any other relationships to one another than the minimal relationship needed to keep such a 'civil society' going."[33]

Those developing an ethic of care argue that relationships of inequality and dependence call for different standards of moral responsibility than the equality presumed by the atomist contractual picture. Many social relations are between unequals, where one party is dependent on the other for some or all of her or his welfare. The relation of parent and child is paradigmatic here, but other hierarchical relations of dependency such as that between teacher and student, or physician and patient, have a similar structure, according to many theorists of an ethic of care. Unlike the relations assumed in the contract model of society, moreover, these unequal relations of dependence are also often not voluntarily entered; they are already constituted relations of kinship or community, which cannot be severed by mutual agreement. The structure of moral obligation and responsibility in such relations operates more through empathy, and through the acknowledgment of pregiven interdependence and connectedness, than through contracts and promises.

Theories of a care ethic have been influential among feminist psychologists and therapists, who have developed theories and practices of service provision and therapy that emphasize empathy and understanding the context of social relationships in which a client's self and problems are embedded.[34] Some of the few drug treatment programs that have been set up specifically to serve pregnant addicts claim to instantiate the values of an ethic of care, as distinct from more confrontational and achievement models they take to be typical of therapeutic techniques.[35] Although there are reasons to praise such efforts, in the next two sections I will also give some reasons to be suspicious of many therapeutic practices for pregnant addicts, including those that explicitly take themselves to be using an ethic of care.

For the most part, discussions of the ethics of care have located this model of obligation and responsibility in face-to-face personal relationships.[36] The values of an ethic of care, however, can and should be extended beyond face-to-face personal relations, to the interconnections of strangers in the public world of social policy and its implementation. A few feminist theorists have suggested that the ethic of care can serve as a general ethical theory to ground a normative conception of politics and policy.[37]

Despite these promising beginnings, feminist ethics in general, and the ethics of care in particular, has done little to apply its insights to the pressing social policy issues of justice and need that face all societies in the world. I think that at the very least such application means interpreting the reasons for welfare and publicly funded social services very differently from the dominant interpretation in the United States.

Public support and assistance for the needy is most often implicitly or explicitly understood as merely beneficent rather than obligatory, except where the person receiving benefits has earned them through her or his productive contribution. Thus, in the United States, unemployment compensation and social security are generally regarded as entitlements, and other forms of public assistance are regarded as handouts, mere charity that the public dispenses at its pleasure and convenience and not because it has a moral responsibility to do so. This distinction in kinds of benefits rests on an implicit contractual model of social relations. The society "owes" welfare to those who have paid for it through working but owes nothing to any others who are needy.[38]

If one substitutes for this model of contractual equality a hierarchical model of social relations in which, by virtue of institutional structures and relations of power, some persons are vulnerable with respect to the actions of others, a different basis for obligation emerges. In relations of inequality, some persons are potentially subject to coercion, to being taken advantage of because they are needy. The privileged and the powerful have a duty to refrain from taking advantage and to protect the vulnerable from the consequences of their compromised situation.[39]

Applying an ethic of care to policy for pregnant addicts means, then, greatly expanded public and private funding for therapeutic drug treatment and social services specifically for pregnant women, mothers, and their children. Such services should include prenatal and obstetrical care, as well as other healthcare. Whether residential or outpatient, such services should include childcare, so that mothers are not inhibited from seeking or staying in treatment, because they have no one to care for their children or do not want to be separated from them. Treatment services for pregnant addicts must be designed with women's lives specifically in mind.[40] For example, programs should directly address the issues of incest, sexual abuse, or battery that are part of the life history of a high proportion of addicted women.[41]

In 1989 Lucia Meijer reported that there was nearly zero funding for such services anywhere in the United States.[42] Since then, both the federal government and a few states have helped develop and provided funding for drug treatment programs specifically designed for pregnant women and mothers. The extent of such services, however, remains pitifully meager. As of fall 1991, for example, Pennsylvania funded four treatment centers providing residential treatment for women and their children in the entire state. The city of Pittsburgh has one of these centers, which houses seventeen women and their children. The state funds a few more outpatient programs, which serve a larger number of women. The Maternal Addiction Program in Pittsburgh, for example, serves about sixty women; one and one-half counselors see these women three times a week in private and group sessions, and the center is unable to provide childcare. In Pittsburgh the ratio of women who need such services to space available may be as high as ten to one, and the problem is probably more dire in other cities.

The United States has been in a period of conservative retrenchment when all forms of publicly supported service provision have been curtailed. We have been moving away from a caring orientation toward needy people. Social problems like poverty and drug abuse have been growing as a result, creating the punitive response toward people with such problems that we see exemplified in some policies toward pregnant addicts. Adopting a seriously caring approach for policy for pregnant addicts may be expensive, although one can argue that taking care of drug-affected babies is more expensive. But publicly supported treatment policies and programs for substance-dependent women, as well as for men, must be on the agenda for a restructured healthcare system in the United States.

FOUCAULDIAN SUSPICIONS OF TREATMENT

Some feminist theorists doubt the usefulness of Foucault's analyses of power and society for understanding women's situations, but many more have found his work important as a tool of feminist analysis.[43] Relying on Foucault's notions of disciplinary power and the confessional discourse of therapies, I argue in this section that there are reasons to be suspicious of many typical aspects of drug treatment therapies from the point of view of feminist values. This disciplinary power can be conceived on a continuum from military-like forms of rules and obedience paternalistically enforced, "for the patient's own good," to more caring, humanistic practices. Many punitive, paternalistic treatment practices and some more caring, humanistic practices are suspicious, I will argue, to the degree that they redefine a client's problem through the categories of expert knowledge; inhibit the client's freedom through surveillance; attempt to normalize her life and behavior, often in ways that reinforce privilege; and individualize the source of her problem and its solution.

As distinct from political and juridical power, according to Foucault, disciplinary power is enacted in the everyday microprocesses of many institutions of state and civil society—schools, factories and other workplaces, the enlightened rehabilitative prison, hospitals, mental institutions, and social service agencies. This power is largely constituted through application of the knowledge of humanistic and social science disciplines—medicine, psychology, social work, criminology, public administration, pedagogy, scientific management. The authority of disciplinary power comes not from commands of a sovereign, upheld and enforced through law, but from the rules that experts claim as natural, the normal structure of operation of human subjects. Disciplinary practices of medical treatment, exercise, therapy, school or workplace examinations, and so forth, aim to constitute subjects in conformity with those norms. Through systems of surveillance and self-examination, disciplinary power enlists the subject's agency in the formation and reformation of her self.[44]

The relation of addicts to the institutions and experts who administer treatment is certainly one of unequal power. Whether she has entered treatment voluntarily or under threat, the addict's situation is usually one of dependence, vulnerability, and need. The relation of power is often obscured by the neutral knowledge and skills providers have and by their real intentions to be helpful and caring. The combination of expertise and care often produces situations of paternalistic power and discipline.

This often means that women in drug treatment programs must obey a set of more or less onerous rules, and often they are subject to various forms of surveillance as well. There is a range of treatment models, some of which are more rigid than others. Programs usually enforce rules that clients must not have drugs on the premises, must remain drug free while in treatment, and must undergo random drug-screening tests. Residential programs frequently have rules about how people should spend their time and what kinds and number of possessions patients may have. Both residential and outpatient programs often discourage the formation of bonds of friendship and especially sexual bonds between clients. Thus programs sometimes have dress codes forbidding "sexually revealing" clothes and do not allow clients to walk alone in pairs. Surveillance by experts may be a normal part of the outpatient experience for pregnant addicts. In the New York City outreach program that allows addicted mothers to take their babies home, provided they go to treatment, for example, mothers must also agree to allow a social worker to visit their homes at least once a week to check on the progress of their babies and the conditions of their homes. Many of the women resent these visits and consider them onerous surveillance.[45] Rarely do drug treatment

programs or other services impose rules or engage in surveillance practices arbitrarily; they usually articulate reasons that involve the good of
the client. This fact does not usually change their being experienced as
imposed disciplines.

Most drug treatment programs claim to enlist the participation of the
client in determining the course of her therapy. Like most social service
practices more generally, however, the introduction of the expert knowledge of social service disciplines often functions to reinscribe her needs
and experience in a foreign language. The normalizing language of
therapy defines her history and the particular attributes of her situation
as a "case," that is, as a particular instance of generalized concepts of
norm and deviance, health and disorder, self-fulfillment and self-de-
struction. The organizations and providers often attach expert labels to
these general conditions and behaviors, which then generate for them
the service response.[46]

The object of treatment is to change behaviors, ultimately to transform the very self of the client. Drug treatment is nearly always medical-
ized insofar as this transformation is conceived as moving the client from
a position of disorder to a position of greater health. When the subject
of such healing is the "mind" or "spirit" rather than the body, however,
these therapeutic norms easily become infiltrated with *social* norms that
function to enforce and reproduce relations of privilege and oppression.
A treatment approach toward pregnant addicts may often work to adjust
her to dominant social norms of being a "good" woman and a "good"
worker, in ways designed to adjust her to the prevailing structures of
domination and exploitation.[47]

There are some parenting standards that pertain to the objective caring that children receive, and mothers can and should be faulted for
neglecting the care of their children. Often, however, superficial and
culturally biased evaluations add to or substitute for such legitimate evaluations. A woman's progress toward normality may be measured according to her development of a demure comportment, a pleasant voice, a
cheerful presence. She may be encouraged to develop modestly feminine habits of personal attire. I spoke with the director of a residential
drug treatment program for women, for example, who mentioned he
and his staff try to teach the women not to dress and wear makeup in a
manner he associated with prostitutes but, rather, to dress them in a
respectably feminine way. Mothers will often be encouraged to develop
mothering and housekeeping styles that may in fact devalue their own
cultural and neighborhood family styles and norms of housekeeping, to
take another example. A woman may "earn" the right to live with her
children by demonstrating a proper self-sacrificing attitude; orienting
her concern away from her own needs and pleasures; adopting a work

ethic where pleasure can and should be delayed, pursued in small amounts, and always kept under control. Much of her therapy will consist in developing her as a competent and compliant worker: developing habits of getting up and getting to work on time, following orders and meeting deadlines, learning proper self-presentation in interview settings, and so on. Drug treatment programs often include a certain amount of job training but usually only for "basic skills" in sorts of low wage work that may be quite sex-typed: a woman will be taught basic secretarial skills, for example.

Caring service providers usually do not consciously aim at adjusting their clients to societal structures of domination and oppression. Institutional racism, sexism, and classism, however, are reproduced partly by the application of unconscious norms and stereotypes in many situations of interaction, especially between social unequals in disciplinary settings. My point here is that it is nearly inevitable for service providers to reproduce these structures as they may condition the lives of pregnant addicts, unless those providers are conscious of how social norms can enter their work and can actively undermine the processes of the reproduction of structures of privilege and oppression.

Drug treatment programs and similar services vary in the manner and degree to which they consciously or unconsciously impose disciplines and surveillances on women and vary in the manner and degree to which they normalize clients and adjust them to dominant structures of privilege and oppression. Many therapists and social workers are critical of the expertise, tendencies toward disrespect and the creation of a punitive atmosphere, and paternalism, which remain the norm in service provision, especially toward those defined as deviant, such as addicts or poor people. Another element that Foucault finds in modern educative and therapeutic practices is much more standard—the use of confessional discourse.

According to Foucault, the genealogy of modern therapeutic practices can be traced to the Christian practice of caring for and making the self by means of a confessional narrative that plumbs the depths of the soul, and seeks to root out illusion and self-deception.

> Each person has the duty to know who he is, that is, to try to know what is happening inside him, to acknowledge faults, to recognize temptations, to locate desires, and everyone is obliged to disclose those things to God or to others in the community and hence to bear public or private witness against oneself.[48]

In traditional and early modern Christianity, the goal of such confessional discourse is the renunciation of the self. Modern therapeutic practices transform and develop these confessional techniques to a new end, the fashioning of a new self. According to Nikolas Rose, twentieth-century therapeutic practices refine and multiply these confessional technologies with the goal of producing a transparently autonomous self, where the individual has internalized the skills and disciplines of self-inspection and self-direction that assure her independence and self-control.[49]

Most of the time clients spend in drug treatment, whether residential or outpatient, they spend in therapeutic talk. Typically a client participates both in individual counseling sessions and in several group sessions per day or per week. Some of these individual and group meetings are educative, for example, focusing on the effects of drug use or on proper nutrition. Much of this individual and group talk, however, is confessional. Its aim is for the patient to discover and express the deep truth about herself. She constructs a narrative of her history that uncovers aspects of herself that account for her drug dependence. Often she finds relationships with others or fears about her capacities that she has been denying, repressing, hiding from herself, which she brings forward through talk and vows to overcome. Group counseling sessions in drug treatment programs are often explicitly modeled on the twelve-step techniques first developed in Alcoholics Anonymous. The confessional model in twelve-step programs is direct. Group members are exhorted to give over their selves to a higher power and plumb their souls' depths while the others bear witness to their discourse. The confessional narrative often includes an element of resolution, a forward-looking conversion toward new understandings and actions, and a construction of the means needed to achieve these goals.

The goal of therapeutic talk in most drug treatment programs is for the patient to bring herself under direction, to make herself an autonomous, independent agent. In this way typical drug treatment programs retain the atomistic and individualizing model of the relation of the person and society that I have argued underlies the punishment approach to pregnant addicts, which I have also argued that a consistent ethic of care rejects.

The problem with the confessional talk typical of drug therapy, as well as most other therapies, is that it tends to be depoliticizing and individualizing. It enlists the patient's own complicity in her adjustment to existing institutions and relations of privilege and oppression, by encouraging her to construct herself, or at best her family, as the source of her pain and her problems. This self-reflective exercise diverts her from locating her life in the context of wider social institutions and problems and also discourages her from forming dialogic bonds with others in relations of solidarity and resistance. The solution to each addict's problems lies solely or primarily in herself, in her ability to develop coping skills, skills for managing her reaction and those around her to the dangers and disturbances that may surround her.[50] Some drug treatment theoreticians and practitioners recognize this depoliticized nature of the therapeutic tradition and have attempted to modify therapeutic practice to include more discussion of the oppressive social causes of personal distress. But an individualized model of self-discovery and conversion remains typical.

I have labeled a typical treatment approach to the problem of pregnant addicts "suspicious" on the grounds developed in this section. To "suspect" them is not to condemn them outright. Support for treatment is still the only viable alternative for a policy approach to the problem of drug-exposed infants. Indeed, some of the causes of surveillance or paternalistic practices in drug treatment programs may lie in insufficient resources for the programs. The grounds for suspicion, moreover, apply to many kinds of therapy and service provision besides drug treatment. What we can learn from Nancy Fraser, Michel Foucault, Nikolas Rose, and some of the others I have referred to is how to view with suspicion precisely those liberal, humanist, service-providing practices that seem to be an alternative to overly dominative practices like criminal punishment. Contemporary structures of domination and oppression appear as often in the bureaucracy of the welfare state as in the prison, although not in the same form.

EMPOWERMENT AS AN ALTERNATIVE

Empowerment is like democracy: everyone is for it, but rarely do people mean the same thing by it. For Jack Kemp, former secretary of Housing and Urban Development, "empowering" poor public housing tenants meant turning over to them the management and/or ownership of the old, deteriorating, and poorly maintained buildings in which they live and providing them with little in the way of resources to help renovate, run, and maintain them. The term "empowerment" appears frequently in literature on the philosophy of social service provision. Although usages vary, I identify two primary meanings. For some therapists and service providers, empowerment means the development of individual autonomy, self-control, and confidence; for others empowerment refers to the development of a sense of collective influence over the social conditions of one's life. I think that the second meaning is better, because it includes both personal empowerment and collective empowerment and suggests that the latter is a condition of the former.

In the previous section I pointed out, following Foucault, that therapeutic services are often sites of the exercise of power in modern societies, which normalize individuals and adjust them to the demands of the dominant oppressive institutions, often with their own complicity through confessional talk. Social service theorists who use the first meaning of empowerment challenge the more overtly dominative forms of power that sometimes appear in drug treatment programs. They challenge models of service provision that make the service provider an expert and authority and that rely on rules and surveillance.[51] They advocate instead what Thomas Wartenberg calls a "transformative" use of power by the service provider in relation to the client. As Wartenberg describes it, in a transformative use of power, the superior exercises power over the subordinate in such a way that the subordinate agent learns certain skills that undercut the power differential between her and the dominant agent. The transformative use of power seeks to bring about its own obsolescence by means of the empowerment of the subordinate agent.[52]

This concept of empowerment fits with a certain parental model of an ethic of care. The parent, teacher, or service provider may exercise some disciplinary power in relation to the child, student, or client, but only for the sake of the development of skills and resources that will lead the client to autonomy and equality. Thus, John L. Forth-Finegan notes that empowerment is "taught by giving choices, and images to hold onto, to help define a self."[53] Some theorists who use empowerment in this sense also derive their conception of the self that is so defined from the self-in-reflection theory of the ethics of care. They argue that a woman's sense of autonomy must be structured not in an effort to separate from others as in many male-oriented concepts of autonomy, but that the autonomous self is established in a context of caring and supportive relationships. For this reason many therapists using this conception of empowerment encourage approaching a client in the context of her family system or other important relationships. Thus Janet L. Surrey defines empowerment as

> the mobilization of the energies, resources, strengths, or powers of each person through a mutual, relational process. Personal empowerment can be viewed only through the lens of power through connection, that is, through the establishment of mutually empathic and mutually empowering relationships.[54]

According to my analysis of the previous section, this sort of caring therapy may not be subject to the more obvious criticisms of disciplinary practices. It nevertheless remains suspect to the degree that it operates with a confessional model of therapeutic talk (as distinct from the dialogical model I will refer to below) where that confessional model encourages the client to look into herself and express her inhibitions and resolutions, while others bear witness. Despite its understanding of the self as constituted in the context of relationships, this meaning of empowerment tends to remain individualistic. It envisions the development of personal skills and resources through which a person can learn to "be on her own," "get on her feet," and be able to cope with the situations and responsibilities she encounters. This meaning of empowerment tends to stop short of a politicized understanding of the social structures that condition an individual's situation and the cultivation of effective action in relation to those structures.

The second meaning of empowerment used by social service theorists, which I endorse, evolves from ideals of participatory democracy, critical self-reflection, and collective action. I define this meaning of empowerment as a process in which individual, relatively powerless persons engage in dialogue with each other and thereby come to understand the social sources of their powerlessness and see the possibility of acting collectively to change their social environment. In this process each participant is personally empowered, undergoes some personal transformation, but in the context of a reciprocal aiding of others in doing so, in order that together they might be empowered to engage in effective collective action.[55]

Empowering treatment involves a kind of talk very different from the therapeutic confessional talk I described in the previous section, which political movements have called "consciousness raising." Confessional therapeutic talk needs other people: the therapist and sometimes fellow confessors. Their function is to encourage the confession, bear witness, and absolve. Confessional talk, however, is monological: even though it requires the presence of others, it remains one individual reciting her individual story. Consciousness-raising talk, by contrast, is dialogical. Through the give and take of discussion, participants construct an understanding of their personal lives as socially conditioned, constrained in ways similar to that of others by institutional structures, power relations, cultural assumptions, or economic forces. The consciousness-raising group "theorizes" this social account together, moving back and forth between individual life stories and social analysis to confirm or disconfirm both. The members of the group propose interpretations of one another's life stories as well as propose accounts of the social structures and constraints conditioning those lives, and these proposals are tested through discussion. Participants in the discussion are equal in the sense that they all have an equal right to speak, an equal right to criticize the accounts of others, and to have their accounts criticized.[56]

Consciousness raising is empowering because it develops in people the ability to be reflective and critical about the situated social basis of individual action. Such reflection and criticism enables people to move from an acceptance of institutional forms as natural and given to seeing them as human constructs that are changeable, however difficult that may be. Especially when this reflection and criticism occurs in dialogue with others, group solidarities can form that portend the further empowerment that can come with collective action. The final aspect of empowerment, then, is organization: the establishment or joining of democratic collectives that foster bonds of solidarity and bring the actions of many individuals together toward some end of social transformation.

Ruth J. Parsons describes a Head Start mothers' program she works in that embodies some of these ideas of empowerment. The mothers' program was started to address the fact that the women's children were identified by the Head Start workers as "discipline problems." Instead of defining this problem as one concerning the mothering practices of the women, however, and developing in them skills to better manage and care for their children, the program encouraged the mothers to come together in free-ranging dialogue about their children and their lives. The women discussed the problems in their neighborhood and their frustration in their interactions with schools, healthcare organizations, and so forth, which made parenting difficult for them. Through this group dialogue, the women began to see ways that they could work together to address some of the community and social problems that pressed on their lives as parents. Together they persuaded local community mental health centers to make home visits and to alter their services in ways the women would find more helpful.[57]

Presumably, drug treatment is a special case of service provision. Substance-dependent women sometimes have lost the ability to function in daily life at a basic level, and they are usually self-deceiving about their dependence and are often emotionally damaged from physical or psychological abuse. These special circumstances perhaps make it more difficult to provide empowering services for them than for women like those described by Parsons, but with sufficient care and resources it should be possible to do so. Many drug treatment professionals are aware of tendencies to normalize and individualize in therapeutic practice and aim in their own practice for more dialogical relationships with clients. But as Joel Handler points out, the good intentions of individual providers are not enough to make drug treatment programs or other social services empowering.[58] The structure, rules, and institutional relationships of programs in many cases must be redesigned to produce more institutional equality between providers and clients and to connect provider activities in treatment programs with wider community activity. I will close with some general proposals for how designers of drug treatment programs might think about the structure of those programs.

I have discussed why drug treatment programs for pregnant addicts should provide prenatal and obstetrical services, childcare, and gender-specific counseling that addresses issues of sexual abuse. But several other structured program elements are necessary to make services empowering. Many of these are not specific to services for women or mothers but should apply to all service provisions that aim to empower. Although a few drug treatment programs contain some of these elements, my research leads me to believe that programs containing all of them are almost nonexistent.

First, programs should structure at least some therapeutic group sessions on the dialogic model of consciousness raising, whose goals are for the group collectively to identify social sources of individual pain and habit in structures of power and privilege. Such consciousness-raising dialogue can also seek to cultivate a positive culture of gender, racial, and/or class solidarity.[59]

Second, programs should include structured client participation and evaluation of the program, including the evaluation of individual providers. If programs have rules that clients must follow, then clients should participate in making the rules. Rather than merely asking clients for suggestions about services or encouraging them individually to voice complaints, programs can have regular periods of structured self-evaluation, in which client representatives formally and collectively participate. The power hierarchy between providers and clients can be reduced, finally, by formal evaluation of providers by clients, perhaps similar to the way that students now evaluate teachers in most colleges. My research leads me to believe that client participation in rule making and the formal evaluation of programs and providers is extremely rare.

Third, meaningful work is another element of empowering programs. Those addicts who have careers or satisfying jobs can be encouraged to continue them while in treatment. Others should be provided meaningful work, by which I mean work that issues in recognizable results, that develops the skills of workers, and from which workers derive significant benefits. Drug treatment programs, even those serving unemployed persons or person working sporadically in unskilled jobs, do not usually include meaningful work. Such programs could try to link with community development programs in order to provide such work. For example, in many cities, nonprofit development agencies rehabilitate dilapidated housing using primarily the labor of future low-income residents, trained and supervised by skilled workers.

My fourth suggestion, linked to the last, is that empowering drug treatment programs need to be part of a wider network of participatory community organizations in which people work to politicize their needs and address community problems, much in the situation Ruth Parsons describes. Dialogue about the social sources of individual problems and the formation of bonds of group solidarity is merely abstract if those who discover such problems are not organized to take action to address them. The dominant tendency in drug treatment programs is still to isolate clients from community networks and for programs themselves to be self-contained. The goal of removing clients from the influence of those who would encourage them to continue their drug use is laudable. But this goal is better achieved by linking drug treatment with broader strategies of community control over networks and services through a set of interlocking institutions.

Chapter V

REFLECTIONS ON FAMILIES IN THE
AGE OF MURPHY BROWN:
ON JUSTICE, GENDER, AND SEXUALITY

IN MAY 1992 Murphy Brown, a situation-comedy character, gave birth cantankerously to a strapping baby boy before millions of television viewers. To the amazement and amusement of many of us, the next day U.S. Vice President Dan Quayle denounced Murphy Brown in a speech to the Commonwealth Club in San Francisco. She's gone too far when she has a baby with no father. An independent woman such as this is a dangerous role model.

It is no coincidence that Dan Quayle's speech came as America was rocketing from the experience of its greatest disorder since the 1960s: the uprising in Los Angeles. Normalcy was suspended, chaos reigned, fear and anger gripped our cities. The world was turned upside down: African American street-gang members appeared on national television as authoritative news analysts.

Dan Quayle's castigation of Murphy Brown worked as an appeal to the basis of all order, The Family. The Family means original unity and comfort, a presocial, pastoral state of nature without encounter and conflict with strangers. It means an orderly hierarchy of father, mother, and children, where authority is clear and each knows his or her place and duties. Appeal to The Family evokes visceral feelings of comfort and security. As I will discuss below, The Family draws a clear boundary between legitimate and illegitimate, but like all boundaries it is arbitrary. Evocation of danger to or dissolution of The Family conjures up fears of identity loss, exposure, extreme vulnerability—what Quayle called "lawless social anarchy."

Whenever uttered in America today the decrying of single motherhood would have a racial subtext, but in the context of the disorder of Los Angeles, which threatened to spill into the entire nation, the text was not very sub. The root cause of the riots in Los Angeles is the breakdown of the family in the ghetto. Black women irresponsibly, shamelessly, have babies without fathers; they sponge off taxpayers and can't give the kids a decent life. Being only mothers, they cannot discipline their sons, who run loose on the streets with guns and torches. The Law of the Fathers is our only hope against being swallowed in the conflagration. "Children need love and discipline. They need mothers and fathers. A welfare check is not a husband. The state is not a father. . . . Bearing babies irresponsibly is simply wrong."[1]

As apparently intended, Dan Quayle's speech launched a summerlong presidential campaign debate on "family values." What might have looked like solid ground for the status quo and conservatism turned out to be pretty muddy terrain. While both major parties quietly colluded in letting the issue of racism in the cities sink back into its normal rumbling silence, and tacitly agreed that single mothers are a social problem, polls bounced around about what good families are and the policies to support them. While Colorado voters approved of an antigay referendum, for the first time in American history a party's candidate for president explicitly supported some rights for gay men and lesbians (though not marriage). The same candidate was able to turn Republican opposition to family leave against them, and to tie the issue of family values to economic recovery.

In the indomitable American way, the drama climaxed on television. There is a general rule in American journalism that the press is not supposed to report on events that are about to occur. But in the third week of September 1992 this cardinal rule was flagrantly broken, as media eyes focused on the still-to-come fall season premier of *Murphy Brown*. *Time* magazine featured Candice Bergen, who plays Murphy Brown, on its cover, sporting a "Murphy Brown for President" button. On the morning before the evening of the great season premier, no less a publication than the *Wall Street Journal*—so staid and respectable that it never prints photographs, only artist-rendered sketches—printed an editorial on "Murphy Brown's Baby." It too lambasted the fictional Murphy and resounded Quayle's alarm at poor single mothers. "Not many disagree now," it said, "that the best cure for childhood poverty is a live-in dad."

The trope of The Family and its invocation as the signifier of order touches such deep chords in the American heart that for many years radicals have been in a rhetorical retreat from the brazen calls for the abolition of marriage and the pluralization of life-styles that were typical of the late 1960s and 1970s, and also typical of earlier Emma Goldman types of radicalism. Those of us who seek to undermine the oppressions of straight women, gay men and lesbians, and people of color of both sexes and sexual orientations, however, should do what we can to break the mystical hold of The Family on people's minds. As the terrain becomes more slippery, we may get a foothold for change; and we may also get mud in our eyes.

In this essay I consider how issues of gender and sexuality should be analyzed as issues of justice. Applying some of my previous work on justice, I argue that the dominant distributive paradigm of justice is not well suited for conceptualizing many of the issues of justice most central for feminists, issues involving sexuality, reproduction, and family. Those few theorists of justice who do analyze issues of justice and family tend to presuppose the institution of marriage as given, and I will argue that their reliance on the distributive paradigm can account for this.

A feminist theory of justice should criticize the institution of marriage itself, on the grounds that it draws an arbitrary line between legitimate and illegitimate relationships and accords special privileges to the former. Thus I consider what a conception of families should be that does not specifically privilege some relationships, but rather extends the privileges, protections, and obligations currently restricted to married couples and their children to other kinds of relationships. Law, policy, and social practice should break the linkages that currently exist among heterosexual coupling, partnership, parenting, and property rights. The Family should be deconstructed into a series of rights and obligations.

Justice, Gender, and Sexuality

In recent years certain feminist philosophers, such as Susan Okin, Joan Tronto, Marilyn Friedman, and Sara Ruddick, have questioned the assumption, held by many feminists, that justice should be opposed to care, or that concepts of justice cannot serve feminist moral theorizing about family, sexuality, and personal relations.[2] This development in feminist moral theory is overdue, in my opinion. As the primary political virtue, justice should be central to feminist moral theory and politics. As Susan Okin rightly and forcefully argues, moreover, the history of male theorizing about justice ignores male domination and male privilege as issues of justice, largely because they wrongly assume that family relations are prior to or outside of the realm of social relations to which issues of justice apply. The issues of sexual liberation, reproductive rights, sexual division of labor, equality in family relations, and so on, which are central to feminist politics, must be understood as issues of justice. This implies, I suggest, a need to rethink the meaning of social justice beyond the distributive paradigm that dominates in contemporary Anglo-American philosophical approaches to justice.

In *Justice and the Politics of Difference* I have defined and criticized this distributive paradigm. It assumes that all questions of justice are about the distribution of social benefits and burdens among individual and groups. These benefits and burdens may be tangibly measurable, such as income received or tax paid. But distributive theorists also speak of intangibles like power and self-respect as goods distributed among agents, a way of speaking about power and self-respect that I believe wrongly reifies relations and processes.[3]

Due to the rejection of the concept of justice as relevant to the specific moral and political concerns of feminism, there are very few philosophers who have considered moral issues of gender as issues of justice. Most of the few who do analyze gender issues as issues of justice work within the distributive paradigm. James Sterba, for example, restricts his understanding of issues of justice to the distributive questions of equal opportunity and welfare. He argues that a feminist conception of justice conceives human traits as evenly distributed across sexes, and that this implies a transformation of the family in such a way that there would be no gender-specific roles in it.[4]

Susan Okin's is probably the best-known and most thorough account of issues of gender and justice. After criticizing important male theorists of justice, including Rawls, for ignoring issues of justice in the family, she modifies Rawls's theory of justice as fairness to apply to relations between men and women in the family. When radically applied, she argues, Rawls's principle of equal liberty and equal opportunity must imply an abolition of a gender division of tasks and status. Most particularly, the sexual division of labor that allocates primary responsibility for household labor and child rearing to women must be eliminated. While such reforms require change in attitudes and behavior of most men and many women, they also imply specific and far-reaching changes in both government and social policy—to support child-care services, parental-leave policies, and more flexible and family-sensitive public workplace policies.

In extending Rawls's conception to the family, Okin relies on a distributive paradigm of justice. The social injustice that women suffer consists in our having fewer benefits and more burdens in the general pattern of social distribution.

> Political power and office, hard work, money and commodities, security—
> Are any of these things evenly distributed between the sexes? In each case,
> the assignment of women to the functional role of actual or potential wife
> and mother, and primary parent, to basic or at least periodic dependence
> on a man, has a great deal to do with the fact that women, in general,
> benefit less from the benefits and are burdened more by the burdens in the
> distribution of social goods than are men.[5]

There is no denying the claim that women suffer distributive injustice. Issues of distribution are important issues of justice, and this is as true for questions of gender justice as for other kinds of questions. But it is a mistake to reduce all issues of justice to issues of distribution, for two primary reasons. First, the distributive paradigm tends either to distort or to ignore issues of justice not easily conceived of in distributive terms. Second, the distributive paradigm tends to presuppose institutional structures within which distributions take place as given, without bringing the justice of those institutional structures themselves into question.

The distributive paradigm conceives all issues of justice as packages of goods that are possessed by individuals. With this paradigm philosophers and political actors tend to focus on issues like the distribution of property, income, or jobs as the primary issues of social justice. When applied to feminist issues, this focus places in the foreground issues of equal opportunity, the distribution of positions, tasks, economic and social resources between men and women, but ignores or obscures many issues of gender justice that are not so obviously distributive. Thus neither Sterba nor Okin, for example, includes issues of sexuality and reproduction in discussions of gender and justice. I believe this omission can be traced at least partly to their applying a distributive understanding of justice.

One can argue that what is most original about contemporary feminist politics is its raising the most private and personal realms of sexuality and reproduction as public issues of social justice. The systematic harms and inhibitions brought upon women as individuals and as a group by prostitution, pornography, rape, incest, and sexual harassment cannot obviously be conceived as distributive inequalities. These entail systematic issues of justice that are broadly speaking cultural: concerning the organization of sexual practices, the meanings attributed to them, and the representational and symbolic forms associated with sexuality.

Some of the injustices suffered by men and women who wish to form sexual partnerships with people of their own sex can perhaps be conceived in distributive terms. Conceiving injustice toward gay men and lesbians in terms of discrimination, that is, the denial of benefits on arbitrary grounds, uses a distributive concept. But many gay men and lesbians find this too narrow an understanding of their oppression. Violence, stereotyping, stigma, and similar oppressions are not well covered by a distributive paradigm; issues of justice and sexual orientation also turn on the cultural meanings of masculinity and femininity and, like the above issues of the sexual oppression of women, the representational and symbolic forms associated with sexuality.

Justice in procreative and parenting relations is equally ill conceived in distributive terms. Selma Sevenhuijsen argues that the attempt to apply Rawlsian principles of justice to child-custody disputes yields absurd results. For cases where parents dispute about who will have primary custody over their children or about what rights the noncustodial parent will have, it is not at all clear what can be seen as distributed. Conceiving the children as objects to be distributed among parents surely disrespects those children. But it is also conceptually weird to think of rights as the subject of distribution. Justice in custody disputes instead concerns attention to the concrete relationships between parents and children, and the most appropriate way to create enforceable rights to foster and facilitate the most beneficial set of intimate relations.[6]

Many other contexts of reproduction and parenting raise issues of justice not fruitfully conceptualized as involving the distribution of some kind of goods. Practices of contraception, abortion, surrogate pregnancy, in vitro fertilization, lesbian and gay parenting, and so on raise complex issues of justice and policy questions of how law and bureaucracy should morally conceive and structure relationships, a set of questions not assimilable into a distributive understanding of justice.

When philosophers or political actors try to raise issues of justice not obviously about the distribution of goods, they usually try to reconceive them in terms of costs and benefits distributed among social actors. Such reconceptualization, however, often distorts what is at stake in questions of justice when they are about decision-making power, the definition of social positions and their relations and obligations, or culture and life-style.

The recent U.S. Supreme Court decision on abortion rights can illustrate this distorting effect. Many hailed *Planned Parenthood v. Casey*, which the Court decided in June 1992, as a great "compromise," because it managed to conceive the abortion issue in "more or less" terms. States may have an interest in making abortion more costly, whether in time, money, or emotional stress, but they are not permitted to raise those costs "unduly." Through this supposedly middle-of-the-road mechanism the Court has allowed an issue of decision-making power and access to services to be complexly reconceived distributively as a large series of different rights. The decision has greater impeding consequences on young, poor, and rural women, thus following and reinforcing existing distributive inequalities.[7]

The second and perhaps more important problem with the distributive paradigm of justice is that by focusing on the allocation of benefits and burdens within institutional structures, it obscures those institutional structures at the same time that the paradigm assumes them as given. Thus it fails to evaluate the justice of the institutions themselves that provide the conditions and practices that both produce the benefits and burdens and define the social positions among which they are allocated. For example, many contemporary discussions of social justice ask whether justice permits or requires taxing the rich in order to meet the basic needs of the poor. This distributive way of formulating issues of economic justice presumes without making explicit a social structure with divisions between rich and poor, never asking whether this structure itself is just.

Discussion of gender justice that focus on the distribution of benefits and burdens between men and women frequently assume the institutions of marriage and normative heterosexuality as given, and within which distributions occur. Thus Okin, for example, writes as though the primary issue of gender justice is the distribution of household and child-rearing tasks, and the distribution of paid work, between a husband and wife.[8] It is certainly not Okin's intention to be heterosexist, and indeed in several passages in her book she refers to gay and lesbian couples as important models of egalitarian relationships.[9] Nor certainly does she intend to suggest with Dan Quayle that married mothers are better than unmarried ones. My suggestion is that because she considers the distribution of labor and resources within the family as the primary issue of gender justice, she tends to presuppose as given the dominant family norms that privilege marriage without calling their justice explicitly into question.

To summarize, distribution is only a part, albeit an important part, of the social circumstances that feminist principles of justice should evaluate. Issues of justice also include decision-making power, the definition of social positions with their relations and obligations, and culture, which are not reducible to distribution. A broader conception of justice takes not fairness but liberation as its ultimate ideal. This broader conception says that social justice concerns the degree to which a society contains and supports the institutional conditions necessary for all its members to develop and exercise their capacities, express their experiences, and participate in determining their actions and the conditions of their actions. Injustice consists in oppression and domination, which often involve distributive inequality or deprivation, but also involve cultural and relations inhibitions and harms.

WHAT'S WRONG WITH MARRIAGE?

In *Of Woman Born*, Adrienne Rich distinguishes between the institution of motherhood as a structure that systematically oppresses women, on the one hand, and the practices, joys, loves, and pains of particular mothers in particular contexts, on the other.[10] She condemns the institution of motherhood as oppressive and morally backward but urges that mothers and the practices of mothering are often good, useful, and not adequately supported.

Rich's concept of compulsory heterosexuality[11] can point to a similar distinction between the institution of marriage, on the one hand, and particular relationships of love and commitment between particular men and women, on the other. In what follows I argue that the

institution of marriage is fundamentally unjust and should be eliminated. This argument does not condemn long-term relationships of
sexual love and affective commitment between men and women. Such
relationships, however, ought not to have the special privileges and legitimacy they currently have. As my argument proceeds it will become clear
that I believe that the elimination of the special privileges of marriage
entails not removing the state from relationships, but rather reconstituting the meaning of family and thereby extending the privileges that marriage now confers on some people to many other relationships.

But just what is marriage? Taking a cue from the "family values" debate, we can say that marriage is the keystone of The Family as defining
order and legitimacy. The institution of modern marriage normatively
links the regulation of sexuality, procreation, and property. Legally marriage has always been male sexual rights over women, the private rights
of a particular man over the sexual behavior of a particular woman. The
institution of marriage is still the cornerstone of patriarchal power. Important feminist treatises have shown how practices like prostitution,
pornography, rape, and sexual harassment are either part of or derived
from this institution of marriage, and I will not repeat those arguments
here.[12] The important point for my argument is that marriage contains
a notion of the sexual rights that men have over women, which rights
men often appear to assume in other relationships.

Marriage is also an exclusive institution, the enforcement of heterosexuality, inasmuch as it is defined by most legal jurisdictions as the legal
union of a man and a woman, and necessarily one of each.[13] An alleged
justification of this exclusivity is sometimes that marriage is linked to
procreation.[14] Thus marriage defines The Family by defining parental
rights and excluding others from parental relationships. Marriage,
finally, is linked to property and economic stability. Historically, of
course, a major function of marriage has been the preservation or enlargement of property.

One might claim that the definition and linkages of marriage that I
have just expressed no longer correspond to the social realities of advanced industrial Western societies. The truth in this objection motivates
the argument of this essay and the urgency of a "family values" debate.
But in sorting out the terms of this debate we should be clear on how the
institution of marriage, as distinct perhaps from the practices of relationships, remains a significant regulator of social norms, that is, the establishment of respectability and legitimacy. This is so in all three areas—
sexuality, procreation, and property.

Many states in the United States still do not recognize marital rape as
a crime. Even where rape in marriage is criminalizable, moreover, many
juries refuse to recognize that forced sex in marriage, or even in relation-

ships like marriage, is a legal wrong. These facts show that the definition of marriage as male sexual property rights over women is alive and well.

While heterosexual sex outside of marriage has become much more common and accepted in the last twenty-five years, moreover, the Murphy Brown debate shows that marriage still generally regulates the norms of procreation. A child born out of wedlock may no longer be legally registered as a bastard, but dominant norms sill treat such behavior as deviant or pathological. A woman can still lose her job or otherwise be punished for bearing a child on her own, and some courts will uphold such actions.[15] Unmarried heterosexual couples who have been in a sexual and affectionate relationship more often than not decide to get married when they desire to have children. While there are positive legal reasons for making such a decision, involving protections for the children and for the parents in relation to the children in case the relationship dissolves, for most the entrance to legal marriage also carries an aura of settledness and respectability.

While marriage is a formal alliance of property today only for the few in Western societies, entering marriage and setting up a Family entails major consumption activities for those who can afford them. Marriage continues to be associated with property in the form of a privately owned home, along with large and expensive consumer items.[16]

The institution of marriage retains the major social function of conferring legitimacy on people and relationships. Thus marriage, as the keystone of The Family, stands for order itself because it draws a boundary. It creates an unambiguous line between the licit and the illicit. It reproduces this order by granting privileges to those who fall on one side of the line and stigmatizing those who fall on the other side.

Even today the privileges of marriage are many, and we should not need reminding. Marriage entails privileges of property and income—privileges of ownership and inheritance, insurance benefit, credit access, specific tax privileges, social security benefits, survivors benefits for spouses of veterans, immigration privileges.[17] Marriage usually confers rights in relation to children, though the privileges of biological parentage sometimes snarl up this benefit. Married people have a privileged access to reproductive technologies, both to aid and to curtail reproduction. They are the preferred clients of adoption services. Marriage gives people the privilege of gaining access to, taking care of, and signing consent forms for their spouses housed in bureaucratic institutions like hospitals, treatment centers, rest homes, or prisons.

The other side of the privileges of marriage is its oppressions. The institution of marriage privileges heterosexual couples and oppresses homosexual couples, and this certainly is one of its major functions.[18] Few gay men or lesbians have chosen to challenge legally the restriction of marriage to heterosexual couples. Until recently U.S. courts routinely rejected such challenges. Frequently the courts give no reasons for excluding homosexuals from the rights and privileges of marriage other than asserting that marriage is *by definition* a union of one man and one woman.[19] The 1993 decision of the Hawaiian Supreme Court was a landmark because it argued that a ban on same-sex marriage violates constitutional protections to due process and called for reasons why the state has a compelling interesting in limiting marriage to heterosexual couples. As of this writing, most observers expect a trial court to be unable to argue such a compelling interest. In response to fears that states may allow gay men and lesbians legally to marry, the United States Congress has made explicit some of the privileges the federal government confers on married people by withholding them from same sex couples.

In the age of Murphy Brown it is important to observe, however, that lesbian and gay households are by no means the only families that suffer stigma and disadvantage by being excluded from the privileges of marriage. In 1989 nearly 25 percent of all children in the United States and more than half of all African American children lived with one parent. The large majority of these parents are women. Single-mother households have been increasing rapidly as a result of increased divorce, decreased remarriage after divorce, and increased births without marriage. From a statistical point of view, then, families headed by women have become normal.

Neither social policy, social attitudes, nor social theory treats female-headed households as legitimate, however. The woman who voluntarily or involuntarily lives with children alone must not only contend with employers and public bureaucracies that assume parents have the assistance of coparents, but also face serious stigma. Both never-married and divorced mothers commonly face employment, credit, and housing discrimination.

Even among those who call themselves liberals, moreover, public-policy discussion usually treats single motherhood as an aberration and social pathology. Liberals and conservatives in policy discussion often share the judgment that the best cure for the poverty, stress, and discrimination that many single mothers face consists in getting or keeping them married. Thus William Julius Wilson's otherwise progressive social democratic program for addressing the problems of poor people argues for a jobs policy targeted at men so that they can marry poor single mothers and support their children.[20] Because nearly one-quarter of single-parent families live in poverty, William Galston argues that child-oriented family policy must favor marriage. Thus he calls for legal changes that would make divorce more difficult.[21]

Rates of out-of-wedlock births and divorce may well be a sign that some men and women are taking their family commitments less seriously than they should, especially their commitments to children, preferring to indulge their own desires. But the rise in single motherhood also signals the refusal by many women to tolerate the infidelity, subservience, and battering that too many wives put up with in the past. It appears that increasing proportions of never-married or divorced mothers prefer not to be married, moreover, even though they must deal with low wages, welfare bureaucracies, difficulties of parenting alone, and stigma.[22] Surely it is a gross infringement on liberty to send mothers the message that they should get and stay married, whether they like it or not, or face poverty, discrimination, stigma, and even in some cases punishment.

The institution of marriage, finally, tends to oppress unmarried people who wish to set up a household or otherwise be thought of as family. Friends or relatives who wish to set up a common household are often forbidden or discouraged from doing so by zoning laws or housing construction presuming and enforcing a small nuclear family. Efforts at deinstitutionalization and independent living for people with developmental or emotional disabilities have often been stymied by this prejudice about who is a proper family. Four mildly retarded men may have formed bonds of mutual caretaking and companionship in a common household, but zoning rules against "group homes" may impede their living together. The Americans with Disabilities Act of 1990 finally provided some redress for such obstacles.

Rights of personal access and tax privileges are often not extended to grandparents, brothers and sisters, cousins, or nonkin household members who share resources and care for one another. This fact makes marriage and the nuclear family unjust to racial and ethnic groups where extended-family caretaking is the norm.[23]

I conclude that the institution of marriage is irreparably unjust. Its original and current meaning is to solidify male power in relation to women, and to draw an arbitrary line around legitimate relationships. Its historical function has been to use women as a means of forging alliances among men and perpetuating their "line." Today, when those functions are diminished but hardly absent, marriage's injustice consists primarily in its discriminatory granting of privileges. Marriage privileges specific ways of living and variously inhibits, stigmatizes, and penalizes other ways of living. A basic principle of liberal justice is that societal norms should regulate the rights and obligations of exchanges, relationships, and institutional structures, without privileging some particular ways of life. The institution of marriage violates this principle, with oppressive

and disadvantaging consequences for many people. If we are not to privilege particular relationships or ways of life, then what it means to be a
family must be redefined and pluralized.[24]

LEGAL REFORM AND CULTURAL REVOLUTION IN FAMILIES

Any project of defining runs the risk of simultaneous over- and underin-
clusion—of ruling out some aspects of social reality one means to include, or including some one means to exclude. This is especially so in
defining family, where we wish to broaden the concept beyond that of
heterosexual coupling through legal marriage, but not make it so broad
that any and all relationships become familial. Mindful of these problems, in redefining family we should aim at a rough-and-ready character-
ization of attributes, some but not all of which should be present to call
a relationship family. We need a concept of family that understands the
"family resemblances" among families, that there are overlapping but
not always shared attributes among them, and that perhaps families admit to degrees.[25]

In this spirit, I define family as people who live together and/or share
resources necessary to the means of life and comfort; who are committed
to taking care of one another's physical and emotional needs to the best
of their ability; who conceive themselves in a relatively long-term, if not
permanent, relationship; and who recognize themselves as a family.
Family are the ones who care for you when you are sick, and for whom
you care when they are sick. Family members are mutually obliged to
remember one another's birthdays, the ones on whom we dump our
troubles. Family entails commitment and obligation as well as comfort:
family members make claims on one another that they do not make on
others. I am obliged to consider the lives of my family members when
deliberating about a career move, but I am not obliged to consider the
lives of others.

I cannot imagine a society without families in this sense. Children
flourish in families in this sense, a relatively small group of committed
intimates that help them develop a sense of self. Many adults choose not
to live in families so defined, for at least part of their lives; they choose to
live alone or in more loosely defined collectives. But at other times of
their lives most adults want families for the same reason that children
need them: they help provide a rooted sense of self and mutual, concrete caring.

The Family as defined through the institution of marriage normatively
links a series of relationships that can and should be deconstructed. The
Family in that conception implies a two-parent, heterosexual couple living with their genetic biological children and sharing resources. A re-

conceptualization of family must break this series of implications. I shall argue that most of the rights, privileges, and obligations that in current law fall to married couples and biological parents should be disconnected and extended to other kinds of relationships in legally generalized forms. Before taking up that argument, however, let me consider briefly some other approaches to legal reform in family relationships. These include getting the law out of relationships, encouraging private contracts for relationships, and a functional approach to family law.

Some people conclude from arguments like those I have made that justice requires not privileging any ways of living that law and state policy should be removed entirely from defining and regulating family relations. I used to conclude this myself. If families are private and personal, and the state and law are general, public, and quintessentially impersonal, then simple logic seems to dictate that the two should have nothing to do with each other. While there are reasons to demand that state institutions be far less intrusive than they currently are in some families, particularly poor families, today, the removal of all legal definition, relation, and adjudication of family relationships would not serve justice, for several reasons.

The law must define and be prepared to help adjudicate the ambiguities, issues, and conflicts that may arise among family members or former family members. The most important of such claims and obligations concern children. The state and law must provide protections for children just in case particular adults are not protecting them or dispute about their relationships to children. Legal regulation of families is also necessary to protect adults who are vulnerable within families, either because of choices they have made that render them economically dependent or because they are old, ill, or disabled. As I will discuss further below, even in the absence of conflict or neglect, families often need various kinds of state support and recognition to promote the flourishing of their members. As Martha Minow argues, even when the state draws a boundary between itself and families, it functions to regulate both sides of the boundary. Withdrawing state regulation will not promote the freedom of families; instead we need legal norms that are able to conceptualize rights in a way that attends to and responds to the context of particular relationships.[26]

Some people suggest that the best way to guarantee such particularity is by encouraging people to draw up private contracts delimiting the precise terms of their relationship as they define it. While I think that individuals should be able to make contractual agreements about what they consider private affairs if they choose, and to a large degree people have this ability today, a private contractual approach to family law reform has several problems, both practical and philosophical.

The ability to draw up the terms of a private contract about intimate relations presupposes class privilege. Many people cannot afford the services of a lawyer for such purposes; many people do not understand enough about legal language and possibilities to know what they would want to put into a contract. Private contracts spelling out particular terms of intimate relations, moreover, can work only for adults; relations between adults and children must be regulated by other means.

Perhaps even more important, intimate relationships are too open-ended and multifaceted to come under contractual agreements. People who live together, commit themselves to care for one another, raise children together, have a more complex, many sided, and unpredictable relationship than do those who enter a business contract, for example. In many situations it is impossible to predict what their life situation, resources, feelings, or relationship with children will be in ten years. This unpredictability and changeability partly accounts for why courts sometimes invalidate private contracts concerning intimate relations.

This point leads to a philosophical objection, that the framework of contract thinking is simply inappropriate, even immoral, when applied to intimate relations. Where contract conceptualizes relations as a product of explicit and voluntary agreement, family relations are often not chosen. Even where a relation was chosen at one time, aspects of vulnerability, dependency, and commitment often develop in families that are not explicitly chosen. The framework of contracted relations, moreover, is possible only against the background of more fundamental kinds of social bonds, of which families are an important kind.[27]

A third approach discussed in family law as an alternative to the existing legal biases that privilege family relations incorporating marriage is the functional approach. Relations that function as familial in people's lives may often emerge or develop that do not fit the normal rules of family, but still ought to be recognized in order to do justice to individuals in situations of dispute or need. Thus courts and other state agencies should be able to operate according to general criteria of such functions to determine particular family rights and obligations. As with family contracts, I think there should be room in legal and policy reasoning for such a functional notion of the family. But a functional approach to family cannot substitute for formal rules delimiting familial rights and obligations, and formal means of declaring family membership. Relying solely on a functional understanding of family would be costly and possibly intrusive, since every case that came before courts or bureaucracies would have to involve an investigation into the actual nature of a particular intimate relation. It would also leave potential disputants too much at the mercy of a particular official's interpretation of the meaning of family functions.

Reform in family law, as I conceive it, would specify general rules and standards of family relationships, but at the same time deconstruct the legal obligations and privileges currently associated with marriage. The chain of implications must be broken that starts with heterosexual rights of sexual intercourse, to connect this with joint property, shared resources, and the right to expect support, and also connects sexual rights with exclusive rights and exclusive obligations regarding children. Issues of sexual rights, property and resources, procreation and parenting, that is, should be more disconnected.

As I discussed earlier, the institution of marriage still contains the assumption that a man has sexual rights over a woman. As Foucault argues, a major meaning of the modern family is the regulation of sexuality and the definition of sexual rights. But sexuality is indeed an area where state and law should keep out. The idea of sexual rights should become incoherent. No one, that is, whatever kind of relations they are in with another, ever at any time should be in a position where they do not have a right to say no to sex. While sexual love can be an important element in some family relationships, legal rules and standards about families should assume nothing about sex, and certainly should not require any demonstration of sexual intimacy. Sex is neither a necessary nor a sufficient condition for families.[28]

The legal and cultural abolition of the idea of sexual rights, and the formal disconnection of sex from family, would truly be a revolutionary change. The patriarchal idea that men have sexual rights over women with whom they are intimate continues to bias the justice system against the victims of acquaintance rape, or even against victims of sexual harassment. The assumption remains strong, moreover, that a family implies that some member of the household has regular sex with another member of the household. Promotion of gay male or lesbian households as families, for example, often does little to challenge this assumption of sex as a necessary condition for family, even though it is not uncommon for the domestic partner of a gay man or lesbian to be a different person from his or her current lover or lovers. The assumption that sex is an essential attribute of families disqualifies as families household forms that many people live as families, such as single-parent families. The assumption that familial relations are or ought to be sexual, moreover, may discourage the formation, development, or recognition of some kinds of families that some people need or want, as in my example earlier of the mentally disabled men. Finally, while I have no evidence to support it, I have a hunch that the patriarchal assumption of sexual rights in families is a source of child sexual abuse.[29]

The concept of domestic partnership has been a creative proposal for addressing the exclusion of gay men and lesbians from the benefits of marriage, and some cities and private companies have adopted the concept to a limited degree. As a method of deconstructing marriage, I would propose that a concept like domestic partnership be universalized. By a simple process of legal registration, any adults should be able to register as domestic partners. I do not even see a reason that only two adults should be allowed to register together as partners, though because of state or employer benefits that partnership would confer, I think it might be reasonable to declare a limit to the number of persons who can register as domestic partners to one another.

Domestic partnership, in the universalized and enlarged form that I conceive it, would carry all the current rights and obligations of marriage having to do with property, support, resources, and access to one another in institutionalized settings—rights of joint ownership, inheritance, to be carried on medical and life insurance policies; immigration rights; rights to visit partners housed in hospitals or prisons; rights to be consulted in treatment options; rights to sign consent forms for; and rights to claim continued resource support at the time of partnership dissolution. Domestic partnership, however, would imply nothing about sex. While heterosexual lovers and homosexual lovers might wish to enter domestic partner relations, so also might sisters or unrelated persons wishing to establish a long-term shared household but who are not sexually involved.

Family law should of course be especially directed at the purposes of nurturing and protecting children. Reproductive and parental rights are currently attached to marriage, and this link too should be deconstructed. All adults, whatever their personal life circumstances, should have equal access to reproductive technologies. Adoption services should not be allowed to discriminate against categories of persons. At the time of the birth of a child, certain people will declare themselves parents of that child, or the child will be given up for adoption. Usually the biological mother of the child will be one of these persons, but the mere fact of her giving birth ought not to make her a parent. Similarly, while I am inclined to agree that something should be done to make men more accountable for the procreative consequences of their sexual activity, the mere fact of being the genetic father of a child should not automatically give a person rights and obligations in relation to that child.[30] For one thing, this can force a mother to have continued contact with a man she no longer wishes to know. Contrary to currently dominant legal norms, it should be possible for the declared parents of a child to be of any sex.[31]

Nor should the law assume, as it currently does, that a child can have only two parents. The controversies about the rights of birth mothers who have contracted to bear a child for another couple have raised in a new and unique way the question of whether more than two people can have parental rights and obligations in relation to a child. Increased divorce and remarriage have also necessitated raising this question. No legal forms can prevent the hurt and confusion that divorce produces for many children. If a child forms a domestic relationship with a new adult that enters her household, however, who wishes to take on the commitment to parent her, that adult should be legally able to become her parent without her having to give up a legal relation with a parent she already has.

But what is this legal relation of parent? While the legal status of parent entails certain rights that courts may decide vary with circumstances—control over health care, religious education, custody or visitation rights for parents who do not have primary custody rights, and so on—I conceive that parenthood primarily involves responsibilities. To declare oneself a parent is to promise to support a child to the best of one's ability, both materially and emotionally, until the child reaches adulthood. Thus while I reject the idea that genetic fathers should be forced to support the children of their issue, fathers or mothers who have taken on the commitment of parenting by declaring themselves parents can be made to pay even if they divorce the other parent(s) and leave the household. The idea of "child-first" divorce polices is sensible in this respect. Courts should make child support awards to a large degree by calculating what the child needs to have a decent life. More vigorous enforcement of postdivorce child-support responsibilities than currently exists, such as attaching paychecks, is consistent with a more universal and just family policy.

If courts consistently ruled for child-support awards that put the needs of children first, however, they might sometimes unfairly burden parents who have left a household, most often men, who would because of these constraints be unable to form or enter new families or make other life choices. For this and other reasons, the welfare of children should be deconstructed from marriage in a final sense: we should not assume that a married couple is solely responsible for the welfare of their biological children. If children are the future of a society, then all the adult members of a society have some responsibility to support all the children. While declared parents would have primary responsibility for the material and emotional support of children, many if not all parents require extensive social supports in carrying out those duties, and nonparents should contribute significantly to such supports.

A just policy of family pluralism would consist not in the state's remaining neutral among family forms, treating them all according to the same rules no matter what their attributes, but rather would positively differentiate among some kinds of families for the sake of providing them with the support that will make them flourish equally with others.

In principle all families need social supports to flourish and be appreciated, but some more than others. I will conclude by briefly discussing such social support issues for two categories of families: families of people with disabilities, and single-parent families.

Even with the passage of the Americans with Disabilities Act, our society has very far to go before it appreciates people with disabilities. Parents of people with disabilities often need a great deal of financial and social support for their families to flourish; while some such financial and social support is available to such parents today, too often parents feel that they must fight for every dime, that they must struggle with service providers over the nature of services, and that the level of support they receive is inadequate. As I have mentioned already, adults with disabilities ought to be able to form families of their own, outside their parents' homes and outside institutionalized settings, if they wish. But they often need financial and social supports in their family settings that others do not require. Empowering people with disabilities to form families includes their being able to parent. Perhaps not all people with disabilities are able to raise children, and many do not wish to try. Many people with disabilities can successfully parent, however, with sufficient financial and social support.[32]

As I discuss in more detail in the following chapter, justice requires respecting families headed by women alone. Children of single mothers are more likely to be poor than are other children. The children of a single parent, however, often have an earlier sense of independence and more companionate relations with their parent than do other children. Parenting alone, on the other hand, is harder than parenting with a partner or partners, which can lead to lack of time and other stresses that make the children's lives less peaceful and stable than they might be if there were more than one adult in the home.

A just and liberal society would have abortion and contraception programs and access of a sort that would aim to ensure that every child a woman bears is a wanted child. If we had such policies in the United States today, there would probably be far fewer single mothers. But there would still be many, either because women chose to bear children on their own, or because parents would continue to separate.

Social justice requires that single-parent families be valued and appreciated and given the social support they need to flourish. Among such social support policies are pay equity schemes to equalize women's wages with men's, expanded welfare support, and vastly expanded child-care subsidies, including child-care services to enable teenage mothers to continue with school. The United States could also emulate some European countries in developing "mothers' houses," where single mothers live in private apartments but also have opportunities for shared cooking and child minding.[33]

I have argued that a distributive paradigm of social justice tends to bias the thinking of those who think about gender justice away from issues of sexuality and reproduction. Because dominant approaches to justice consider how benefits and burdens should be distributed within institutions, moreover, theorists of justice and family usually assume the institution of marriage as given. Feminists must question the justice of the institution of marriage itself. Declaring marriage unjust then requires a feminist theory of justice to conceptualize legal frameworks for family relations that deconstruct the series of relations currently joined in the legal framework of marriage and family. Family justice, finally, implies social policies that appreciate plural family forms and provide social support for families, especially for those families with special needs.

Chapter VI

MOTHERS, CITIZENSHIP, AND INDEPENDENCE:
A CRITIQUE OF PURE FAMILY VALUES

IN HIS IMPORTANT BOOK, *Liberal Purposes*, William Galston argues against the commonly held position that state action and policy is or ought to be neutral among ends. He demonstrates that, despite their professions of liberal neutrality, the most important liberal theories presuppose non-neutral accounts of the human good and cannot help but do so. Liberal theory and practice rely on value judgements about human well-being that are largely independent of individually defined tastes and interests—for example, judgments of health, comfort, and aesthetic satisfaction. Liberal principles and programs take for granted the need to pursue specific ends, such as security, the relief of misery, and the development of the capacities of children. Promoting these ends entails valuing some institutions, character traits, and actions more than others, moreover, and sometimes implementing state policies that encourage or require some and discourage or forbid others.[1]

I agree with Galston's general argument that law and public policy cannot and should not be neutral among ends and legitimately ought to encourage in its citizens the virtues consistent with the social good. I find disturbing, however, a particular inference that Galston draws from this position, namely that the liberal state ought to privilege the "intact two-parent" family. This particular family structure, he argues, best promotes the welfare of children and enables them to become good citizens. The state is therefore justified in implementing policies that encourage marriage and discourage divorce and single motherhood. This paper criticizes Galston's position.

Galston's position on family values is widely shared by liberals and conservatives, both in the United States and in other liberal democracies. Galston's argument for the moral preeminence of the intact two-parent family has both an empirical and a normative aspect. I first examine some of his empirical claims that divorce and single motherhood have bad social consequences and show that the evidence is much more ambiguous than he allows. I concentrate on the normative dimensions of Galston's argument, which hinge on the citizen virtue of independence. Review of the role of the norm of independence in modern political theory reveals it as male biased and operative in relegating dependent people and their usually female caretakers to an inferior status.

Contrary to Galston, promoting equal citizenship requires abandoning the idea that those who are not self-sufficient are of lesser worth. On the contrary, public policy should provide social support to promote the autonomy of people who need help from others. Only such an abandonment of the norm of independence understood as self-sufficiency can grant equal citizenship to at-home caretakers and people who, for whatever reason, are unable completely to support or take care of themselves. Liberals must affirm a plurality of family forms as valid ways of life. By virtue of its structure, no one family form is inherently better at realizing the values of family life. I conclude by discussing some general implications of this argument for public policy.

ARE DIVORCE AND SINGLE PARENTHOOD CAUSES OF POVERTY AND DISABILITY?

In arguing for the moral superiority of stable marriage, Galston distinguishes what he calls intrinsic traditionalism from functional traditionalism. Intrinsic traditionalism promotes particular institutional forms and individual behavior simply because they conform with past practice, the precepts of religion, or the commands of some other authority adhered to without reason or criticism. Functional traditionalism, on the other hand, "rests its case on asserted links between certain moral principles and public virtues or institutions needed for the successful functioning of a liberal community. So, for example, an intrinsic traditionalist might deplore divorce as a violation of divine law, whereas a functional traditionalist might object to it on the grounds (for which considerable empirical evidence can be adduced) that children in divorced families tend to suffer the kinds of economic and psychological damage that reduce their capacity to become independent and contributing members of the community" (p. 280).

If a plausible link can be established between a particular family form and the ability of children to take their place as good citizens—independent and contributing members of the community—Galston asserts, then this justifies the state's preference for that family form and perhaps even limits the liberty of adults to raise children under other conditions. Just as parental freedom does not include the right to beat or starve your child, or to treat your child in a manner that will impede normal development, so "you are not free to act in ways that will lead your child to impose significant and avoidable burdens on the community" (p. 252). Consequently, the freedom of parents should be subordinate to the state aim of raising good citizens. "My focus is on what must be a key objective of our society: raising children who are prepared—intellectually, physically, morally, and emotionally—to take their place as law-abiding and independent citizens. Available evidence supports the conclusion that on balance, the intact two-parent family is best suited to this task" (p. 285).

The divorce rate in the United States jumped very significantly between 1970 and 1975, peaked in 1981, and since then has been declining back to the 1975 level of 4.7 divorces per 1,000 married couples per year.[2] The number of children affected by divorce has remained roughly constant since 1975, at around 1 million each year. Galston claims that there is strong evidence to support the claim that divorce causes lasting emotional distress in children. He cites a study by Wallerstein and Blakeslee for this evidence. They followed about sixty children of divorce for ten years and claimed to find that the experience of divorce in adolescence causes a lack of confidence and an inability to sustain relationships in adulthood.[3] This study has been criticized for its small sample, the fact that all the subjects were in therapy at the start of the study, and the fact that there are no comparisons with children from intact families.[4]

A wider look at the literature reveals a much more ambiguous picture of the effects (or lack of effects) of divorce on the capacities and character of children. Some demographic studies show greater risk of school drop-out, career and income disadvantage, and greater rates of teen pregnancy for children of divorce than for children of stable marriage, but others find few differences on a range of academic, developmental, emotional, and health measures. Some longitudinal studies find poorer adjustment for adolescent children of divorce, but others find no relationships.[5] Where differences between children of divorce and those from intact families on measures of well-being are found, they are usually rather small. One meta-analysis of ninety-two mostly American studies finds children of divorce to have only slightly lower levels of well-being than those from intact families.[6]

Where children of divorce do suffer emotional damage, moreover, it may be that family conflict, rather than divorce itself is the cause. A ten-year study recently released in Australia found no significant differences between children of divorce and children of continuing marriage in level of academic achievement, career success, or ability to enter and maintain intimate relationships. It found that emotional distress tended to be associated with family conflict, whether it resulted in divorce or not, and that even the effects of conflict are offset by a strong relationship between the child and at least one of the parents.[7]

One of the policy recommendations that Galston makes for regulating family life for the sake of raising good citizens is to make divorce more difficult to obtain. Given the very mixed record on the effects of divorce on children, surely it is questionable that the state has a legitimate right to limit the liberty of unhappily married adults to sever their relationship. If family conflict, instead of divorce itself, is a likelier cause of emotional distress in children, moreover, encouraging parents to stay together when they don't want to may cause more harm in children than allowing them to divorce in as simple and peaceful a manner as possible.[8]

Galston argues that not only divorce but also single parenthood, whether the parent has been married or not, is bad for children. In 1992, 26 percent of families with children in the United States were headed by single parents; only 4 percent of all families were headed by unmarried men, while 22 percent were headed by unmarried women.[9] Many single-parent families are created by divorce; in 1992, 14 percent of American children lived with a divorced or separated mother only. Because so much of family values discourse is laced with race, I will note that 22 percent of black children were living with a divorced or separated mother, and 13 percent of white children.[10]

Recent discussions of family values, however, focus more on single-mother families created by births to unmarried women. Galston is not alone in suggesting that this "illegitimacy" is on the rise and is destroying the moral fabric of society. So let us dwell for a moment on the facts about births to unmarried women. In 1990, 26 percent of all births in the United States were to unmarried women. Contrary to the image that "illegitimacy" is a black phenomenon, 56 percent of these women were white, and 41 percent were African American.[11] Again contrary to popular image, the rate of births to unmarried black mothers has been falling in the last twenty years and rising very significantly among white mothers. The proportion of births to unmarried African American mothers is still far higher than to unmarried white mothers, but the gap has been steadily narrowing. The proportion of births to unmarried mothers in relation to all births has been rising significantly in the last decade, largely because married couples are having significantly fewer children.[12]

Popular imagery also assumes that most unwed mothers are black teenagers. There was a significant decline in births to unmarried black teenagers from 1970 to 1986, however, and births to unmarried white teenagers more than doubled during the same period. The proportion of teens among unwed mothers has been declining steadily, moreover; in 1990 more than two-thirds of births to unwed mothers were women 20 years and older. Birth rates among unmarried white women between the ages of 30 and 34 doubled between 1980 and 1987; among all other races there was only a modest increase in this age bracket.[13]

Thus unwed motherhood has become a mainstream American phenomenon, not confined to any particular age, race, or educational attainment. Divorce when children are present increased significantly in the 1970s but has leveled off in the 1980s and occurs among all races, ages, regions, and income groups. As a result of all these trends, some people estimate that, among children born in the late 1970s, 42 percent of whites and 86 percent of blacks will spend some time in a single-parent family.[14] The single-parent family form, primarily of single mothers, is common in American society, and increasingly common in many other societies in the world today.

Galston claims that the single-parent family is bad for children. He and others suggest that children of single parents have less emotional and intellectual support, and receive less supervision, than do children in two-parent families.[15] It is certainly plausible to claim that parenting is easier and more effective if two or more adults discuss the children's needs and provide different kinds of interactions for children. It does not follow that the second adult must be a live-in husband, however, and some studies have found that the addition of any adult to a single-parent household, whether a relative, lover, or friend, tends to offset single-parent tendencies to relinquish parental decision making too early.[16]

While Galston claims that the evidence is clear that single-parent families are worse for children than intact two-parent families, many others find the evidence to be more ambiguous. It seems more likely that single-parent families are better for children in some respects and not better in others. For example, while adults in single-parent families tend to spend less time supervising homework, at the same time single parents are less likely to pressure their children into social conformity and are more likely to praise good grades.[17] Children in single-mother households may suffer disadvantages associated with stress on that one parent, but there may also be advantages to single-parent families, such as a greater closeness between parent and child or greater emotional maturity than children have in two-parent families.[18] Growing up in a single-parent family may be a handicap, but having numerous siblings in a two-parent family is also a handicap. Since single parents have fewer children, these two family forms may be comparable in their consequences for children.[19]

Galston's main reason for claiming that single parenthood is bad for children, however, is less contestable. Children in single-mother families are much more likely to be poor than families headed by men. In 1990, 44.7 percent of woman-maintained households with children were in poverty, compared with about 7.7 percent of male-headed households. Black single mothers are more likely to be poor, but white single mothers are also at high risk; in 1990, 48 percent of black female-headed households were poor, and 27 percent of white female-headed families.[20] More than half of single mothers with a high school education or less are poor, regardless of their race or age.[21]

The primary income for most of these children comes from their mothers. Court-ordered child support awards averaged only $2,100 per family in 1985, and many fathers failed to pay.[22] The primary cause of the poverty of children in single-parent households is women's lack of earning power. In 1990, the median weekly earnings for women twenty-five years and over was $400, compared with $539 for men.[23] About 40 percent of women maintaining households alone are full-time year-round workers, and another 27 percent work seasonally or part-time. But more than 21 percent of families headed by employed women have incomes below poverty, compared with 4 percent of families headed by an employed man.[24] Jenks estimates that, if we wanted to ensure that every full-time employed single mother could live a life of minimum subsistence for herself and two children on her earnings alone, we would have needed a minimum wage of $9.00 per hour in 1988. Unless the woman has a college degree, she is likely to earn more like $6.50 per hour, and if she does not have a high school diploma she earns an average of $4.10 per hour.[25]

One-third of all single mothers do not participate in the official labor force. (There is no way of telling how many of these earn income in informal markets, and many of them do.) Some cannot get jobs, because jobs are not available to match their skills or because they lack skills. Some believe that they will be better mothers if they can nurture and supervise their children at home, even though they will be poor. Many lack access to decent child care or cannot afford it at the low wage they can earn. Some reason that living on state subsidy will be better for their children than accepting employment at or near minimum wage with no benefits, especially since as workers they must pay for clothes, transportation, child care, and other expenses they would not have if they did not have paid employment. Even so, less than 60 percent of poor children were subsidized by welfare in 1986, down from nearly 86 percent of poor children in 1973.[26] Despite racist myths, only about 31 percent of welfare recipients are African American, a proportion that has remained constant in the last twenty years.[27]

Because of the undeniable fact that children of single-mother families are economically disadvantaged, many of them severely, Galston argues that the single-parent family form is itself a bad family form. He recommends marriage as the cure for childhood poverty. "It is no exaggeration to say that the best anti-poverty program for children is a stable, intact family" (p. 285). Given that over 40 percent of poor families are married-couple families, this certainly is an exaggeration.

Still, on average adult men of all races earn more than women, and white men earn on average about one and one-third times what white women earn.[28] Galston is right, moreover, to claim that most families today need two wage earners "to maintain even a modestly middle-class way of life" (p. 285). Most children who are economically well-off, therefore, depend on two adult incomes. Because couples usually choose to allocate household and child-rearing responsibilities to women, however, many married women work only part-time. This fact, in combination with the fact that men are usually able to earn significantly more than women, means that most economically well-off women and children depend on a male wage to keep them out of poverty.

Marriage Preference Reinforces
the Subordination of Mothers

Now let us proceed to examine Galston's normative argument for the superiority of the intact two-parent family. Single-parent families are a less desirable family form, according to Galston, and public policy ought to take action to discourage their existence. Galston takes pains to deny that his position is an attack on single parents. Such a proposition would be "insulting to the millions of single parents who are struggling successfully against the odds to provide good homes for their children" (p. 285). Nor does he believe that mothers ought to have primary responsibility for child welfare. Indeed, he rightly believes that fathers who leave mothers alone with children and pay little or no child support are a major social problem. In evaluating Galston's arguments about desirable family structure, however, I will focus on single mothers, because the vast majority of single-parent households are headed by women. I will assume that the only empirical case to be made for the claim that single-parent families are undesirable is that they are more likely to be poor than two-parent families.

Many women parent alone because they have inadequate access to contraception and abortion or because their husbands have chosen to the leave the household. Many women of all ages, however, choose to bear children without husbands. Women initiate an increasing proportion of divorces, moreover, and increasing numbers of divorced mothers are not seeking remarriage. Galston's position on the moral superiority of the two-parent family implies that the choices of these mothers are morally wrong, not for reasons of intrinsic traditionalism, but for the functional traditionalist reasons concerning the duty of parents to maximize the welfare of children. Here is how I reconstruct Galston's argument to that conclusion.

Society through the state has a direct and fundamental interest in the raising of good citizens. A good citizen possesses liberal virtues, which are courage, law-abidingness, loyalty, independence, tolerance, willingness to work and delay gratification, adaptability, and the ability to discern the rights of others (pp. 221–24). Two-parent families are best able to inculcate these virtues, whereas single-mother families are less likely to do so. Therefore women should refrain from having children out of wedlock; mothers should put the interests of their children above their own and not divorce their husbands in order to pursue greater happiness for themselves, and in circumstances where they have not chosen single motherhood, mothers should try to get husbands. Thus public policy should regulate family behavior, providing disincentives for less worthy lifestyles and actions, and incentives for the more worthy. In what follows I shall show that this argument entails continuing the patriarchal tradition which denies women, and in particular mothers, full citizenship.

Galston identifies independence as one of the primary liberal virtues, because the liberal society is characterized by individualism. Public policy should prefer intact two-parent families because these best nurture such independence.

> To individualism corresponds the liberal virtue of independence—the disposition to care for, and take responsibility for, oneself and avoid becoming needlessly dependent on others. Human beings are not born independent, nor do they attain independence through biological maturation alone. A growing body of evidence suggests that in a liberal society, the family is the critical arena in which independence and a host of other virtues must be engendered. The weakening of families is thus fraught with danger for liberal societies. In turn, strong families rest on specific virtues. Without fidelity, stable families cannot be maintained. Without a concern for children that extends well beyond the boundaries of adult self-regard, parents cannot effectively discharge their responsibility to help form secure, self-reliant young people. In short, the independence required for liberal social life rests on self-restraint and self-transcendence—the virtues of family solidarity. (p. 222)

This is a rather thin and vague definition of independence, but from this and other passages I infer that independence here means primarily having a well-paid secure job sufficient to support oneself and one's children at a level that can enable them to develop the capacities and acquire the skills to achieve such jobs themselves, and can also provide enough savings so that one does not become dependent on those children or others when one is too old to work.

The major problem with single motherhood, as I construe Galston's argument, is that single mothers tend often not to be independent in this sense; that is, they are poor or close to poor and often depend on government subsidy to meet some or all of their needs and those of their children. I noted earlier that the primary reason for this is that women's wages frequently are far lower than men's and that affordable child care is often unavailable.

I have no doubt of Galston's commitment to sexual equality, including pay equity. Nor do I doubt that he deplores men who dominate women in the household. An argument for the superiority of intact two-parent families, he says, does not entail a return of women to the status of barefoot in the kitchen; sound families today need mothers as well as fathers in the workforce. He does not note that in most families with two wage earners there is a great disparity between the male and the female wage, either because the mother's full-time work is less well paid than the father's, or because the mother works part-time so that she can also take primary responsibility for caring for the children and doing household work. Most economically well-off women and children are economically dependent on a man.

In the absence of explicit attention to the facts of gender inequality and male domination, and their implications, Galston's argument for the moral superiority of stable marriage comes to this. Mothers should subordinate themselves to and be dependent on men, even if they would rather parent on their own, for the sake of nurturing the independence of their children. Independence is a paragon virtue of liberal citizenship, but a mother's virtue entails dependence on a man. The independence they nurture, moreover, is primarily in their male children, since their female children are likely to grow up to be mothers. This argument implies that mothers are less than full citizens in the liberal society.

Now Galston would surely deny that he intends that mothers should subordinate themselves to men. But in the absence of explicit consideration of gender inequalities in earning power and household division of labor, preferring stable marriage over divorce and single motherhood amounts to calling for mothers to depend on men to keep them out of poverty, and this entails subordination in many cases. As Susan Okin powerfully argues, men and women tend not to have equal power in families, and the unequal power derives to a significant extent from the unequal wages that men typically bring into the household.[29] Men fail to take equal responsibility for housework and child care, often doing little of either, because they have the power not to. Women therefore often work many more hours than their husbands at tasks that are undervalued. More often than not men are primary decision makers in a household, not because the women are passive and traditional, but because they depend on their husband's income. Women's lives are disrupted and friendships torn by following the male wage earner to another job. Finally, their subordination and dependence puts women at risk of battery and rape, which far too many suffer at the hands of their husbands. Many women nevertheless stay in battering relationships for a long time because they economically depend on their batterers and believe that it is best for their children to keep the family "intact."

A gender-neutral theory of family values ignores the fact that, in the current gender structure, stable marriage means that women are often dependent on men and often suffer power inequality and various degrees of domination by men both in and outside the home. It ignores the fact that, for many mothers, leaving marriage and choosing not to enter marriage is not a frivolous and selfish pursuit of pleasure, but a matter of escaping unjust subordination. In the absence of attention to this unjust gender structure, Galston's argument replicates the male centeredness of modern political theory's conception of citizenship. Liberal and republican political theorists in the early modern period more explicitly recommended the subordinate and dependent status of wives and mothers.[30] The actual unit of liberal or republican society is the household, not the individual person. The male head of household exhibits the virtue of independence, supporting dependent mothers and children. The citizen virtue of mothers does not entail independence but, rather, the virtues of caring and sacrifice necessary for nurturing children to be good citizens.

INDEPENDENCE, DEPENDENCE, AND CITIZENSHIP

In the tradition of modern political theory, independence is the citizen virtue of the male head of household and property owner. The bourgeois citizen meets his own needs and desires, and those of his dependents, by means of self-sufficient production on his property and by means of independent contract to buy and sell goods. This social organization depends on a distinction between private and public. Productive activity of meeting needs and desires is organized privately, with dependent wives overseeing their day-to-day provision, and the raising of children. This frees the male head of household to conduct the contract business that will enlarge his property and to meet with other independent citizens to discuss affairs of state.[31]

Independence is an important citizen virtue in the modern democratic republic, because it enables citizens to come together in public on relatively free and equal terms. If every citizen meets the needs of himself and his dependents through his own property, then citizens are immune to threats or particularist influence by others on whom they depend for their livelihoods. With independence in this sense they may deliberate on equal terms and consider the merits of issues in terms of the general good.[32]

Thus the citizen virtue of independence also entails personal autonomy, a sense of self-confidence, and inner direction, as well as the ability to be reflective, not swayed by immediate impulse or blind emotion in the making of political argument. Paradoxically, such autonomy and personal independence is thought to require the loving attention of particularist mothers who devote themselves to fostering this sense of self in their children. Attentive love disqualifies the nurturers of the individuality and autonomy of citizens from the exercise of citizenship, however, because the character of mothers tends to be emotional and oriented to particular needs and interests instead of to the general good. A sexual division of labor is thus appropriate and fitting, between noncitizen women who are emotionally attached to men and children whose autonomy they foster by nurturing their particular individuality, and citizen men who have become autonomous and independent thinkers thanks to the loving care of mothers, who exercise autonomous political judgment for the general good.[33]

Galston's statement of the virtue of independence departs from this modern understanding of the importance of independence as a virtue. As I quoted earlier, he defines independence as "the disposition to care for, and to take responsibility for, oneself and avoid becoming needlessly dependent on others" (p. 222). Unlike the tradition, Galston does not construct independence as a means to the end of promoting rational political judgment by free and equal citizens. His picture of the polity distinguishes between leaders and citizens, and it seems that only leaders will make public policy decisions. The primary virtue of citizens in this division is that they be moderate in their demands on leaders; they should demand no more from their government than they are willing to pay for in taxes and be self-disciplined enough to accept painful measures when their leaders judge that they are necessary (see pp. 224–25).

Instead of a means to the end of political autonomy, in Galston's account it seems that the primary purpose of independence is to minimize public spending. Divorce and single parenthood, he suggests, cause the poverty, crime, and disability that make people depend on public spending to meet their needs. "The consequences of family failure affect society at large. We all pay for systems of welfare, criminal justice, and incarceration, as well as for physical and mental disability; we are all made poorer by the inability or unwillingness of young adults to become contributing members of society; we all suffer if our society is unsafe and divided" (p. 286).

Although it is a far cry from the old property-based meaning of economic independence, as I noted above, Galston appears to follow contemporary liberal common sense in identifying independence with having a well-paid secure job. On his scheme of liberal virtues, persons who are independent in this sense are more virtuous than those who are not.

I wish now to question this commonsense valuation of independence, however, as a measure of the value or virtue of citizens.

Normatively privileging independence in this sense, and making it a primary virtue of citizenship, implies judging a huge number of people in liberal societies as less than full citizens. First, there are those unable to care for themselves alone, and thus who depend on others to meet some or all of their needs: children, frail old people, many people with physical and mental disabilities, sick and injured people. Most of us are dependents of this sort at some time of our lives, and many of us for a good part of our lives. Second, there are those people, usually women, who care for dependents of this sort, dependency workers. Most dependency work takes place outside paid employment, in the home. Thus those who do this work must be supported by others to have their material needs met. Though they do vital, often difficult and time-consuming work, dependency workers are often not independent in Galston's sense. Privileging independence as a citizen virtue thus amounts to defining dependency workers as second-class citizens.[34]

Holding independence as a norm not only renders dependent people and their caretakers second-class citizens, but it also tends to make them invisible. Dependent people and their caretakers come to be defined outside public social relations, marginalized to a private realm beyond the interaction of free and full citizens with one another. Such marginalization renders dependent people and their caretakers more abjectly dependent than they would if they were acknowledged as equal citizens and received the kind of social support that would enable them to be as independent as possible and participate in civic and political life.

As women have joined the labor force in large numbers, the expectation that every person should be an independent worker has become more general. Thus the stigma attached to dependency has increased.[35] Ironically, during this same period it has become increasingly difficult for many people to have well-paid secure jobs, because employers have closed down basic manufacturing enterprises and rely increasingly on part-time and seasonal work.

Independence, I suggest, should not be thought of as a basic citizen virtue. But this contradicts many people's stated values. If you ask children, or people in wheelchairs, or old people, or women on welfare, what they want for their lives, they will all say that they wish to be independent. In order to respect their experience and at the same time recognize people's need for support, I suggest that we must distinguish two meanings of independence.

The first is autonomy: within the bounds of justice, to be able to make choices about one's life and to act on those choices without having to obey others, meet their conditions, or fear their threats and punishments. The second is self-sufficiency: not needing help or support from anyone in meeting one's needs and carrying out one's life plans. The modern republican linkage of citizenship with independence tied these two. If you were not a self-sufficient property holder, then you were subordinate to a property holder in order to have your needs met and thus could not be a full citizen. But egalitarian social movements claimed equal citizenship for servants, wage workers, and wives. The extension of citizenship to formerly subordinate people meant that the link between self-sufficiency and autonomy had to be broken. The ability of workers and wives to think for themselves in politics and to make their own decisions about their lives and actions, however, had to be guaranteed by laws that protected them from the power of employers and husbands on whom they were dependent for their livelihoods.

Autonomy should be considered an important moral value in the liberal society. Respecting individuals as full citizens means granting and fostering in them liberties and capacities to be autonomous—to choose their own ends and develop their own opinions. It also means protecting them from the tyranny of those who might try to determine those choices and opinions because they control resources on which citizens depend for their living.[36]

In contemporary society, however, most people experience this kind of dependence. Most people depend directly or indirectly on the owners of capital for their living. Whole communities depend on employment in a local manufacturing plant and the retail markets that employment generates. When the owner shuts down the plant, furthermore, he says that he is dependent on the world market, on the relation of the dollar to the yen, and must compete with cheaper goods made in Korea. The ideal of independence as self-sufficiency, perhaps a worthy ideal in Thomas Jefferson's America, has become inoperative in today's world of intricate economic interdependence.

Independence as self-sufficiency has come to mean in most people's minds what I have suggested that it means for Galston—having a well-paid secure job—even though this is not self-sufficiency in Jefferson's sense. I have suggested that privileging independence in the newer sense has the consequence of marginalizing many people—women who take care of children or old people at home, sick people, people who for whatever reason cannot find work, or whose wages are too low to provide subsistence. Wealthier liberal societies usually do not allow these people to starve or die of exposure. But they usually limit the autonomy of those to whom they provide aid and support. People who depend on public subsidy or private charity to meet some or all of their needs must often submit to other people's judgments about their lives and actions—where they will live, how they will live, how they will spend money, what they will do with their time. Thus citizens judged self-sufficient have a right to autonomy, but those who are not independent in this sense often have their autonomy limited in many ways. I submit that this makes them second-class citizens. Too many single mothers fall in this category, and contemporary rhetoric and policy proposals seem determined to deprive them further of their autonomy.

In a liberal polity, independence as being able to make choices about one's life without coercion or threat should be thought of as a liberal right, respected equally in all citizens. Independence in the sense of thinking for oneself and making rational judgments about the public good, should be thought of as a liberal virtue; the society is likely to be better governed and more democratic if its citizens think critically and express themselves honestly. Contemporary liberal welfare societies still often tend to recognize a right of autonomy only for those who can meet their needs entirely through private employment. But a humane liberal society should affirm that, in order to be autonomous in both the sense of deciding what to do with one's life and formulating one's own opinions, most people require material and social support, and that some people require more support than others.[37]

CITIZEN RESPONSIBILITIES TO CONTRIBUTE TO SOCIETY

Galston would be likely to criticize my claim that independence of choice and thought requires social support for focusing too much on citizen rights and not enough on citizen responsibilities. He thinks that a client, demand-oriented view of citizenship has weakened the expectation that citizens will attend to the public good as well as their own. While citizens have rights to basic liberty, respect, and tolerate from their fellow citizens and from the state, they have the reciprocal responsibility to contribute meaningfully to the social fabric. The state can rightfully expect such contributions from healthy adult citizens, and can rightfully punish and stigmatize noncontributors.

Galston is quite right to expect that citizens should contribute to the social good and should be given equal opportunity to contribute. He is wrong, however, to identify making a social contribution with being independent in the sense of having a job. The following passages suggest this identification of making a contribution with having a job.

> This conception of contribution opportunity applies not only to the availability of jobs for adults but also to the availability of adequate opportunities for children and youth to develop their capacities to contribute. (p. 185)

> Contribution has both quantitative and qualitative dimensions. Key quan-
> titative variables include sacrifice, effort, duration, and productivity. The
> key qualitative variable is the importance of different functions as defined
> either by the community as a whole or (more typically) by some socioeco-
> nomic entity within the community. (p. 186)

In other words, the worth of a person's social contribution is usually
measured by how much wage or salary that person earns at a job. Galston
is hardly alone in identifying making a significant social contribution
with having a good job. This is the stuff of popular common sense. It is,
however, an incorrect and unjust identification.

Although they do overlap, having a good job and being a contributing
member of society are not equivalent concepts. Most of us can think of
lucrative jobs and businesses that we judge contribute little to society,
except perhaps notches in the gross national product, and that may be
positively harmful. Two of my candidates are designing sugary cereal ads
to be aired on Saturday morning cartoons and working as a lobbyist for
the tobacco industry. Just what sorts of activities count as contributing is
of course contestable, but most people would agree that some jobs do
not contribute to the social good, even though they may contribute to
some particular ends.

More important, perhaps, most of us would agree that people can
make important social contributions that either do not get paid or receive a token payment disconnected from their social worth. Good art,
literature, and philosophy, for example, are notoriously poor sellers in
the market. Every society must publicly subsidize its cultural production.

Most relevant to the citizen status of mothers, dependency work
makes a vast and vital social contribution. As already mentioned, most
caring for children, sick people, old people, and people with disabilities
is performed unpaid by women in the home. In American society, as in
many others, when these usually female dependency workers are paid in
social services agencies, the wages often keep the workers below the poverty line. A just society would recognize dependency work as the significant social contribution it is by giving those who do it decent material
comfort.[38]

Community organizing and service provision represent a final category of social contribution outside the labor market. Much of the infrastructure of civic life in American society today, which keeps the society
minimally democratic, participatory, and critical, and also does much to
preserve what social bonds there are, is done by volunteers or very low
paid and dedicated workers: neighborhood crime watches, rape crisis
centers, environmental cleanup crews, AIDS prevention and support
groups, consumer information lobbies, political issue and advocacy

groups, and so on. Poor people, especially poor single mothers, participate in such service providing and organizing activity to an extent that
seriously belies the stereotype of the welfare loafer.[39] Many people believe that having the state directly organize political participation and
social service provision both is inefficient and tends wrongly to infringe
on civil and political freedom. Thus people who do these things—and a
healthy liberal democratic society needs a great many more people doing them than we have in the United States today—must depend on
public resources for their ability to make these social contributions.

I agree with Galston that society ought to encourage all its citizens to
engage in useful social contributions to the extent that they are able.
Many children, old people, people with little training, and people with
physical and mental disabilities would be able to contribute more to social life than their circumstances allow them today if the norm of the
self-sufficient hale and healthy male adult worker did not hold sway. A
more just society would provide the home help, child care, transportation, workplace accommodation, and flexible work hours that would enable more of these people to make meaningful contributions. Many people should contribute through private paid employment. But many of
the activities that are basic to a healthy liberal democratic society—
cultural production, caretaking, civic and political organizing, the building and maintenance of decent affordable housing—are not and never
will be profitable in the private market. Many of these activities, moreover, are not best performed in state bureaucratic jobs. They are best
performed privately and autonomously, but the people who do them
must be socially supported in a decent life.

Pluralist Family Values and Public Policy

I have agreed with Galston that the idea of liberal neutrality is a fiction
and that it is appropriate for public policy to promote particular ends
and goods. Among such ends and good, some belong to family life:
privacy, intimacy, responsibility, caring for particular others, and leisure-
time play. In addition to these, there are particular family values important for children's welfare: attentive love; nurturance to emotional, intellectual, and moral maturity; relative stability and orderly change.

There are family values, the ends and purposes of family life, and individual virtues that enact them. There is no doubt that some families better instantiate them than others. Along with many others today using
family values rhetoric, however, Galston is wrong to assert that a particular *kind* of family best embodies these values for children—the intact,
two-parent, by implication heterosexual, family. These family values can
and often are realized in a plurality of family forms: gay and lesbian

families,[40] single-parent families, blended families, nuclear families, extended families.

Public policy should promote and encourage the ends and purposes of families. Contrary to what Galston argues, however, public policy should not *prefer* particular means of realizing these ends. It is wrong, that is, for public policy to encourage particular family forms and discourage others. For the sake of protecting children and other household members, the state can properly intervene in or punish particular actions or inactions within families, especially violence and serious willful neglect, but this is quite different from punishing or favoring families based on their composition alone. Such preference is simply discrimination, inconsistent with liberal pluralist principles of giving children equal respect whatever their culture or way of life.

Attitudes and institutional assumptions that are unfairly biased toward heterosexual two-parent families put burdens and stresses on many families that others do not face, which sometimes make it more difficult for them to raise children well. Injusticies in the economic system and workplace structures prevent many families, including many single-parent families, from giving their children material comfort and the resources they need to develop their capacities. In light of such prejudices and unjust inequalities, the primary way that public policy should promote family values is by facilitating material and social supports to enable all families to be as excellent as possible. I will conclude by briefly discussing several policy areas affected by this argument.

Reproductive Freedom

Many people respond to calls for appreciation and support for single-mother families that women simply should not have babies that they cannot raise in material comfort on their own. Many single women who do have babies, of course, have inadequate access to contraception and abortion. Policies that truly enabled women to be heterosexually active without having to bear unwanted children would thus probably reduce the need for publicly supporting children.

Reproductive freedom goes both ways, however. People should be free to have children as well as not to have them. In a crowded world each additional child makes for social costs; thus everyone has a moral obligation to ask whether they should bring another child into the world. The decision of an upper-income married couple to have their third child may be morally questionable from this point of view. A liberal society that claims to respect the autonomy of all its citizens equally should affirm the freedom of all citizens to bear and rear children, whether they are married or not, whether they have high incomes or not.

Father Obligations

Many argue that it is unfair for mothers to bear responsibility for financial support of children alone and that fathers ought to be made to pay. In principle I agree. Court-ordered child support obligations of divorced fathers should be much more vigorously enforced, and children-first divorce policies should make these awards larger than they usually are now, when the father earns a good income. Forcing unwed mothers to name fathers of their children is problematic under liberal principles, however, because it may subject the women to harassment or threat of violence from the man she names or force her into a long-term relation with a man she wishes not to see. Trying to force low-income fathers to pay child support they do not have, moreover, will not raise the standard of living of children.

Welfare Reform

Proposals under consideration in the U.S. Congress would require mothers receiving welfare to work at government-sponsored and subsidized jobs and might drop her from all support if she does not find a private-sector job in two years. Such a plan would reinforce gender inequality by creating a new kind of gendered, two-tiered workforce.[41] Pay in these jobs would be at minimum wage or less, thus keeping women and their children well below poverty level. In the absence of a general full employment program, moreover, subsidizing jobs for some poor people is likely simply to remove opportunities for other poor people. The proposal to force a mother to get a welfare check, moreover, gives no recognition or accommodation to the demands and contribution of the work she must do caring for her children. At best, it will force her to put even very small children into inadequately funded child care centers whose workers are paid poverty wages; at worst, it will force her to go to a job even when she has no one to care for her children. Expecting welfare recipients to find a private sector job within two years, finally, presumes that their inability to do so is a sign of their failure rather than a labor market failure.

Full Employment and Guaranteed Income

Capitalism has some virtues, but after three hundred years it should be clear that one of them is not employing all able-bodied people at decent wages. A liberal capitalist society can expect all citizens to make contributions only if it makes opportunities available to everyone at a level of compensation sufficient to support themselves and their children in a decent life. Where the private labor market does not have enough jobs for all those able and willing to work, the public sector should provide useful work at a decent wage.

Either employers should be required to raise their wages so that every worker can live at least a minimally decent life moreover, or public funds should supplement the incomes of poorly paid workers.[42] Part of any such wage adjustment policy should be efforts to raise wages for typically female jobs to levels more typical of decently paid men's jobs. A liberal democratic society that gives equal respect to all citizens, moreover, would institute a guaranteed income policy that guaranteed public support to all able-bodied persons to make social contributions that the private market only poorly supports: for example, care of dependents, whether inside or outside the home, provision of social service, building and maintaining affordable housing, community enhancement and empowerment organizing, and the facilitation of citizen participation in civic and political activities.

Within such a full employment and guaranteed income framework, dependency work done in the home ought to be recognized as a social contribution. As much as possible, families ought to be able to choose to care for their young children, elderly or disabled relatives, and close friends, in their homes; they should not be forced to do so, however, by lack of good affordable alternative care. People who do dependency work, whether in or outside the home, should be materially supported. Public policy should promote flexible work hours in private and public jobs, moreover, so that dependency workers can combine their home-care responsibilities with out-of-home contributions. If dependency work were recognized and supported in these ways, many men would probably do more of it.

Mothers' Houses

People who parent alone by choice or circumstances should be respected as equal citizens. Even with adequate material support, however, it is more difficult for many people to raise children on their own than cooperatively with others. One way to recognize and appreciate single-mother families is to promote living arrangements for them that ensure privacy and at the same time facilitate cooperation and support in child-rearing responsibilities. Some liberal democratic governments have promoted or supported such cooperative living arrangements among single mothers.[43]

I have argued that a family-values rhetoric that finds married-couple families the most morally valuable fails to recognize mothers as equal citizens. Holding independence in the sense of self-sufficiency as a primary norm of citizenship accounts for this devaluation of women, who in the current gender structure are double disadvantaged by poor wages and primary responsibility for society's dependency work. A society that recognizes all its members as equal citizens and expects them all to make meaningful contributions must recognize and support the contribution of dependency work and publicly support many other opportunities for making social contributions.

Chapter VII

HOUSE AND HOME:
FEMINIST VARIATIONS ON A THEME

FOR MILLENNIA the image of Penelope sitting by the hearth and weaving, saving and preserving the home while her man roams the earth in daring adventures, has defined one of Western culture's basic ideas of womanhood. Many other cultures historically and today equate women with home, expecting women to serve men at home and sometimes preventing them from leaving the house. If house and home mean the confinement of women for the sake of nourishing male projects, then feminists have good reason to reject home as a value. But it is difficult even for feminists to exorcise a positive valence to the idea of home. We often look forward to going home and invite others to make themselves at home. House and home are deeply ambivalent values.

In this essay I sort through this ambivalence. On the one hand, I agree with feminist critics such as Luce Irigaray and Simone de Beauvoir that the comforts and supports of house and home historically come at women's expense. Women serve, nurture, and maintain so that the bodies and souls of men and children gain confidence and expansive subjectivity to make their mark on the world. This homey role deprives women of support for their own identity and projects. Along with several feminist critics, furthermore, I question the yearning for a whole and stable identity that the idea of home often represents. Unlike these critics, however, I am not ready to toss the idea of home out of the larder of feminist values. Despite the oppressions and privileges the idea historically carries, the idea of home also carries critical liberating potential because it expresses uniquely human values. Some of these can be uncovered by exploring the meaning-making activity most typical of women in domestic work.

Instead of following one line of argument, I aim here to weave together several thematic threads. All of them wind around meanings of subjectivity or identity. I begin by noting Martin Heidegger's equation of dwelling with the way of being that is human, and note his division of dwelling into moments of building and preservation. Despite his claim that these moments are equally important, Heidegger nevertheless seems to privilege building as the world-founding of an active subject, and I suggest that this privileging is male-biased.

Luce Irigaray makes explicit the maleness of Heidegger's allegedly universal ontology. Man can build and dwell in the world in patriarchal culture, she suggests, only on the basis of the materiality and nurturance of women. In the idea of "home," man projects onto woman the nostalgic longing for the lost wholeness of the original mother. To fix and keep hold of his identity man makes a house, puts things in it, and confines there his woman who reflects his identity to him. The price she pays for supporting his subjectivity, however, is dereliction, having no self of her own.

Irigaray writes about the association of house and home with a male longing for fixed identity in a timeless tone. The property acquisition she describes men as engaging in as a means of substituting for the lost mother, however, is probably best thought of as characteristic of bourgeois society, whose values became hegemonic in the twentieth century in the West, and increasingly in the world. Thus I explore the specific attachment of personal identity to commodified houses and their contents, in order to find another angle of critique of the longing for home.

Before entering a critique of Simone de Beauvoir's devaluation of housework, I digress to tell the story of one bad housekeeper: my mother. The purpose of this gesture is to commemorate, but also to describe in concrete terms how disciplinary standards of orderly housework and PTA motherhood continue to oppress women, especially single mothers.

Like Irigaray, Beauvoir describes women's existence as deprived of active subjectivity because their activity concentrates on serving and supporting men in the home. Unlike Irigaray, however, Beauvoir materializes this account by reflecting on the sexual division of labor. Because she accepts a dichotomy between immanence and transcendence and identifies all of women's domestic labor with immanence, however, Beauvoir misses the creatively human aspects of women's traditional household work, in activities I call preservation.

That aspect of dwelling which Heidegger devalues thus provides a turning point for revaluing home. Preservation makes and remakes home as a support for personal identity without accumulation, certainty, or fixity. While preservation, a typically feminine activity, is traditionally devalued at least in Western conceptions of history and identity, it has crucial human value.

I next challenge a group of feminist texts whose writers all reject the idea of home as inappropriately totalizing and imperialist. Essays by Biddy Martin and Chandra Mohanty, Teresa de Lauretis, and Bonnie Honig all argue that longing for home expresses an oppressive search for certainty and attachment to privilege. Although I accept much of their analysis, I question the wholesale rejection of an ideal of home for feminism. While values of home do indeed signal privilege today, analysis of those values and commitment to their democratic enactment for all can have enormous critical political potential in today's world. In addition to preservation, those values include safety, individuation, and privacy.

DWELLING AND BUILDING

Dwelling, says Martin Heidegger, is man's mode of being. Habitual human activity reveals things as meaningful, and through dwelling among the meaningful things people have a place for themselves. Dwelling and building, Heidegger says, stand in a circular relation. Humans attain to dwelling only by means of building. We dwell by making the places and things that structure and house our activities. These places and things establish relations among each other, between themselves and dwellers, and between dwellers and the surrounding environment. But we only build on the basis of already dwelling as the beings whose mode of being is to let things be, to think and reveal them.[1]

Building has two aspects, according to Heidegger: cultivating and constructing. One mode of building consists in cherishing, protecting, preserving, and caring for, whose paradigm is agriculture, the cultivation of the soil. "Building in the sense of preserving and nurturing is not making anything" (BDT, 147). Thus to remain, to stay in place, is an important meaning of dwelling. "To dwell, to be set at peace, means to remain at peace within the free, the preserve, the free sphere that safeguards each thing in its nature. The fundamental character of dwelling is this sparing and preserving" (BDT, 149).

After introducing this duality of building, as preservation and construction, Heidegger's text leaves preservation behind to focus on construction. A curious abandonment, in light of the above claim that preservation is fundamental to dwelling. To describe the human mode of being in the world, Heidegger dwells on the heroic moment of place through creative activity that gathers the environment into a meaningful presence.

We can dwell only in a place. Edifices enclose areas with walls and link areas by planes, thus creating locations. Walls, roofs, columns, stairs, fences, bridges, towers, roads, and squares found the human world by making place.[2] Through building, man establishes a world and his place in the world, according to Heidegger, establishes himself as somebody, with an identity and history. People inhabit the world by erecting material supports for their routines and rituals and then see the specificity of their lives reflected in the environment, the materiality of things gathered together with historical meaning.[3] If building in this way is basic to the emergence of subjectivity, to dwelling in the world with identity and history, then it would appear that only men are subjects. On the whole, women do not build.

Even today, when women have moved into so many typically male activities, building houses and other structures remains largely a male activity in most parts of the world.[4] In building industries, a woman with a hard hat is still a rare sight. Nowhere in the world do women participate in the building trades in more than very small numbers. Perhaps even more significantly, men dominate the ranks of those who make building decisions—corporate boards of directors, architects, planners, engineers. Even in some of the most egalitarian households, the work of building and structural maintenance falls most often to men.

In many traditional societies of Africa and Asia, women were the home builders. But peasants all over the world have migrated to cities and towns because capitalism and environmental destruction have made it nearly impossible in many places to live off the land in traditional ways. Many rural and urban development projects include programs where people build the houses in which they will live. Despite the fact that poorer households in developing countries are very often headed by women, they rarely participate in these house-building projects. Either they do not have title to land on which to build because of male biases in property laws; or the development project has simply assumed that men are more natural builders and thus have designed construction projects with men in mind. Frequently women's income and assets are so low that they cannot qualify for the credit necessary to participate in building projects.[5]

If building establishes a world, if building is the means by which a person emerges as a subject who dwells in that world, then not to build is a deprivation. Those excluded from building, who do not think of themselves as builders, perhaps have a more limited relation to the world, which they do not think of themselves as founding. Those who build dwell in the world in a different way from those who occupy the structures already built, and from those who preserve what is constructed. If building establishes a world, then it is still very much a man's world.

Women as a group are still largely excluded from the activities that erect structures to gather and reveal a meaningful world. It will be women's world as much as men's only when women participate as much in their design and founding. But the male bias of building also appears in the devaluation of that other aspect of building Heidegger discusses, preservation, a devaluation to which his own philosophy tends. For a distinction between constructing and preserving, as two aspects of building and dwelling, is implicitly gendered. Later I will pick up the thread of this concept of preservation, to argue that much of the unnoticed labor of women is this basic activity of meaning maintenance. First we shall explore further the masculinism implicit in a philosophy of existence that takes building as world founding, by way of a bridge from Heidegger to his feminist follower and critic, Luce Irigaray.

Building, says, Heidegger, gathers together dispersed surroundings, which have no center apart from the artifice around which they are oriented. The house in the woods gives to the trees and lakes a placement. The bridge across the river gathers the shores, revealing a nexus of relationships, a context. But man's building, Heidegger points out, occurs on the foundation of already dwelling. Man is enveloped by being, finds himself as already having been at home in nature, which building reveals as already surrounding. This revealing of the world itself depends on a prior ground that sustains and nurtures.

With such a move Heidegger believes himself to be sublating modern Western philosophy, and its specifically technological orientation. Descartes and those who come after him have the hubris to think of man as self-originating, the thinking subject as the master and representor of being. They have forgotten the humility of the ancients, who understand better the placement of mortals in a nature on which they depend, whose thoughtful tending and preserving is the lot of mortals. Man builds for the sake of dwelling, to make himself at home, in respect to the prior elements that envelop and nourish him, which his building gathers and reveals.

WOMAN AS NOSTALGIC HOME

Luce Irigaray names the gendering already present in Heidegger's worlding of the world: Man builds for the sake of dwelling, to make himself at home, on the basis of Woman as already always positioned as the enveloping nurturing presence of nature. For man, woman is always mother, from whose dark womb he emerges to build solid structures in the light of day, with whose light he returns to look in the caverns with the speculum. In lovemaking he seeks to return to the enclosing warmth of the original union with the mother. The patriarchal gender system allows man a subjectivity that depends on woman's objectification and dereliction; he has a home at the expense of her homelessness, as she serves as the ground on which he builds.

Everyone is born in loss. Ejected from the dark comfort of the mother's body, we are thrown into a world without walls, with no foundation to our fragile and open-ended existence. Speaking mortals must come to terms with this separation from the mother, to find and form meaning and identity for ourselves, without foundation or certainty. In patriarchal culture, according to Irigaray, the gender system of masculinity and femininity makes it possible for man to come to terms with this loss by never really dealing with it; instead, he attempts to return to the lost home of the womb by means of woman.

Man deals with the loss by building, in order that he may recover his dwelling. He seeks to make himself a home to stand in for the lost home. Through building he gathers the amorphous and fluid elements into solid structure. Through projecting outward he makes objective works where he can see himself reflected. He makes and affirms himself as subject through building and making. In this objectifying self-reflection woman serves as material both on which to stand and out of which to build, and women likewise serve as a primary object for reflecting himself, his mirror.

> Man's love is teleological. It aims for a target outside them. It moves toward the outside and the constitution, on the outside, within that which is outside themselves, of a home. Outside of the self, the tension, the intention, aims for a dwelling, a thing, a production. Which also serves men as a third part and stake.

> To *inhabit* is the fundamental trait of man's being. Even if this trait remains unconscious, unfulfilled, especially in its ethical dimension, man is forever searching for, building, creating homes for himself everywhere: caves, huts, women, cities, language, concepts, theory, and so on.[6]

Building is for the sake of dwelling, gathering together natural material and element into a determinate place. In the patriarchal gender scheme, woman serves as the construction material (ESD, 103–107), and as the *place* within which man dwells. His self-affirming subjectivity is possible because she supports and complements his existence as both an origin of his creativity and the product in which he can see his self reflected. She serves as the material envelope and container of his existence. "She is assigned to be place without occupying place. Through her, place would be set up for man's use but not hers. Her jouissance is meant to 'resemble' the flow of whatever is in the place that she is when she contains, contains herself"(ESD, 52).

The form of man's self-affirmation in this gender system is *nostalgia,* a longing for the return to a lost home. Man puts woman in her place, so that he can return to the original maternal home. Nostalgia is this recurrent desire for return, which is unsatisfiable because the loss is separation, birth, mortality, itself. Nostalgia is a flight from having to come to terms with this loss, by means of constant search for a symbolic substitute for lost home. Man yearns nostalgically for an original union with the

mother within safe walls of warmth. In women men look nostalgically to
return to their own lost home; thus they fail to face women as subjects
with their own identities and need of covering.

> He arrests his growth and repeats, endlessly, searching for the moment
> when the separation of memory and forgetting was lost to him. But, the
> more he repeats, the more he surrounds himself with envelops, containers,
> "houses" which prevent him from finding either the other or himself. His
> nostalgia for a first and last dwelling prevents him from meeting and living
> with the other. (ESD, 142)

Man seeks nostalgically to return to the lost home by making buildings
and putting things in them that will substitute for that original home. He
creates property, things he owns and controls. But because the property
doesn't satisfy the longing for lost home, he is launched on an acquisitive
quest for more property. In this acquisitive economy women serve as raw
materials, caretakers, and goods themselves to be traded. Her role is to
be the home by being at home. Her being home gives him comfort and
allows him to open on the expanse of the world to build and create. For
her, however, the placement is an imprisonment.

> Centuries will perhaps have been needed for man to interpret the meaning
> of his work(s): the endless construction of a number of substitutes for his
> parental home. From the depths of the earth to the highest skies? Again
> and again, taking from the feminine the issue or textures of spatiality. In
> exchange—but it isn't a real one—he buys her a house, even shuts her up
> in it, places limits on her that are the opposite of the unlimited site in which
> he unwillingly situates her. He contains or envelopes her with walls while
> enveloping himself and his things in her flesh. The nature of these enve-
> lopes is not the same: on the one hand, invisibly alive, but with barely visible
> limits; on the other, visibly limiting or sheltering, but at the risk of being
> prison-like or murderous if the threshold is not left open. (ESD, 11)

Since woman functions for man as the ground of his subjectivity, she
has no support for her own self. She is derelict. She too must deal with
the same loss as he, with the abandonment of mortality, radical freedom,
and groundlessness, and the expulsion from warmth and security of the
mother's body. By means of her, man makes for himself a home to substitute for this loss. He creates by holding her as his muse, he rests by having her serve his needs at home. Her only comfort is to try to derive her
satisfaction from being in the home, the Other. She tries to take her
subjectivity from her being-for-him. She tries to envelop herself with dec-
oration. She covers herself with jewelry, makeup, clothing, in the attempt to make an envelope, to give herself a place. But in the end she is

left homeless, derelict, with no room of her own, since he makes room for himself by using her as his envelope.

If building establishes a world, if building is the means by which a person emerges as a subject who dwells in that world, then not to build is a deprivation. In the patriarchal gender system, men are the builders and women the nurturers of builders and the ornaments placed within their creations. As homeless themselves, women are deprived of the chance to be subjects for themselves. Language, says, Heidegger, is the house of being. Men not only build material shelters, temples, bridges to gather the environment into a place. Masculine subjects are also the founders of civilization itself, those who name things and construct the theories and epics in which their meanings are preserved over generations. According to Irigaray, woman's place in language is a sign of her dereliction, of her inability to attain to the position of subject for herself.

The question for postmodern living is whether an end to such exploitation requires rejecting entirely the project of supporting identity and subjectivity embodied in the patriarchal ideology of home. The feminist writers with whom I engage in Section VI answer this question affirmatively. While I accept many of their reasons for leaving home, I wish to explore another possibility. Is it possible to retain an idea of home as supporting the individual subjectivity of the person, where the subject is understood as fluid, partial, shifting, and in relations of reciprocal support with others? This is the direction in which I find Irigaray pointing to an alternative to the desire for fixed identity that historically imprisons women. Before thematizing an alternative concept of house and home, however, I want to explore more of its questionable aspects.

COMMODIFIED HOME

Irigaray's rhetoric invokes a (patriarchal) universality. Her images of women's enclosure in the house, a house in which man arranges his possessions to satisfy his desire to substitute for the lost security of the womb, presuppose a specifically modern, bourgeois conception of home. The subject that fills its existential lack by seeing itself in objects, by owning and possessing and accumulating property, is a historically specific subject of modern capitalism. Economic and psychosocial processes collude in the twentieth century in particular to encourage the expression of a subject that fulfills its desire by commodity consumption.[7] While this consumer subject is best realized in advanced industrial societies, its allure has spread around the globe. House and home occupy central places in this consumer consciousness as the core of personal property and a specific commodity-based identity.[8] Radical critics of the allure of home rightly find this link of home and identity to be a source of quietism and privilege. The commodified concept of home ties identity to a withdrawl from the public world and to the amount and status of one's belongings.

In many societies, both historically and today, people do not "live" solely in a house. There are huts and cottages reserved for certain life activities, such as sleeping, making love, and giving birth, but dwelling in a wider sense occurs outdoors and/or in collective spaces, both sheltered and not. In rural Botswana, for example, this individual private "home" is outdoor space enclosed by a fence, within which stand small houses for different family members and different activities. When the family grows they build another little house. Preparing food, cooking, eating, washing, child's and adult's amusements all usually occur outdoors. If these families move to a small apartment in the city, they often have difficulty adjusting their lives.[9]

In many societies "home" refers to the village or square, together with its houses, and dwelling takes place both in and out of doors. While few societies fail to distinguish status partly by the size and artfulness of the individual houses, in many societies houses are rather small and plain and do not function very much as status symbols. They and their contents are only minor sources of identity. In many of these societies people take their personal pride more from collective buildings, such as churches or meeting houses. They invest creative energy into erecting and decorating these buildings with carvings, columns, statues, paintings, and fine furnishings. The celebrated carvings of the Maori people, for example, belong for the most part to the collective meeting houses on the *marae* of each clan. Even in modern capitalist cities some people "live" more in their neighborhood or on their block than in their houses. They sit in squares, on stoops in bars and coffee houses, going to their houses mostly to sleep. The bourgeois sensibility of civic privatism, however, finds such street living disorderly and threatening. In "better" neighborhoods and communities people discretely and privately sit behind their houses, leaving the streets to teenagers.

Under these modern circumstances, home tends to be restricted to the living space of house or apartment. Personal identity is linked to commodified home in specific ways. The house is the primary place of consumption itself. Freedom consists in release from work and public responsibility in activities of leisure, pleasure, and consumption. The house or apartment is the site of many of these activities, filled with comfortable furnishings and gadgets.

Commodified home supports identity not only as the site of consumer freedom, but as the mark of one's social status. The size, style, and especially location of the house, along with its landscaping and furnishing, establish the individual's location in the social hierarchy. Everyone knows which are the better houses or apartments, better streets, better neighborhoods, better communities, and the aspiration for upward mobility is often expressed in the desire to move house from one neighborhood or community to another.

Attachment to home as status symbol and investment opportunity creates and perpetuates a market competition in which most people are losers. The project of maintaining good "property values," and not simply a comfortable living space, produces or exacerbates racial and class exclusion, which condemns a majority to inferior housing while a few reap windfall profits. To the extent that housing status is also associated with lot size and building size, attachment to house as status also maldistributes land and living space, giving too much to some people and wrongly crowding others. The social and economic organization of commodified housing thus makes the value of home a privilege, and constructs many as relatively or absolutely deprived.

In this commodified construction of personal achievement and lifestyle, the house often becomes an end in itself. The goal of a dream house sets workers working and keeps workers working, fearing job loss, working overtime. The consumer-driven desire of civic privatism tends to produce political quietism because people invest their commitment into their private life, which needs even greater income to fuel it.[10] Women have entered the labor force in mass numbers partly because one person's income is no longer sufficient to pay for the house; ironically, all the adults now stay away from the house for most hours of the week in order to earn the money for the house in which they invest their sense of self.[11]

Fantasy feeds consumer desire that fuels this privatist identity attached to house and home. Whatever our actual living conditions, we can buy the dream of a beautiful home in magazines. Along with sex, sports, and clothes, house and home are million-dollar magazine subjects. The magazines offer countless sets on which one can imagine one's life staged. Dining rooms, airy and light, diaphanous curtains revealing a sunny garden beyond the French doors. Solid living rooms, tasteful painting on the walls, a grand piano in the corner, massive leather couches. Cozy bedrooms, fluffed with pillows, lace, and comforters. A kitchen for grand cuisine, with a double-door refrigerator, forty feet of smooth, uncluttered wooden counter, and copper cookware hanging from the ceiling. The rooms in house magazines are nearly always empty of people, thus enabling us to step into their spaces.

The house magazines often sing with nostalgia. Rustic house in the woods, old wood, antique furniture, leaded glass windows. New tiles and floorings are reminiscent of the turn of the century. The dream house often evokes the image of the cozy traditional cottage.[12] Even when the images do not explicitly evoke the past, they often are calculated to produce a longing for a way of life gone by or which might have been as nostalgic. These home images also whisper of stillness, rest.

The attachment of personal identity of commodified home is not specifically gendered. Men and women are equally prone to assess their status and self-worth according to the things they have. The commodified home does have some specific consequences for women, however. The reduction of home to living space can confine women even more than before, especially when suburban development reduces whole townships to living space. Making the house and its furnishings an indicator of personal and family status, moreover, can increase the pressure on women to be good housekeepers, not for the sake of nurturance, efficiency, or hygiene, but for the sake of appearances.

INTERLUDE: MY MOTHER'S STORY

The dream of a house in the suburbs became my mother's nightmare.

My daddy left our Flushing apartment each morning in one of his three slightly different grey flannel suits and took the subway to midtown Manhattan. An aspiring novelist turned insurance underwriter, he was moving slowly but steadily up the corporate ladder. I imagined his office as Dagwood's, and his boss as Mr. Dithers.

My sister and I tripped out to school each morning, in the horrid saddle shoes our mommy made us wear, and she stayed home with the little baby boy. A perfect picture of '50's family bliss, with one flaw: my mother didn't clean the house.

Our two-bedroom apartment was always dirty, cluttered, things all over the floors and piled on surfaces, clothes strewn around the bedroom, dust in the corners, in the rugs, on the bookcases; the kitchen stove wore cooked-on food. I never invited my friends into my house. If they came to the door and peered in I told them we were getting ready to move. Mostly my friends did not care, since we played in the alleys and hallways, and not in each other's houses.

My mother spent her days at home reading books, taking a correspondence course in Russian, filling papers with codes and calculations. She seemed to me an inscrutable intellectual. But she also played with us—authors, rummy, twenty-questions, with gusto—and sang and sang, teaching us hymns and old army songs. Sometimes on a Saturday she hauled out the oils and sat her little girls down to model, and then let us make our own oil paintings. From my mommy I learned to value books and song and art and games, and to think that housework is not important.

It was 1958. My mother had to stay home with her children even though she had worked happily in a Manhattan magazine office before we were born, even though she spoke three languages and had a Master's degree. I was mortified then by her weirdness, sitting in her chair reading and writing, instead of cooking cleaning and ironing and mending like a real mom. Later, after she died in 1978, I read her refusal to do housework as passive resistance.

Like most of the Joneses (well, more likely the Cohens) on our block, my mommy and daddy dreamed of owning a house in the suburbs. They dragged us three kids all over the state of New Jersey looking at model homes in new developments. Back in Flushing, they poured over house-plan sketches, looked at paint samples, calculated mortgage costs. Finally we settled on one of the many mid-Jersey developments built on filled-in wetlands (called swamps at that time). From the four models available my parents chose the mid-priced split-level. My sister and I chose the blue for our room and my three-year-old brother pointed to the green patch on the sample chart. Many Sundays we drove the more than hour-long trip to watch the progress of the house: foundation, frame, walls, grass.

Finally we moved. This was happiness. We were the Cleavers. We bought a ping-pong table for the game room. My sister and I went careening on the streets on our bikes. Then my daddy died—quickly, quietly, of a brain tumor.

My mother was devastated. She relied on us for what comfort there could be in this wasteland of strangers in four types of model homes. At first the neighbors were solicitous, bringing over covered dishes, then they withdrew. The folks at church were more helpful, offering rides to the insurance office or church. My mommy drank, but never on Sunday morning. My sister and I went to school sad, my brother stayed home with our mother, who had less motive than ever to clean the house. We were not poor once the insurance and social security money came, just messy.

But one spring day a uniformed man came into my class and called my name. He escorted me to a police car where my brother and sister were already waiting. Without explanation, they drove us to a teen-reform home. No word from or about our mommy, where she was, why we were being taken away. Slowly I learned or inferred that she had been thrown in jail for child neglect. Daughters do not always defend their mothers accused of crimes. Being one to please authorities, and at eleven wanting to be knowing and adult, I believe that I told stories to confirm their self-righteousness, of how I did most of the cooking and how my mother did not keep house.

A woman alone with her children in this development of perfectly new squeaky clean suburban houses. She is traumatized by grief, and the neighbors look from behind their shutters, people talk about the disheveled way she arrives at church, her eyes red from crying. Do they help this family, needy not for food or clothes, but for support in a very hard time? A woman alone with her children is no longer a whole family, deserving like others of respectful distance. From my mother's point of view there was no difference between child-welfare agents and police. A woman alone with her children is liable to punishment, including the worst of all for her: having her children taken from her.

Neglect. The primary evidence of neglect was drinking and a messy house. We ate well enough, had clean enough clothes, and a mother's steady love, given the way she gave it: playing ping-pong, telling bible stories, playing twenty-questions. We were a family in need of support, but we children were not neglected.

After two months we were reunited, moved back to our grey split-level. My sister and I rode our bikes on the street again, played kickball and croquet with the neighbor kids. My mother was determined to prove she could manage a household by suburban standards, so she did what she thought she had to—called an agency for live-in maids.

One day a thin fourteen-year-old black girl arrived at the door, fresh from North Carolina. We gave her my brother's room and he moved in with my mommy. I felt a strange affinity with this shy and frightened person, who sobbed so quietly in her room. She was not prepared for the work of housekeeping. She and I worked together to prepare the packaged macaroni and cheese. We sorted laundry, silently sitting across from each other, for she did not know who's things were who's. We hardly talked; she told me the barest facts about her life. I see her standing on the landing in a cotton summer dress, a Cinderella figure holding a broom and wistfully sweeping. She quit within two weeks, and the house was not any cleaner.

So we glided through the summer, playing punch ball and tag with the kids in the terrace. My mother went to the city frequently to look for work. In August she took us out to buy three pairs of new shoes, for my brother would start kindergarten. School began, my mother was off to work, my twelve-year-old life seemed rosy enough.

Until one day in early fall I came home from school to find a police sign nailed to my door. A fire. A smoldering ember in my mother's slipper chair had ignited and sent out flames, the neighbors had summoned the fire department. I used their phone to call a family friend to come and get us kids—I wasn't going to any reform school again. There was not much damage to the house, they had caught the fire early, but when breaking in to douse it they had seen the papers strewn about and dust on the floor and beer cans. My mother was arrested again.

We lived with those family friends for a year. Every three months a box of clothes arrived for us from the Department of Social Services—I loved the discovery of what they thought we ought to be wearing. After they let my mommy out of jail and rehab we visited her every couple of months in an impersonal office for an hour or so. She hugged us and cried, and told us of her job in the city and the new cleaning lady, Odessa. As I plummeted into adolescence and my brother entered his seventh year, there was a crisis in our foster home: our foster father died suddenly of pneumonia. Headed now only by a woman, our foster family instantly became a bad environment for us; they shipped us back to my mother without warning. Her family reunited again, my mother wasted no time packing up and moving us all back to the safe indifference of New York City.

Waves of grief rolled up from my gut when, ten years after my mother died, I saw the movie *Housekeeping*.

HISTORICITY, PRESERVATION, AND IDENTITY

Beauvoir on Housework

Simone de Beauvoir's *The Second Sex* still stands as one of the most important works documenting women's oppression, because it describes the typical life and dilemmas of women so graphically. One cannot read Beauvoir's descriptions of domestic labor without appreciating how endless the work is, how oppressive.

> Such work has a negative basis: cleaning is getting rid of dirt, tidying up is eliminating disorder. And under impoverished conditions no satisfaction is possible; the hovel remains a hovel in spite of women's sweat and tears: 'nothing in the world can make it pretty.' Legions of women have only this endless struggle without victory over the dirt. And for even the most privileged the victory is never final.
>
> Few tasks are more like the torture of Sisyphus than housework, with its endless repetition. The clean becomes soiled, the soiled is made clean, over and over, day after day. The housewife wears herself out marking time: she makes nothing, simply perpetuates the present.[13]

Beauvoir's account of the oppressions of domestic work fits in the frame of her general account of women's situation as confined to immanence, whereas man exists as transcendence.

> The fact is that every human existence involves transcendence and immanence at the same time; to go forward, each existence must be maintained, for it to expand toward the future it must integrate the past, and while intercommunicating with others it would find self-confirmation. These two elements—maintenance and progression—are implied in any living activity, and for *man* marriage permits precisely a happy synthesis of the two. In his occupation and in his political life he encounters change and progress,

he senses his extension through time and the universe; and when he is tired
of such roaming, he gets himself a home, where his wife takes care of his
furnishings and children and guards the things of the past that she keeps in
store. But she has no other job than to maintain and provide for life in pure
unvarying generality; she perpetuates the species without change, she en-
sures the even rhythm of the days and the continuity of the home, seeing to
it that the doors are locked. (p. 430)

In the existentialist framework Beauvoir uses, transcendence is the
expression of individual subjectivity. The subject expresses and realizes
his individuality through taking on projects—building a house, organizing a strike, writing a book, winning a battle. These projects, which may
be individual or collective, are determinate and particular contributions
to the world of human affairs. Transcendence also expresses a mode of
temporality. The living subject is future oriented; the future is open with
possibility, which generates anxiety at the same time as its openness and
possibility restructure the meaning of the present and the past. Human
existence is historical in this framework, in that it is structured by creative deed and always must be structured by future deeds.

In Beauvoir's scheme, immanence expresses the movement of life
rather than history. Life is necessary and very demanding. Without getting food and shelter and caring for the sick and saving babies from
harm there is no possibility for transcendence and history. The activities
of sustaining life, however, according to Beauvoir, cannot be expressions
of individuality. They are anonymous and general, as the species is general. Thus if a person's existence consists entirely or largely of activities
of sustaining life, then she or he cannot be an individual subject.
Women's work is largely confined to life maintenance for the sake of
supporting the transcending individual projects of men and children. As
in Irigaray's account, for Beauvoir man's subjectivity draws on the material support of women's work, and this work deprives her of a subjectivity
of her own.

The temporality of immanence is cyclical, repetitive. As the movement
of life it moves in species time unpunctuated by events of individual
meaning. The cycles go around, from spring to summer to fall to winter,
from birth to death and birth to death. Beauvoir describes the activity of
housework as living out this cyclical time, a time with no future and no
goals.

Beauvoir has an entirely negative valuation of what she constructs as
woman's situation, a negative valuation of the activity of giving meaning to and maintaining home. She is surely right that much of what we
call housework is drudgery, necessary but tedious, and also right that
a life confined to such activity is slavery. But such a completely nega-

tive valuation flies in the face of the experience of many women, who devote themselves to care for house and children as a meaningful human project. If Irigaray is correct, of course, many women pour their soul into the house because they have no other envelope for the self. But it seems too dismissive of women's own voices to deny entirely the value many give to "homemaking." Following Irigaray, we can reconstruct core values from the silenced meanings of traditional female activity. Because she relies on the dichotomy of transcendence and immanence to conceptualize women's oppression, Beauvoir misses the historical and individualizing character of some of the activity associated with the traditional feminine role, which in the above quotation she calls "guarding the things of the past that she keeps in store." Giving meaning to individual lives through the arrangement and preservation of things is an intrinsically valuable and irreplaceable aspect of homemaking.

Homemaking

Beauvoir is surely right that the bare acts of cleaning bathrooms, sweeping floors, and changing diapers are merely instrumental; though necessary, they cannot be invested with creativity or individuality. She is wrong, however, to reduce all or even most domestic work to immanence. Not all homemaking is housework. To understand the difference we need to reconsider the idea of home, and its relation to a person's sense of identity. Home enacts a specific mode of subjectivity and historicity that is distinct both from the creative-destructive idea of transcendence and from the ahistorical repetition of immanence.

D. J. Van Lennep suggests that we can learn what it means to inhabit a space as "home" by thinking about forms of shelter that are not home; he suggests that we consider why a hotel room is not a home. A hotel room has all the comforts one needs—heat, hot water, a comfortable bed, food and drink a phone call away. Why, then, does one not feel at home in a hotel room? Because there is nothing of one's self, one's life habits and history, that one sees displayed around the room. The arrangement is anonymous and neutral, for anyone and one no one in particular.[14]

A home, on the other hand, is *personal* in a visible, spatial sense. No matter how small a room or apartment, the home displays the things among which a person lives, that support his or her life activities and reflect in matter the events and values of his or her life. There are two levels in the process of the materialization of identity in the home: (1) my belongings are arranged in space as an extension of my bodily habits and as support for my routines, and (2) many of the things in the home, as well as the space itself, carry sedimented personal meaning as retainers of personal narrative.

(1) Home is the space where I keep and use the material belongings of my life. They are mine—or ours, when I live together with others—because I/we have chosen or made them, and they thus reflect my needs and tastes. Or they have found their way into my home as inheritance or gifts or perhaps even by accident, but then I have appropriated them. The home is not simply the things, however, but their arrangement in space in a way that supports the body habits and routines of those who dwell there. The arrangement of furniture in space provides pathways for habits—the reading lamp placed just here, the television just here, the particular spices on the rack placed just so in relation to this person's taste and cooking habits. Dwelling, says Lennep,

> is the continuous unfolding of ourselves in space because it is our unbroken relation with things surrounding us. It is human existence itself which constitutes space. We simply cannot do otherwise. The things which surround us present themselves in a quality of space which we ourselves are as those who live in space. The pronoun "my" in the expression "my room" does not express my possession of it, but precisely a relation between me and the room, which means that my spatial existence has come about.[15]

Edward Casey carries this insight further in his idea of the body forming "habit memories" in the process of coming to dwell in a place. One comes to feel settled at home in a place through the process of interaction between the living body's movement to enact aims and purposes and the material things among which such activities occur. The things and their arrangement bear witness to the sedimentation of lives lived there. The home is an extension of and mirror for the living body in its everyday activity. This is the first sense in which home is the materialization of identity.

> But more than comfort is at issue in the elective affinity between houses and bodies: *our very identity is at stake.* For we tend to identify ourselves by—and with—the places in which we reside. Since a significant part of our personal identity depends on our exact bodily configuration, it is only to be expected that dwelling places, themselves physical in structure, will resemble our own material bodies in certain quite basic respect.[16]

(2) The process of sedimentation through which physical surroundings become home as an extension and reflection of routines also deposits meaning onto things. Material things and spaces themselves become layered with meaning and personal value as the material markers of events and relationship that make the narrative of a person or group.

The meaningful things in my home often have stories, or they are characters and props in stories. I was a little boy in Japan and I picked out that statuette on my own. Those gashes in the top of the chest show the time I got mad at my mother and went at the chest with a pair of scissors. There's our son's room, still with the trophies he won and the books he read in high school. The things among which I live acquired their meaning through events and travels of my life, layered through stories, and the wordless memories of smells, rhythms, and interactions. Their value is priceless: often worthless even on the yard sale market, the arrangement of these things in rooms is what I would mourn with the deepest grief if they were destroyed by fire or theft.

The activities of homemaking thus give material support to the identity of those whose home it is. Personal identity in this sense is not at all fixed, but always in process. We are not the same from one moment to the next, one day to the next, one year to the next, because we dwell in the flux of interaction and history. We are not the same from one day to the next because our selves are constituted by differing relations with others. Home as the materialization of identity does not fix identity, but anchors it in physical being that makes a continuity between past and present. Without such anchoring of ourselves in things, we are, literally, lost.

Preservation

Homemaking consists in the activities of endowing things with living meaning, arranging them in space in order to facilitate the life activities of those to whom they belong, and preserving them, along with their meaning. Things are made or chosen for the house—furniture, pictures, draperies. Traditionally and today women furnish and decorate houses more than men. Often a home reflects a woman's taste and sensibility, often, the style and image she projects of herself and her family. The decor of a poor or modest home usually reflects this meaning-giving impulse as much as the homes of more wealthy people—she bought fabric for the window curtains that she made by hand, she painted or covered the chairs.

That is the photograph of my grandmother, who died before I was born, and it hung over the piano in every apartment and house we lived in while I was growing up; when my mother died it was the first thing I took home. The history embodied in the meaningful things of the home is often intergenerational. Traditionally women are the primary preservers of family as well as individual histories. Women trace the family lines and keep safe the trinkets, china cups, jewelry, pins, and photos of the

departed ancestors, ready to tell stories about each of them. I am suggesting that a main dimension for understanding home is time and
history.

Beauvoir, like Sartre, tends to associate historicity with futurity. So she
considers the oppression of women to consist in our being inhibited
from the creative activity of bringing new things into being.

> The male is called upon for action, his vocation is to produce, fight, create
> progress, to transcend himself toward the totality of the universe and the
> the infinity of the future. But marriage does not invite the woman to tran-
> scend herself with him—it confines her to immanence, shuts her up within
> the circle of herself. (p. 448)

This focus on futurity, on the unique moment when the human actor
brings something new into the world, makes Beauvoir ignore the specifically human value of activities that, as she puts it, guard the things of
the past and keep them in store. She implicitly collapses the activities
that consist in preserving the living meanings of past history into her
category of immanence. This conflation prevents her from seeing the
world-making meaning in domestic work. The particular human meanings enacted in the historicality of human existence depend as much on
the projection of a past as of a future.

Hannah Arendt's distinction between labor and work is similar to
Beauvoir's distinction between immanence and transcendence. Labor
consists in the grinding activity of doing what is necessary to meet needs
and maintain life. Its temporality is repetitive and cyclical because the
products of labor are always consumed by the needs of life, and thus they
leave no lasting monuments. Work, on the other hand, is that individualizing activity that makes a world of permanent historical objects—temples, squares, great books, lasting political constitutions. For Arendt too,
a quintessential moment of human meaning and individuality is that of
founding—erecting the city, establishing the republic.[17] But as soon as
the deeds of founding are accomplished, as soon as the heroic work of
the artist, statesman, or planner are recognized and celebrated, a new
task comes into play: preservation.[18]

Earlier I cited Heidegger's claim that building has a dual aspect: constructing and preserving. But even his discussion of the correlation of
dwelling with building drops the thread of preservation and concentrates
on the creative moment of constructing. It is time to pick up the threads
of preservation in order to understand the activities of homemaking. Traditional female domestic activity, which many women continue today,
partly consists in preserving the objects and meanings of a home.

Homemaking consists in the activities of endowing things with living
meaning, arranging them in space in order to facilitate the life activities

of those to whom they belong, and preserving them, along with their meaning. Dwelling in the world means we are located among objects, artifacts, rituals, and practices that configure who we are in our particularity. Meaningful historical works that embody the particular spirit of a person or a people must be protected from the constant threat of elemental disorganization. They must be cleaned, dusted, repaired, restored; the stories of their founding and continued meaningful use must be told and retold, interpreted and reinterpreted. They must also be protected from the careless neglect or accidental damage caused by those who dwell among and use them, often hardly noticing their meaning as support for their lives. The work of preservation entails not only keeping the physical objects of particular people intact, but renewing their meaning in their lives. Thus preservation involves preparing and staging commemorations and celebrations, where those who dwell together among the things tell and retell stories of their particular lives, and give and receive gifts that add to the dwelling world. The work of preservation also importantly involves teaching the children the meanings of things among which one dwells, teaching the children the stories, practices, and celebrations that keep the particular meanings alive. The preservation of the things among which one dwells gives people a context for their lives, individuates their histories, gives them items to use in making new projects, and makes them comfortable. When things and works are maintained against destruction, but not in the context of life activity, they become museum pieces.

The temporality of preservation is distinct from that of construction. As a founding construction, making, is a rupture in the continuity of history. But recurrence is the temporality of preservation. Over and over the things must be dusted and cleaned. Over and over the special objects must be arranged after a move. Over and over the dirt from winter snows must be swept away from the temples and statues, the twigs and leaves removed, the winter cracks repaired. The stories must be told and retold to each new generation to keep a living, meaningful history.

It would be a mistake, however, to conceive of the identity supported through this preservation of meaning in things as fixed. There are no fixed identities, events, interactions, and the material changes of age and environment make lives fluid and shifting. The activities of preservation give some enclosing fabric to this ever-changing subject by knitting together today and yesterday, integrating the new events and relationships into the narrative of a life, the biography of a person, a family, a people.

Preserving the meaningful identity of a household or family by means of the loving care of its mementos is simply a different order of activity from washing the unhealthy bacteria out of the bathroom. As Beauvoir rightly says, the latter is general, the abstract maintenance of species life.

The former, however, is specific and individuated: the homemaker acts
to preserve the particular meaning that these objects have in the lives of
these particular people. The confusion between these acts and the level
of immanence is perhaps understandable, because so many activities of
domestic work are both simultaneously. The homemaker dusts the
pieces in order to keep away the molds and dirts that might annoy her
sinuses, but at the same time she keeps present to herself and those with
whom she lives the moments in their lives or those of their forebears that
the objects remember. She prepares the sauce according to her
mother's recipe in order physically to nourish her children, but at the
same time she keeps alive an old cuisine in a new country.

Thus the activity of preservation should be distinguished from the nostalgia accompanying fantasies of a lost home from which the subject is
separated and to which he seeks to return. Preservation entails remembrance, which is quite different from nostalgia. Where nostalgia can be
constructed as a longing flight from the ambiguities and disappoint-
ments of everyday life, remembrance faces the open negativity of the
future by knitting a steady confidence in who one is from the pains and
joys of the past retained in the things among which one dwells. Nostalgic
longing is always for an elsewhere. Remembrance is the affirmation of
what brought us here.[19]

We should not romanticize this activity. Preservation is ambiguous; it
can be either conservative or reinterpretive. The same material things
sometimes carry the valences of unique personal identity and status privilege. By using my grandmother's china I both carry the material memory of childhood dinners and display the class position of my family history. I spoke once to a woman committed to restoring and preserving
her grandmother's Victorian southwestern ranch house, fully mindful of
her grandmother's passive participation in the displacement of Native
Americans from the land. The house has the history whether she
chooses to live in it or not. The moral and political question for her is
how she constructs her own identity and tells the stories of her family to
her children. Homemaking consists in preserving the things and their
meaning as anchor to shifting personal and group identity. But the narratives of the history of what brought us here are not fixed, and part of
the creative and moral task of preservation is to reconstruct the connection of the past to the present in light of new events, relationships, and
political understandings.

Given the cruelties of the histories of persons and peoples, remembrance and preservation often consists in the renewal of grief or rage. A
Jewish survivor of the Holocaust keeps safe the small and tattered mementos of her long dead parents. A city debates whether to demolish or
preserve the two-hundred-year-old slave auction block that once stood in
its center; after much political struggle in which many African Ameri-

cans, among others, demand its preservation, the city decides to leave it as a painful memorial of slavery. Some of the meaning preserved in things that anchor identity can be summed in the words "never again."

Preservation of the history that supports a person's identity by means of caring for and arranging things in space is the activity of homemaking still carried out primarily by women in the West, and in many other cultures as well. Such homemaking is not done exclusively by women, but to the degree that women more than men attend more to family and community ties in everyday life, the activities of preservation tend to be gender specific. Through these same activities, moreover, as I have already begun to indicate, the identity of groups and peoples is preserved. Especially in this late modern world where public administration and corporate standardization tend to drain individualized meaning from politics, schooling, and work, home and neighborhood retain meaningful importance as primary bearers of cultural identity and differentiation. For many migrants who wish to succeed in their new land, for example, their home is the primary place of the expression of cultural identity and continuity with their native lands.[20]

In many premodern or non-Western societies, I pointed out earlier, home is not confined to houses. Often the spaces of village squares, meeting halls, or mountain tops are more the home of the people in a group than are their individual shelters. The activities of preservation of the meaningful things that constitute home are important here as public acts of the group: maintaining collective spaces, guarding and caring for statues and monuments. For some traditional societies this preservative work is highly regarded, the responsibility of priests and elders. Modern Western societies also perform such public acts of preservation, but they are less often noticed or valued.

Such collective preservative activities continue in the interstices of modern urban societies today in the activities of civic clubs, neighborhood organizations, and religious institutions. When cities commemorate buildings as historic landmarks and stage periodic historically tinged festivals, they are also often performing the self-sustaining actions of preservation. These projects of keeping the meaning of past events and characters by maintaining material thus are not confined to things with positive feeling. In modern Western societies these public activities of preservation are also often coded as feminine, the devalued responsibility of "preservation ladies" who drink tea and look through moldy records, and often it is women in fact who seek to maintain or recover, interpret and reinterpret the historical meaning of places.[21]

Beauvoir is right to link her account of women's oppression with domestic work, but not entirely for the reasons she has. A sexual division of labor that removes women from participation in society's most valued and creative activities, excludes women from access to power and resources, and confines women primarily to domestic work is indeed a source of oppression. Much of typically women's work, however, is at least as fundamentally world-making and meaning-giving as typically men's work. Especially modern, future-oriented societies devalue this work, at the same time that they depend on its continued performance for the nurturance of their subjectivity and their sense of historical continuity. We should not romanticize this activity. Like the other aspects of home that I have discussed, preservation is ambiguous; it can be both conservative and reinterpretive, rigid and fluid. To the extent that it falls to women to perform this work for men and children, just as they perform the work of cooking and washing for them, without men's reciprocation, then women continue to serve as material for the subjectivities of men without receiving like support for themselves. Equality for women, then, requires revaluation of the private and public work of the preservation of meaningful things, and degendering these activities.

Contemporary Feminist Rejection of Home

I have been arguing that the value of home is ambiguous, and that feminists should try to disengage a positive from an oppressive meaning of home. If women are expected to confine themselves to the house and serve as selfless nurturers, and as those who automatically expand their domestic tasks when economic retrenchment rebounds on families,[22] then house and home remain oppressive patriarchal values. To the extent that both men and women seek in their homes and in the women who make them a lost unity and undisturbed comfort, moreover, the idea of home fuels a wrongful escapism. Values of homemaking, however, underlie the affirmation of personal and cultural identity, which requires material expression in meaningful objects arranged in space that must be preserved.

A chain of recent interlinked essays elaborates an argument that feminists should reject any affirmation of the value of home. Biddy Martin and Chandra Mohanty launched this discussion in their reading of Minnie Bruce Pratt's reflections on growing up as a privileged white woman in the American South.[23] Teresa de Lauretis then commented on Martin and Mohanty, enlarging their insights about the connection between home and identity.[24] Most recently Bonnie Honig criticizes what she perceives as a privileged position of withdrawal from politics that the idea of home affords, and she enlarges de Lauretis's ideas about decentered identity and feminist politics.[25]

All these essays express a deep distrust of the idea of home for feminist politics and conclude that we should give up a longing for home. Although I agree with much in their critiques, in this section I argue that while politics should not succumb to a longing for comfort and unity, the material values of home can nevertheless provide leverage for radical social critique. Following bell hooks, I shall suggest that "home" can have a political meaning as a site of dignity and resistance. To the extent that having home is currently a privilege, I argue, the values of home should be democratized rather than rejected.

All of these writers suspect a tendency they perceive among feminists to seek a home in a sisterhood with women. Home is a concept and desire that expresses a bounded and secure identity. Home is where a person can be "herself"; one is "at home" when she feels that she is with others who understand her in her particularity. The longing for home is just this longing for a settled, safe, affirmative, and bounded identity. Thus home is often a metaphor for mutually affirming, exclusive community defined by gender, class, or race.[26]

Feminist analysis reveals that this feeling of having a home as a bounded identity is a matter of privilege. Recall Irigaray's claim: man's ability to have a home, to return to his original identity, is achieved by means of the dereliction of woman as she provides the material nurturance of the self-same identity and the envelope that gives him his sense of boundary. In the feminist texts I am exploring here, the privilege of home the writers refer to is less a specifically gender privilege, and more a class and race privilege. Martin and Mohanty interpret Pratt's text as revealing how the sense of security and comfort that Pratt experienced as a child was predicated on the exclusion of blacks and lower-class whites at the same time that they were invisibly present as workers producing the comforts of home. Bonnie Honig argues that the sense of home as a place where one is confident who one is and can fall back on a sense of integrity depends on a vast institutional structure that allows such a luxury of withdrawal, safety, and reflection for some at the expense of many others who lose out in the global transfer of benefits. Home is here constructed in opposition to the uncertainties and dangers of streets and foreign territories where various riff-raff hang out in less than homey conditions.

> "Being home" refers to the place where one lives within familiar, safe, protected boundaries, "not being home" is a matter of realizing that home was an illusion of coherence and safety based on the exclusion of specific histories of oppression and resistance, the repression of differences, even within oneself.[27]

In his study of the construction of modern Western imperialist culture through interaction with the culture of the places constructed as colonies, Edward Said similarly suggests that the material comfort of bourgeois home derives from the material and discursive exploitation of distant colonies. Through a reading of Jane Austen's *Mansfield Park*, Said argues that a British sense of settled bourgeois home depended quite specifically on the nationalist enterprise of empire. Austen makes it plain, says Said,

> that the values associated with such higher things as ordination, law, and property must be grounded firmly in actual rule over and possession of territory. She sees clearly that to hold and rule Mansfield Park is to hold and rule an imperial estate in close, not to say inevitable, association with it. What assures that domestic tranquility and attractive harmony of one is the productivity and regulated discipline of the other.[28]

The women writers we are examining all conclude from these considerations that feminist politics should reject the idea of home. In giving up the idea of home, feminism is consistently postcolonial, exposing the illusion of a coherent stable self or a unified movement of women. A more honest and open attitude toward the world recognizes the plural identities of each of us and that a politics that recognizes and affirms differences cannot draw safe borders for the self.

> When the alternatives would seem to be either the enclosing, encircling, constraining circle of home, or nowhere to go, the risk is enormous. The assumption of, or desire for, another safe place like "home" is challenged by the realization that "unity"—interpersonal and well as political—is itself necessarily fragmentary, itself that which is struggled for, chosen, and hence unstable by definition; it is not based on "sameness," and there is no perfect fit.[29]

According to de Lauretis, feminism must make a shift in historical consciousness that entails

> a dis-placement and self-displacement: leaving or giving up a place that is safe, that is "home"—physically, emotionally, linguistically, epistemologically—for another place that is unknown and risky, that is not only emotionally but conceptually other; a place of discourse from which speaking and thinking are at best tentative, uncertain, unguaranteed.[30]

Bonnie Honig argues specifically against the use of "home" as a means of withdrawing from politics into a place of more certain principle and integrity. Feminist politics should be prepared to face dilemmas to which there are no simple responses. Longing for home is the effort to retreat into a solid unified identity at the expense of those projected and excluded as Other.

> The dream of home is dangerous, particularly in postcolonial setting, because it animates and exacerbates the inability of constituted subjects—or

nations—to accept their own internal divisions, and it engenders zealotry, the will to bring the dream of unitariness or home into being. It leads the subject to project its internal differences onto external Others and then to rage against them for standing in the way of its dream—both at home and elsewhere.[31]

Martin and Mohanty, de Lauretis, and Honig are right to criticize the bourgeois-dominative meaning of home, and earlier sections of this essay have explicated why. They are also right to fear the nostalgic seductions of home as a fantasy of wholeness and certainty. Through a reading of Irigaray, I have also elaborated on this claim. They are right, finally, to suggest that the attempt to protect the personal from the political through boundaries of home more likely protects privilege from self-consciousness, and that the personal identities embodied in home inevitably have political implications. I have also explored this undecidable difference between the personal and the political in preserving the meaning of things. These writers make persuasive analyses of the depoliticizing, essentialist, and exploitative implications that the idea of home often carries.

While agreeing with much of this critique, I have also argued that home carries a core positive meaning as the material anchor for a sense of agency and a shifting and fluid identity. This concept of home does not oppose the personal and the political, but instead describes conditions that make the political possible. The identity-supporting material of home can be sources of resistance as well as privilege. To the extent that home functions today as a privilege, I will argue later, the proper response is not to reject home, but to extend its positive values to everyone.

bell hooks expresses a positive meaning of "home" for feminism. She agrees with Martin and Mohanty, de Lauretis, and Honig, that "home" is associated with safety and the making of identity. She gives a positive and political meaning, however, to these functions of "home." Appealing to the historic experience of African American women, she argues that "homeplace" is the site of resistance to dominating and exploiting social structures. The ability to resist dominant social structures requires a space beyond the full reach of those structures, where different, more humane social relations can be lived and imagined. On hooks's view, homeplace uniquely provides such safe visionary space. The mutual caring and meaningful specificity provided by homeplace, moreover, enables the development of a sense of self-worth and humanity partially autonomous from dominating, exploiting, commercial or bureaucratic social structures. Thus hooks agrees with the feminist critics of "home" that home is a site of identity; whereas they criticize a search for pregiven,

whole, and apolitical identity, however, hooks finds homeplace to be the
site for a self-conscious *constructed* identity as a political project of criticism and transformation of unjust institutions and practices.

> Historically, African American people believed that the construction of a
> homeplace, however, fragile and tenuous (the slave hut, the wooden
> shack), had a radical political dimension. Despite the brutal reality of racial
> apartheid, of domination, one's homeplace was the one site where one
> could freely confront the issue of humanization, where one could resist.[32]

Thus hooks reverses the claim that having "home" is a matter of privilege. "Home" is a more universal value in her vision, one that the oppressed in particular can and have used as a vehicle for developing resistance to oppression. As long as there is a minimal freedom of homeplace, there is a place to assemble apart from the privileged and talk of
organizing; there is a place to preserve the specific culture of the oppressed people. The personal sense of identity supported in the site and
things of a homeplace thus enables political agency.

hooks emphasizes this political value of homeplace as the place of the
preservation of the history and culture of a people, in the face of coloniz-
ing forces of the larger society. This project of preservation and remembrance, I have argued, above, is very different from the nostalgic longing
for home that Martin and Mohanty, de Lauretis, and Honig rightly suspect. Preservation and remembrance are historical. Colonized people
can project an alternative future partly on the basis of a place beyond
dominance that is preserved in everyday life. hooks herself seeks in her
essay to remember the African American mothers and grandmothers
who have preserved generations of homeplace, distinct African American cultural meanings in stories, foods, songs, and artifacts.

> I want to remember these black women today. The act of remembrance is
> a conscious gesture honoring their struggle, their effort to keep something
> for their own. I want us to respect and understand that this effort has been
> and continues to be a radically subversive political gesture. For those who
> dominate and oppress us benefit most when we have nothing to give our
> own, when they have so taken from us our dignity, our humanness that we
> have nothing left, no "homeplace" where we can recover ourselves.[33]

HOME AS A CRITICAL VALUE

The criticisms of the idea of home I have reviewed dwell primarily on a
temptation to reject or reconstruct conflict and social difference by creating safe spaces in politics. Nationalism is an important and dangerous

manifestation of this temptation, in romanticizing "homeland." The positive idea of home I have advocated is attached to a particular locale as an extension and expression of bodily routines. Nationalism attempts to project such a local feeling of belonging onto a huge territory and "imagined community" of millions,[34] and in so doing creates rigid distinctions between "us" and "them" and suppresses the differences within "us." Other attempts to project an ideal of home onto large political units are just as damaging. A useful response to such idealizations of politics as a search for home, however, is to emphasize the radical potential of values that attend to the concrete localized experience of home, and the existential meaning of being deprived of that experience.

Having the stability and comfort of concrete home is certainly a privilege. Many millions of people in the world today do not have sufficient space of their own to live by themselves or with others in peace. They do not have the time or space to preserve much of the history and culture of their family and community, though only refugees and the most desperately destitute are unable to try. With upwards of 500 million refugees and other homeless people in the world, that deprivation is serious indeed. Even if people have minimal shelter of their own, moreover, they need a certain level of material comfort in their home for it to serve as a place of identity-construction and the development of the spirit of resistance that hooks discusses. In this way having a home is indeed today having a privilege.

The appropriate response to this fact of privilege is not to reject the values of home, but instead to claim those values for everyone. Feminists should criticize the nostalgic use of home that offers a permanent respite from politics and conflict, and which continues to require of women that they make men and children comfortable. But at the same time, feminist politics calls for conceptualizing the positive values of home and criticizing a global society that is unable or unwilling to extend those values to everyone. There are at least four normative values of home that should be thought of as minimally accessible to all people. These stand as regulative ideals by which societies should be criticized.

(1) Safety—Everyone needs a place where they can go to be safe. Ideally, home means a safe place, where one can retreat from the dangers and hassles of collective life. It is too much to ask, perhaps even in the ideal, that everyone can be safe anywhere. The potential for violence and conflict cannot be eradicated from the world. But it is not too much to ask that everyone have a home in which they can feel physically safe and secure.

Today we are frighteningly, horribly far from this simple goal. For too many women and children, their houses do not enclose them

safely, but threaten them with violence from the men who live there
with them. Too many poor peasants and barrio dwellers in the world
cannot sleep peacefully in their homes without fear that paramilitary
squads will rouse them, rape them, shoot them, or carry them away in
the dark. If anything is a basic need and a basic liberty, it is personal
safety and a place to be safe. Yet ensuring such safety at home is an
arduous and complex matter, one that seems too daunting for the will
of the late twentieth century. We must be ashamed of a world in which
safety at home is a privilege, and express outrage at any stated or implied suggestion that such a need and liberty is too expensive for any
society to meet.

(2) Individuation—A person without a home is quite literally deprived
of individual existence.[35] However minimal, home is an extension of the
person's body, the space that he or she takes up, and performs the basic
activities of life—eating, sleeping, bathing, making love. These need not
all be done in the same place or behind closed doors, in a house. But the
individual is not allowed to be if she does not have places to live and to
perform the activities of life, with basic routine and security. As I have
already outlined in the concept of homemaking, moreover, people's existences entail having some space of their own in which they array
around them the things that belong to them, that reflect their particular
identity back to them in a material mirror. Thus basic to the idea of
home is a certain meaning of ownership, not as private property in ex-
changeable goods, but in the sense of meaningful use and reuse for life.
Even the monk has a cell of his own in the collective life of the monas-
tery; even in crowded families with little space there is usually an effort
to allocate each person a corner of his own where he can sleep and put
the things he calls his own. Where this is not possible it nevertheless
remains as an ideal.[36]

(3) Connected with the value of individuation is privacy. A person
does not have a place of her own and things of her own if anyone can
have access to them. To own a space is to have autonomy over admission
to the space and its contents. Some feminists doubt the value of privacy,
because they associate this idea with the "private sphere," to which
women have been historically confined. But there are crucial differences
in the two concepts. Privacy refers to the autonomy and control a person
has to allow or not allow access to her person, information about her,
and the things that are meaningfully associated with her person. The
traditional "private sphere," on the other hand, confines some persons
to certain realm of activity and excludes them from others. As a value,
privacy says nothing about opportunities for the person to engage in
activity. It only says that whatever her social activities, a person should

have control over access to her living space, her meaningful things, and information about herself.[37]

Feminists have been suspicious of a value of privacy also because traditional law has sometimes appealed to a right of privacy to justify not interfering with autocratic male power in the family. Because of a supposed right of privacy, the law should turn a blind eye to marital rape or battering. But perhaps the most important defense against this legitimation of patriarchal power is an insistence that privacy is a value for individuals, not simply or primarily for households. Anita Allen argues that if we insist on privacy as a value for all persons as individuals, then the extent to which women deserve privacy at home and elsewhere, and do not have it, becomes apparent.[38] The appeal to privacy as a value thus enables social criticism.

Some might claim that appeal to a value of privacy is ethnocentric, because the idea of privacy is a Western idea. Scholars disagree on the question of whether non-Western societies both historically and today have held a value of privacy. My cursory reading of that literature leads me to conclude that there is often, if not always, a form of respect for the physical person of another and for some kind of spaces associated with the person. In stratified societies, such respect may be restricted to those in the upper strata. This does not mean that such a value does not exist in the society, but rather that it is held as a privilege. I am arguing here that certain values associated with home, among them control over access to one's person and personal space, be made available everyone: to the degree that non-Western and premodern societies, as well as modern societies, do not democratize privacy, then I am indeed criticizing them.

Thus while it seems to me that an ideal of respect for the personal space of others is not restricted to Western societies, one can argue that conceptualizing this idea in terms that we call privacy is Western. The concept of privacy is a relatively recent development of positive law based in rights. The concept of rights to privacy extends law to relations of interaction among private individuals or between private agents, as well as between the state and individuals. Thus I wish to suggest that there are long-standing ideas and practices analogous to privacy in many societies, and that to the degree that positive law and social policy have evolved in those societies, it is not a mistake today to appeal to a value of privacy.

(4) The final value of "home" that should be available to everyone I have already explicated at length in an earlier section: preservation. Home is the site of the construction and reconstruction of one's self. Crucial to that process is the activity of safeguarding the meaningful

things in which one sees the stories of one's self embodied, and rituals of remembrance that reiterate those stories. I have argued that preservation in this sense is an important aspect of both individual and collective identity.

Home is a complex ideal, I have argued, with an ambiguous connection to identity and subjectivity. I agree with those critics of home who see it as a nostalgic longing for an impossible security and comfort, a longing bought at the expense of women and of those constructed as Others, strangers, not-home, in order to secure this fantasy of a unified identity. But I have also argued that the idea of home and the practices of home-making support personal and collective identity in a more fluid and material sense, and that recognizing this value entails also recognizing the creative value to the often unnoticed work that many women do. Despite the real dangers of romanticizing home, I think that there are also dangers in turning our backs on home.

NOTES

CHAPTER 1
GENDER AS SERIALITY

I am grateful to Linda Alcoff, David Alexander, Sandra Bartky, Sonia Kruks, Lynda Lange, Bill McBride, Uma Narayan, Linda Nicholson, Vicki Spelman, and anonymous reviewers for *Signs* for comments on earlier versions of this essay.

1. Elizabeth Spelman, *Inessential Woman*. (Boston: Beacon Press, 1988).

2. Chandra Talpade Mohanty, "Under Western Eyes: Feminist Scholarship and Colonial Discourses," in Chandra Mohanty, Ann Russo, and Lourdes Torres, eds., *Third World Women and the Politics of Feminism* (Bloomington: Indiana University Press, 1991).

3. Judith Butler, *Gender Trouble* (New York: Routledge, 1990).

4. See Susan Bordo, "Feminism, Postmodernism, and Gender-Scepticism," in Linda Nicholson, ed., *Feminism/Postmodernism* (New York: Routledge, 1989), 133–56.

5. For a discussion of the concept of social group in the context of a politics that exposes oppression, see I. M. Young, *Justice and the Politics of Difference* (Princeton: Princeton University Press, 1990), chap. 2.

6. See Lynda Lange, "Arguing for Democratic Feminism: Postmodern Doubts and Political Amnesia," paper presented to the American Philosophical Association, Midwest Division, Chicago, April 1991.

7. Spelman, *Inessential Woman*, pp. 170–78.

8. Ann Ferguson, "Racial Formation, Gender, and Class in U.S. Welfare State Capitalism," in *Sexual Democracy* (Boulder: Westview Press, 1991), 114–15.

9. Cf. Bordo, "Feminism."

10. Diana Fuss, *Essentially Speaking* (New York: Routledge, 1989), 36. She argues, as I read her, that "woman" designates a social position, defined by relations of power and potentially shifting with the context of power and practices. This relationally defined position is itself an epistemological or discursive product of social movement politics that asks specific and unique questions about social practices and relations. "Woman is a position from which feminist politics can emerge rather than a set of attributes that are 'objectively identifiable.' Seen in this way, being a 'woman' is to take up a position within a moving historical context and to be able to choose what we make of this position and how we alter this context. From the perspective of the fairly determined though fluid and mutable positions, women can themselves articulate a set of interests and ground a feminist politics." In a personal correspondence Alcoff has denied being located in the position I am constructing as saying that the category of woman is a product of feminist politics, so I do not include her in the text.

11. Nancie Caraway, "Identity Politics and Shifting Selves: Black Feminist Coalition Theory," paper presented at American Political Science Association, August 1989, 9.

12. For one effort to use Sartre positively for feminist theory, see Julien Murphy, "The Look in Sartre and Rich," in Jeffner Allen and Iris Marion Young, eds., *The Thinking Muse: Feminism and Modern French Philosophy* (Bloomington: Indiana University Press, 1989).

13. Linda Singer, *Erotic Welfare* (New York: Routledge, 1992).

14. Sartre, *Critique of Dialectical Reason*, trans. Alan Sheridan-Smith (London: New Left Books, 1976). Book II, sections 1, 2, and 3, are the most relevant for the concept of group. Sartre in fact distinguishes several levels of group: the group-in-fusion, the statutory group, the organization, and the institution. Each is less spontaneous, more organized and rule bound, and more materialized than the last. All come under the more general definition I am offering here, which is all that is necessary to develop my argument. My summaries of Sartre throughout this paper are quite short and leave out a great deal of detail. I believe they are nevertheless adequate to the text and sufficient for developing my argument.

15. Gayatri Chakravorty Spivak, "French Feminism in an International Frame," in *In Other Worlds* (New York: Methuen, 1987), 151.

16. In terms of Sartre's early work, I am here interpreting seriality as a condition of facticity that helps constitute a situation, but in no way determines action. Action, the having of projects and goals, the realizing of ends, I am saying here, is what constitutes the identities and experiences of persons. Action is situated against a background of serialized existence, which means that it is constrained but neither general nor determined.

17. While Sartre does not thematize race as such, I think he provides grounds for understanding race positioning as seriality. He describes being Jewish as initially belonging to a series. As a social fact or social label, being Jewish in a society that marks or devalues Jews does not name some concept, a set of specific attributes a person must be identified as having in order to be classed as Jewish. In the social relation of being Jewish, there is no separate substance that Jews have in common that makes them Jews. The group label is never real, specific, limited, here; it always names an alien otherness coming from elsewhere, from the facticity of "them," the anonymous others who say things about the Jews, who "know" what the Jews are.

> In fact, the being-Jewish of every Jew in a hostile society, which persecutes and insults them, and opens itself to them only to reject them again, cannot be the only relation between the individual Jew and the anti-semitic, racist society which surrounds him; it is this relation insofar as it is lived by every Jew in his direct or indirect relations with all the other Jews, and in so far as it constitutes him, through them all, an Other and threatens him in and through the Others. To the extent that, for the conscious, lived Jews, being-Jewish (which is his status for *non-Jews*) is interiorized as his responsibility in relation to all other Jews and his being-in-danger, out there, owing to some possible carelessness caused by Others who mean nothing to him, over

whom he has no power and every one of whom is himself like Others (in so far as he makes them exist as such in spite of himself), the *Jew,* far from being *the type* common to each separate instance, represents *on the contrary* the perpetual being-*outside-themselves-in-the-other* of members of this practico-inert grouping. (p. 268)

Sartre also discusses colonialism as a serial social relation, mediated by an anonymous Public Opinion that constitutes racist discourse. He says that the most important thing about racist ideas and utterances is that they are not *thoughts.* Racism as operative in everyday life and as a medium of works and beliefs for reproducing practically congealed social relations of oppression and privilege is not a *system* of beliefs, thought through and deliberated. On the contrary, the racist language is unconsidered, uttered as the obvious, and spoken and heard always as the words of an Other. Everyday repeated stereotypes that Blacks are lazy or more prone to be aggressive, or that they prefer to stay with their own kind, etc.,

> have never been anything more than this system itself producing itself as a determination of the language of the colonists in the milieu of alterity. And, for this point of view, they must be seen as material exigencies of language (the *verbal milieu* of all practico-inert apparatuses) addressed to colonialists as members of a series and *signifying* them as colonialists both in their eyes and in those of others, in the unity of a gathering. . . .The sentence which is uttered, as a reference to the common interest, is not presented as the determination of language by the individual himself, but as his *other* opinion, that is to say, the claims to get it from and give it to others, insofar as their unity is based purely on alternity. (p. 301)

18. Nancy Chodorow, *The Reproduction of Mothering* (Berkeley: University of California Press, 1978).

19. Ann Ferguson develops an important criticism of the ideal of a common woman's or lesbian's identity in her paper, "Is There a Lesbian Culture?" in Jeffner Allen, ed., *Lesbian Philosophies and Cultures* (Albany: State University of New York Press, 1991), 63–88.

CHAPTER II
ASYMMETRICAL RECIPROCITY

I would like to thank David Alexander, Lisa Heldke, Laurie Schrage, Pamela Coughie, Laurence Thomas, and Bill Scheuermann for comments on an earlier version of this essay. I have also benefited from conversations about these ideas with audiences to which the paper was presented at York University, Loyola University, Free University of Berlin, Institute for Philosophy of Vienna, and the Society for Women in Philosophy.

1. Seyla Benhabib, *Situating the Self* (New York: Routledge, 1991).

2. Anita Silvers, "Reconciling Equality to Difference: Caring (f)or Justice for Defective Agents," *Hypatia: A Journal of Feminist Philosophy* (1995).

3. See Joseph P. Shapiro, *No Pity: People with Disabilities Forging a New Civil Rights Movement* (New York: Times Books, Random House, 1993). See also Karen

Fiser, "Philosophy, Disability and Essentialism," in Lawrence Foster and Patricia Herzog, eds., *Defending Diversity: Contemporary Philosophical Perspectives on Pluralism and Multiculturalism* (Amherst: University of Massachusetts Press, 1994), 83–102.

4. Compare Diva Stasvilis, "'Authentic Voice: Anti-racist Politics in Canadian Feminist Publishing and Literary Production," in Genew and Yeatman, eds., *Feminism and the Politics of Difference* (Sydney: Allen and Unwin, 1993).

5. Luce Irigaray, *Speculum of the Other Woman*, trans. Gillian C. Gill (Ithaca: Cornell University Press, 1974).

6. Compare Laurence Thomas, "Moral Deference," *The Philosophical Forum*, 14, 1–3 (Fall–Spring 1992–93: 233–50. Though Thomas is referring primarily to the relation between privileged and oppressed groups in this essay, he also appeals to the unique subjectivity of each person to argue that we cannot put ourselves in one another's position. "No amount of imagination in the world can make it the case that one has the subjective imprimatur of the experiences and memories of another. And an individual's subjective imprimatur makes a very real difference" (p. 235).

7. Compare Laurie Schrage's discussion of Benhabib's notion of reversing perspectives, *Moral Dilemmas of Feminism: Prostitution, Adultery, and Abortion* (New York: Routledge, 1994), 14–18.

8. Melissa A. Orlie, "Thoughtless Assertion and Political Deliberation," *American Political Science Review* 88, 3 (September 1994): 684–95. Elisabeth Spelman makes a similar point about how the effort to take the other person's perspective may be little else than a desire to see oneself reflected in the other person, in her idea of "boomerang perception." See *Inessential Woman* (Boston: Beacon Press, 1988). See also Maria Lugones, "On the Logic of Pluralist Feminism," in Claudia Card, *Feminist Ethics* (Laurence: University of Kansas Press, 1993).

9. Compare Jessica Benjamin, "The Shadow of the Other (Subject): Intersubjectivity and Feminist Theory," *Constellations* 1, 2 (October 1994): 231–55. "If we are to go beyond a conception of a self-enclosed self, if we want to recuperate difference and respect for otherness along with agency, we have to account for the impact of the other on the self—a negation that is at once indeterminate and irreducible to the subject's own mental world, thus not the subject's own constructed Other, even though related and interdependent with it" (p. 239).

10. This notion of moral humility is similar to the idea of "moral deference" expressed by Laurence Thomas in "Moral Deference." People in relatively socially privileged positions, Thomas suggests, owe moral deference to those in "diminished social categories." In moral deference, we assume that the socially diminished people best know and express the experience of those in that social category and the moral judgment of the harm suffered by them. This does not mean that such expressions are incorrigible or cannot be criticized. Rather, it means that those in privileged social categories cannot assume they can imaginatively put themselves in the situation of those in diminished social categories to understand their experience. Instead, they must listen across distance before they make their critical judgments.

Moral humility is not quite the same as deference. In the first case I only admit that I lack knowledge of the other, and in the second I recognize that the other has the knowledge I lack. The two concepts are close, however, and potentially complementary, though not entailed by one another.

11. I derive this account from my reading of Emmanuel Levinas, *Otherwise than Being, or Beyond Essence* (The Hague: Martinus Nijhoff, 1981). For an excellent commentary on the work of Levnias as relevant to a political ethics, see Simon Critchley, *The Ethics of Deconstruction* (London: Blackwells Publishers, 1992). On the notion of the relation of self and other as asymmetrical, see Martin Matustick, *Post-National Identity* (New York: Guilford Press), pp. 190–93. In "The Shadow of the Other (Subject)," Jessica Benjamin also proposes an idea of moral recognition as asymmetrical reciprocity; see pp. 243–48. See also Arne Johan Vetlesen, "Relations with Others in Sartre and Levinas: Assessing Some Implications for an Ethics of Proximity," *Constellations* 1, 3, (January 1995): 358–82.

12. Nancy Love, "Politics and Voice(s): An Empowerment Knowledge Regime," *Differences*, 3, 1, (Spring 1991): 96; compare Stephen White, *Political Theory and Postmodernism* (New York: Cambridge University Press, 1991), 110.

13. Irigaray, *The Ethics of Sexual Difference* (Ithaca: Cornell University Press, 1984), p. 14.

14. Ibid, p. 48.

15. James Tully has interpreted me as claiming in earlier writing that differently situated people cannot understand each other. See Tully, *Strange Multiplicity: Constitutionalism in an Age of Diversity* (New York: Cambridge University Press, 1995), 132–34. I do not believe that I have ever argued that ontological and social difference implies that people cannot understand one another.

16. Sandra Lee Bartky argues for a similar idea of understanding others, but not through identification or taking their standpoint. She draws on Max Scheler's criticism of the idea that sympathy involves imagining the other person's experience in terms of one's own. See Bartky, "Sympathy and Solidarity: On a Tightrope with Scheler," in Diana Meyers, *Feminists Rethinking the Self* (New York: Routledge, 1996).

17. One of the points of Wittgenstein's later philosophy is to challenge the common assumption that the particular meaning of speech-acts derives from or is assimilable to a more general linguistic logic. I am interpreting a stance that says that to understand others we must be able to put ourselves in their place, to see ourselves as symmetrical with them, as making a similar assumption. In *Strange Multiplicity*, James Tully invokes a Wittgensteinian approach to communication to explain how understanding across difference is possible; pp. 103–16, 181–82. Maria Lugones also invokes the metaphor of a game to remind us of the element of the unexpected and surprising involved in being open to understanding others. See "Playfulness, 'World,'- Traveling, and Loving Perception," in Jeffner Allen, ed., *Lesbian Philosophies and Cultures* (Albany: State University of New York Press, 1991), especially 177.

18. Jacques Derrida, *Given Time: Counterfeit Money*, trans. Peggy Kamuf (Chicago: University of Chicago Press, 1992), 12

19. Ibid., p. 41.

20. Habermas, *The Theory of Communicative Action* (Boston: Beacon Press, 1983), vol. 2, part 5.

21. Luce Irigaray, *An Ethics of Sexual Difference* (Ithaca: Cornell University Press, 1993), p. 13.

22. Ibid., p. 74

23. I take the stance of playfulness that Maria Lugones recommends as similar to this concept of wonder. "Playfulness that gives meaning to our activity includes uncertainty, but in this case the uncertainty is an *openness to surprise*. This is a particular metaphysical attitude that does not expect the world to be neatly packaged, rule." Lugones, "Playfulness." On the role of wonder in the communicative relation between groups, see also Tully, *Strange Multiplicity*, 206.

24. Benhabib, *Situating the Self,* 54.

25. Lisa Disch, *Hannah Arendt and the Limits of Philosophy* (Ithaca: Cornell University Press, 1995); "More Truth than Fact: Storytelling as Critical Understanding in the Writings of Hannah Arendt," *Political Theory* 21, 4 (November 1993): 665–94. I find an ambiguity in Disch's interpretation of Arendt along the lines of my discussion below. On the one hand, Disch seems to recommend Arendt's idea of imaginatively putting oneself in the position of everyone else in moral reasoning. On the other hand, I find Disch's explication of Arendt's notion of plurality and publicity in tension with that recommendation, for the reasons I give here.

26. Immanuel Kant, *The Critique of Judgment*, trans. James Cried Meredith (Oxford: The Clarendon Press, 1952), section 40.

27. Hannah Arendt, *The Human Condition* (Chicago: University of Chicago Press, 1958), pp. 52, 57.

28. Orlie, "Thoughtless Assertion," 689.

29. I have learned to think about objectivity in this sort of way from Donna Haraway; see "Situated Knowledges: The Science Question in Feminism and the Privilege of Partial Perspective," *Simians, Cyborgs, and Women* (New York: Routledge, 1991). For a particularly interesting account of objectivity as the enlargement of the circle of one's thinking, see Lisa M. Heldke and Stephen H. Kellert, "Objectivity as Responsibility," ms., Gustavus Adophus College, 1994.

CHAPTER III
COMMUNICATION AND THE OTHER

1. I have begun to develop this idea of communicative democracy in another essay, "Justice and Communicative Democracy," in Roger S. Gottlieb, ed., *Radical Philosophy: Tradition, Counter-Tradition, Politics* (Philadelphia: Temple University Press, 1993), 23–42.

2. Among the writers whom I include as theorists of deliberative democracy are Joshua Cohen, "Deliberation and Democratic Legitimacy," in Alan Hamlin and Philip Pettit, *The Good Polity* (London: Blackwell, 1989), 17–34; Thomas Spragens, *Reason and Democracy* (Durham, N.C.: Duke University Press, 1990); Benjamin Barber, *Strong Democracy* (Berkeley and Los Angeles: University of California Press, 1984), though Barber is not as susceptible to one of the critiques I offer as the others; Cass R. Sunstein, "Beyond the Republican Revival," *Yale Law Journal* 97 (1988): 1539–90; Frank Michelman, "Traces of Self-Government," *Harvard Law Review* 100 (1986): 4–77; Jane Mansbridge, "A Deliberative Theory of Interest Representation," in Mark P. Patracca, ed., *The Politics of Interests: Inter-*

est Groups Transformed (Boulder, Colo.: Westview Press, 1992); John Dryzek, *Discursive Democracy* (Cambridge: Cambridge University Press, 1990); James Bohman, "Democracy and Cultural Pluralism," *Political Theory* 23, no. 2 (1995): 253–79; and James Fishkin, *Deliberative Democracy* (New Haven: Yale University Press, 1991). I also assume Habermas's theory of communicative action as a basis for a theory of deliberative democracy, and some of my criticism is directed at his theory. Later I will refer to some of Michael Walzer's writing as falling within this general approach to democratic theory.

3. Spragens and Bohman both point to the potential irrationality of an interest-based conception of democracy. See also Jack Knight and James Johnson, "Aggregation and Deliberation: On the Possibility of Democratic Legitimacy," *Political Theory* 22, no. 2 (May 1994): 277–98.

4. See John Burke for a particularly bold assertion of the impossibility of moral claims in public life. *Bureaucratic Responsibility* (Baltimore: Johns Hopkins University Press, 1989).

5. James Fishkin is something of an exception here. He argues that there is a tradeoff between political equality and participation. Giving every citizen an equal influence over outcomes, he suggests, precludes deliberation, because in a large-scale democracy this means one person/one vote in aggregated elections and referenda. See *Deliberative Democracy*.

6. Cohen, "Deliberation and Democratic Legitimacy," 22–23.

7. Habermas, *A Theory of Communicative Action*, vol. 1: *Reason and the Rationalization of Society* (Boston: Beacon Press, 1981); Dryzek, *Discursive Democracy*, chaps. 1 and 2.

8. A passage from Habermas's exposition of the function of moral argument shows this unquestioned acceptance of the model of dialogue as competition: "What happens in argumentation is that the success orientation of competitors is assimilated into a form of communication in which action oriented toward reaching understanding is continued by other means. In argumentation, proponents and opponents engage in *competition with arguments* in order to convince one another, that is, in order to reach a consensus. This dialectical role structure makes forms of disputation available for a comparative search for truth. Argumentation can exploit the conflict between success-oriented competitors for the purpose of achieving consensus so long as the arguments are not reduced to mere means of influencing one another." *Moral Consciousness and Communicative Action*, trans. Christian Lenhardt and Shierry Weber Nicholsen (Cambridge, Mass.: MIT Press, 1991), 160.

9. See Lynn Sanders, "Against Deliberation," a paper presented at a meeting of the American Political Science Association, September 1992; she cites studies that show that in juries men talk considerably more than women and are leaders more often. Jane Mansbridge cites studies that show that female state legislators speak less than their male counterparts and that in public meetings women tend more to give information and ask questions, while men state opinions and engage in confrontation. Mansbridge, "Feminism and Democratic Community," in John W. Chapman and Ian Shapiro, eds., *Democratic Community*, Nomos no. 35 (New York: New York University Press, 1991).

10. Anthony Cortese argues that the model of moral reasoning presupposed by Kohlberg and Habermas is ethnocentric and culturally biased and tends to

locate Chicano speaking and reasoning styles lower in its scale; see *Ethnic Ethics* (Albany: SUNY Press, 1990). Charles Henry discusses the tendency of African Americans more than whites to couple emotion and anger with argument, influencing African American styles of public debate; see *Culture and African American Politics* (Bloomington: Indiana University Press, 1990).

11. Michael Walzer, *Interpretation and Social Criticism* (Cambridge, Mass.: Harvard University Press, 1987).

12. Habermas, *Moral Consciousness*, 67.

13. For one statement of this kind of position, see Benjamin Barber, *Strong Democracy*, 197–212.

14. Compare Lynn Sanders, "Against Deliberation"; I have developed an argument similar to this at greater length in chap. 4 of *Justice and the Politics of Difference* (Princeton: Princeton University Press, 1990).

15. I have developed more of such a conception of understanding across difference in another article, "Asymmetrical Reciprocity: On Moral Respect, Wonder and Enlarged Thought" (see chapter 2 of this volume).

16. Alison Jaggar, "Feminist Practical Dialogue," an unpublished typescript; and Patricia Hill Collins, *Black Feminist Thought* (New York: Routledge, 1990), especially chap. 8.

17. Cortese, *Ethnic Ethics*; and Henry, *Culture and African American Politics*.

18. I have arrived at this moment of communication by way of a reading of Emmanuel Levinas's distinction between the Saying and the Said in *Otherwise than Being, or Beyond Essence* (The Hague: Nijhoff, 1981).

19. Upendia Baxi criticizes those who might judge what he calls sycophancy in politics as a symptom of underdevelopment, and calls such a reaction ethnocentric. Sycophancy, or the mutual exchange of flattery and praise, he argues, is an important element in maintaining relationships. To the degree that Western public culture reduces such behavior, he suggests, it impoverishes communication. "What Is Wrong with Sycophancy? A Caveat on Overrationalized Notions of Political Communication," in Bhikhu Parekh and Thomas Pantham, eds., *Political Discourse: Explorations in Indian and Western Thought* (Beverly Hills: Sage, 1987).

20. In "Feminist Practical Dialogue," Alison Jaggar remarks on the importance of such bodily care-taking for promoting the ends of democratic communication.

21. Spragens, *Reason and Democracy* (Durham, N.C.: Duke University Press, 1990), 128.

22. James Bohman, "Emancipation and Rhetoric: The Perlocutions and Illocutions of the Social Critic," *Philosophy and Rhetoric* 21, no. 3 (1988).

23. Barber, *Strong Democracy*, 175.

24. Compare Kathryn Abrams, "Hearing the Call of Stories," *California Law Review* 79, no. 4 (July 1991): 971–1052. Reviewing the use of narrative in feminist legal theory, Abrams argues that narrative serves important argumentative functions.

25. Sanders, "Against Deliberation."

26. Jane Braten, "From Communicative Rationality to Communicative Thinking: A Basis for Feminist Theory and Practice," in Johanna Meehan, ed., *Feminists Read Habermas* (New York: Routledge, 1995).

CHAPTER IV
PUNISHMENT, TREATMENT, EMPOWERMENT

I am grateful to Claire Cohen, Nancy Fraser, Nancy Glazner, Michelle Harrison, Kary Moss, Shane Phelan, Dorothy Roberts, Jana Sawicki, Joan Tronto, Tom Wartenberg, and anonymous referees for *Feminist Studies* for helpful comments on earlier versions of this article. Thanks to Terrence Raferty, Amy Marlo, and Carrie Smarto for research assistance.

1. See Jan Hoffman, "Pregnant, Addicted—and Guilty," *New York Times Magazine*, Sunday, 19, Aug. 1990, 24; some estimate that as many as 11 percent of women in labor test positive for illegal drugs; see Benjamin A. Niel, "Prenatal Drug Abuse: Is the Mother Criminally Liable?" *Trial Diplomacy Journal* 15 (May/June 1992): 129. Kary Moss, of the American Civil Liberties Union Reproductive Rights Project, in a personal communication, dated 8 Apr. 1991, tells me that these governmental statistics are badly sampled and do not adequately distinguish types of drug use.

2. See Michelle Harrison, "Drug Addiction in Pregnancy: The Interface of Science, Emotion, and Social Policy," *Journal of Substance Abuse Treatment* 8 (1991): 261–68. See also Wendy K. Mariner, Leonard H. Glantz, George J. Annas, "Pregnancy, Drugs, and the Perils of Prosecution," *Criminal Justice Ethics* 7 (winter/spring 1990): 30–41.

3. Emmalee S. Bandstra, "Medical Issues for Mothers and Infants Arising from Perinatal Use of Cocaine," in *Drug Exposed Infants and Their Families: Coordinating Responses of the Legal, Medical, and Child Protection System*, ed. Judith Larsen (Washington, D.C.: American Bar Association Center on Children and the Law, 1990). See also Joseph B. Treaster, "Plan Lets Addicted Mothers Take Their Newborns Home," *New York Times*, 19 Sept. 1991, A1, B4.

4. A survey of fifteen southern states by the *Atlanta Constitution* found that 71 percent of the 1,500 people polled favored criminal penalties for pregnant women whose illegal drug use injured their babies; see Mark Curriden, "*Roe v. Wade* Does Not Prevent Criminal Prosecution of Prenatal Child Abuse," *American Bar Association Journal* 16 (March 1990): 51–53. A *National Law Journal* Lexis news service poll found that the majority say a mother should be held criminally responsible when she abuses substances during pregnancy and as a result gives birth to an impaired child. See "Courts Disagree on Mother's Liability," *National Law Journal* 13 (13 May 1991): 30.

5. Curriden, "*Roe v. Wade*," 52; Ellen M. Barry, "Pregnant, Addicted, and Sentenced," *Criminal Justice* 5 (winter 1991): 22–27; Jean Davidson, "Drug Babies Push Issue of Fetal Rights," *Los Angeles Times*, 25 Apr. 1989, sec. I, p. 1.

6. American Civil Liberties Union, Washington Office Memo, 3 Oct. 1989; Dorothy E. Roberts, "Punishing Drug Addicts Who Have Babies: Women of Color, Equality, and the Right of Privacy," *Harvard Law Review* 104 (May 1991): 1419–82.

7. These states are Illinois, Indiana, Minnesota, Nevada, Florida, Oklahoma, Rhode Island, and Utah. See Dorothy Roberts, "Drug Addicted Women Who Have Babies," *Trial* (April 1990): 56–61.

8. Ruth Ann Strickland and Marcia Lynn Whicker, "Fetal Endangerment versus Fetal Welfare: Discretion of Prosecutors in Determining Criminal Liability

and Intent" (Paper presented at meetings of the American Political Science Association, Chicago, August 1992).

9. Alison B. Marshall, "Drug Addiction, Pregnancy, and Childbirth: Legal Issues for the Medical and Social Service Communities," in *Drug Exposed Infants and Their Families*, 31–50; Jan Hoffman and Matthew Burns, "Greenville Woman Sentenced to Prison," *Charleston News and Courier*, Friday, 19 Oct. 1990.

10. Roberts, "Punishing Drug Addicts Who Have Babies"; Deborah S. Pinkey, "Racial Bias Found in Drug Abuse Reporting," *American Medical News* 32 (6 Oct. 1989): 4; Ira S. Chasnoff, Harvey J. Landress, and Mark E. Barrett, "The Prevalence of Illicit Drug or Alcohol Use during Pregnancy in Pinellas Co., FL," *New England Journal of Medicine* 322 (26 Apr. 1990): 1202–7. Despite similar rates of substance abuse among black and white women, black women were ten times more likely to be reported than white women, and poor women were also more likely to be reported.

11. Mark Hanse, "Courts Side with Moms in Drug Cases," *American Bar Association Journal* 18 (November 1992): 18.

12. In June 1989 a survey of five major cities found that there were 304 "boarder" babies, most born to drug-using mothers; Josephine Gittler and Merles McPerson, "Prenatal Substance Abuse," *Children Today* 19 (July-August 1990): 3–7.

13. See Wendy Chavkin, "Drug Addiction and Pregnancy: Policy Crossroads," *American Journal of Public Health* 8 (April 1990): 483–87. These states include Massachusetts, Minnesota, Oklahoma, and Utah; see Roberts, "Punishing Drug Addicts Who Have Babies," 1430; Bonnie I. Robin-Vergeer, "The Problem of the Drug Exposed Newborn: A Return to Principled Intervention," *Stanford Law Review* 42 (February 1990): 745–809.

14. Judith Larson, "Creating Common Goals for Medical, Legal, and Child Protection Communities," in *Drug Exposed Infants and Their Families*, 3–18.

15. Judy Mann, "Cure an Addict, Save a Child," *Washington Post*, 5 Apr. 1991, C3.

16. Treaster, "Plan," A1, B4

17. Cf. Harrison, "Drug Addiction in Pregnancy," 262.

18. Dorothy Dinnerstein, *The Mermaid and the Minotaur: Sexual Arrangements and Human Malaise* (New York: Harper & Row, 1976).

19. See Edwin M. Shur, *Labeling Women Deviant: Gender, Stigma, and Social Control* (Philadelphia: Temple University Press, 1983); allegations of "unfit" motherhood stand against the understanding that when a woman undertakes parenthood she subordinates her own needs, desires, or priorities to the welfare of the child.

20. Roberts, "Punishing Drug Addicts Who Have Babies."

21. Alan I. Trachtenberg, M.D., Testimony to House Select Committee on Children and Families, 19 Apr. 1990, Memo from ACLU; Barry claims that research shows that the threat of incarceration is no significant deterrent on the behavior of substance-dependent women and tends to deter women from getting prenatal care.

22. Andrew Skolnick, "Drug Screening in Prenatal Care Demands Objective Medical Criteria, Support Services," *Journal of the American Medical Association* 264 (18 July 1990). Researchers conclude that care provided in the framework of

support, rather than judgment, can improve the outcome for drug-abusing pregnant women.

23. See *Robinson v. California*, 370 U.S. 660 (1962), cited by Roberts.

24. See Lynn M. Paltrow, "When Becoming Pregnant Is a Crime," *Criminal Justice Ethics* (winter/spring 1990): 41–47; Mariner, Glantz, and Annas, "Pregnancy"; Roberts ("Drug Exposed Infants") argues that prosecutions of drug-addicted mothers infringe on the woman's freedom to continue a pregnancy, which Roberts claims is essential to an individual's personhood and autonomy and impose an invidious government standard for the entitlement to procreate; see esp. 1445–56.

25. See Tamar Lewin, "Hurdles Increase for Many Women Seeking Abortions," *New York Times*, 15 Mar. 1992.

26. See "Substance Abuse Treatment for Women: Crisis in Access," *Health Advocate*, no. 160 (Spring 1989); see also Josette Mondonaro, *Chemically Dependent Women: Assessment and Treatment* (Lexington, Mass.: Lexington Books, 1989), esp. chaps. 1–3.

27. Wendy Chavkin, "Mandatory Treatment for Drug Use during Pregnancy," *Journal of the American Medical Association* 260 (18 Sept. 1991): 1556–61.

28. See Thomas H. Murray, "Prenatal Drug Exposure: Ethical Issues," in *The Future of Children* (Spring 1991): 105–12.

29. Jeffrey Murphy, "Marxism and Retribution," in *Retribution, Justice, and Therapy* (The Hague: D. Reidel, 1979), 93–115.

30. Michel Foucault, *Discipline and Punish* (New York: Pantheon, 1977). In Foucauldian usage "carceral" refers to discipline of the body.

31. Statement of the Board of Trustees of the American Medical Association, "Legal Intervention during Pregnancy: Court-Ordered Medical Treatment and Legal Penalties for Potentially Harmful Behavior by Pregnant Women," *Journal of the American Medical Association* 264 (28 Nov. 1990): 2663–70; cf. Skolnick: Study showed that when pregnant addicts were in a supportive atmosphere and not threatened with punishment, 83 percent of patients who tested positive for drug use agreed to counseling and 61 percent of the women in counseling discontinued their drug use. See also Chavkin, "Drug Addiction and Pregnancy."

32. A literature in philosophy and political theory on the ethics of care has burgeoned that is too vast to enumerate. Carol Gilligan's *In a Different Voice: Psychological Theory and Women's Development* (Cambridge: Harvard University Press, 1982) is the starting point of this work. Other important works in addition to those I will cite below are Seyla Benhabib, "The Generalized and the Concrete Other," in *Feminism as Critique: On the Politics of Gender*, ed. Seyla Benhabib and Drucilla Cornell (Minneapolis: University of Minnesota Press, 1987); *Women and Moral Theory*, ed. Diana Meyers and Eva Kittay (Totowa, N.J.: Rowman & Littlefield, 1986); Marilyn Friedman, "Beyond Caring: The De-Moralization of Gender," in *Science, Morality, and Feminist Theory*, ed. Marsha Hanen and Kai Nielsen (Calgary: University of Calgary Press, 1987).

33. Annette Baier, "The Need for More Than Justice," in *Science, Morality, and Feminist Theory*, 47.

34. The Wellesley College Stone Center for the Study of the Psychology of Women has pioneered transferring the insights of Gilligan and other theorists of

caring into a general theory of self-in-relation that can be applied in therapeutic situations. See Judith V. Jordan et al., *Women's Growth in Connection: Writings from the Stone Center* (New York: Guilford Press, 1991); see also Emily K. Abel and Margaret K. Nelson, eds., *Circles of Care: Work and Identity in Women's Lives* (Albany: SUNY Press, 1990).

35. See Gillian Walker et al., "A Descriptive Outline of a Program for Cocaine-Using Mothers and Their Babies," *Journal of Feminist Family Therapy* 3, no. 3 and 4 (1991): 7–17.

36. Nell Noddings, *Caring: A Feminine Approach to Ethics and Moral Education* (Berkeley: University of California Press, 1984); Lawrence Blum, *Friendship, Altruism, and Morality* (London: Routledge & Kegan Paul, 1980).

37. Virginia Held, "Non-Contractual Society: A Feminist View," in *Science, Morality, and Feminist Theory*, 111–38; Bernice Fisher and Joan Tronto, "Toward a Feminist Theory of Caring," in *Circles of Care*, 35–62; Selma Sevenhuijsen, "Justice, Moral Reasoning, and the Politics of Child Custody, in *Equality, Politics, and Gender*, ed. Elizabeth Meehan and Selma Sevenhuijsen (London: Routledge, 1991), 88–103.

38. See Theodore M. Benditt, "The Demands of Justice: The Difference That Social Life Makes," in *Economic Justice*, ed. Kenneth Kipnis and Diane T. Meyers (Totowa, N.J.: Rowman & Allenheld, 1985), 108–20. Nancy Fraser points out that the distinction between benefits that recipients have rights to and those that are merely gifts of charity is also gendered in the U.S. welfare system, as it is in many others. Such a gender division in social service, she suggests, perpetuates the second-class citizenship of women. See her "Women, Welfare, and the Politics of Need Interpretation," in *Unruly Practices: Power, Discourse, and Gender in Contemporary Social Theory* (Minneapolis: University of Minnesota Press, 1988); see also Carole Patement, "The Patriarchal Welfare State," in *The Disorder of Women: Democracy, Feminism and Political Theory* (Stanford: Stanford University Press, 1989).

39. See Robert Goodin, *Protecting the Vulnerable: A Re-Analysis of Our Social Responsibilities* (Chicago: University of Chicago Press, 1985); see also his *Reasons for Welfare: The Political Theory of the Welfare State* (Princeton: Princeton University Press, 1989), chaps. 5 and 6.

40. G. M. Beschner, B. G. Reed, and Josette Mondonaro, *Treatment Services for Drug Dependent Women* (Washington, D.C.: GPO National Institute on Drug Abuse, U.S. Department of Health and Human Services, 1981).

41. John L. Forth-Finegan, "Sugar and Spice and Everything Nice: Gender Socialization and Women's Addiction—A Literature Review," *Journal of Feminist Family Therapy* 3, no. 3 and 4 (1991): 25; a number of studies find a high correlation between women's substance abuse and a history of sexual abuse.

42. Lucia Meijer, Testimony before House Select Committee on Children, Youth and Families on Substance Abuse Treatment and Women, 27 Apr. 1989, mimeo from ACLU; see also "Substance Abuse Treatment for Women: Crisis in Access."

43. See Nancy Hartsock, "Foucault on Power: A Theory for Women," in *Feminism/Postmodernism*, ed. Linda Nicholson (New York: Routledge, 1990), 157–75; Nancy Fraser expresses skepticism about Foucault's conception of biopower

in her chapter on "Foucault's Body Language: A Posthumanist Political Rhetoric," in *Unruly Practices*. Her papers on women and the welfare state from the same volume, which I will rely on later in this section, however, are informed by Foucauldian insights as well as insights from critical theory. For different views, see Jana Sawicki, *Disciplining Foucault: Feminism, Power, and the Body* (New York: Routledge, 1991); Shane Phelan, "Foucault and Feminism," *American Journal of Political Science* 34 (May 1990): 421–40; Chris Weedon, *Feminist Practice and Poststructuralist Theory* (London: Basil Blackwell, 1987), chap. 5; Sandra Bartky, "Foucault, Femininity, and the Feminization of Patriarchal Power," in Sandra Bartky, *Femininity and Domination* (New York: Routledge, 1990), 63–82; Susan Bordo, "The Body and the Reproduction of Femininity: A Feminist Appropriation of Foucault," in *Gender/Body/Knowledge: Feminist Reconstructions of Being and Knowing*, ed. Susan Bordo and Allison Jaggar (New Brunswick, N.J.: Rutgers University Press, 1986), 13–33.

44. See Foucault, *Discipline and Punish*; see also his *Power/Knowledge* (New York: Pantheon, 1980), 93–108. Mary Rawlinson provides a good summary and analysis of disciplinary power in "Foucault's Strategy: Knowledge, Power, and the Specificity of Truth," *Journal of Medicine and Philosophy* 12 (1987): 371–95.

45. Treaster, "Plan."

46. Nancy Fraser, "Women, Welfare, and the Politics of Need Interpretation," and "Struggle over Needs: Outline of a Socialist Feminist Critical Theory of Late Capitalist Political Culture," both in *Unruly Practices*; Joel Handler, "Dependent People, the State, and the Modern/Postmodern Search for the Dialogic Community," *UCLA Law Review* 35 (August 1988): 999–1113; Ann Weick et al, "A Strengths Perspective for Social Work Practice," *Social Work* 34 (July 1989): 350–54.

47. See Fraser, "Women"; Handler, "Dependent People"; see also Nikolas Rose, *Governing the Soul: The Shaping of the Private Self* (New York: Routledge, 1990), 224–37.

48. Michel Foucault, *Technologies of the Self*, ed., Luther H. Martin, Huck Gutman and Patrick Hutton (Amherst: University of Massachusetts Press, 1988), 40; cf. Foucault, *History of Sexuality* (New York: Random House, 1978), 1: 60–67.

49. Rose, *Governing the Soul*, esp. chaps. 16–20.

50. See Fraser, "Women, Welfare, and the Politics of Need Interpretation"; Ellen Luff, "Using First Amendment and Title VII to Obtain Woman-Centered Drug/Alcohol Treatment Programs," *Proceedings of the Second Conference of the Institute for Women's Policy Research* (Washington, D.C.: Institute for Women's Policy Research, June 1990), 1–7; Bette S. Tallen, "Twelve-Step Programs: A Lesbian Feminist Critique," *NWSA Journal* 2 (summer 1990): 390–407.

51. See Patricia Pasick and Christine White, "Challenging General Patton: A Feminist Stance in Substance Abuse Treatment and Training," *Journal of Feminist Family Therapy* 3, no. 3 and 4 (1991): 87–102; Judy Kopp, "Self-Observation: An Empowerment Strategy in Assessment," *Social Casework: The Journal of Contemporary Social Work* 70 (May 1989): 276–79.

52. Thomas Wartenberg, *Forms of Power: From Domination to Transformation* (Philadelphia: Temple University Press, 1990), chap. 9.

53. Forth-Finegan, "Sugar and Spice," 36.

54. Janet L. Surrey, "Relationship and Empowerment," in *Women's Growth in Connection*, 164.

55. For statements of this sort of meaning of empowerment, see Ruth J. Parsons, "Empowerment: Purpose and Practice Principle in Social Work," *Social Work in Groups* 14, no. 2 (1991): 7–21; Lorraine M. Gutierrez, "Working with Women of Color: An Empowerment Perspective," *Social Work* 35 (March 1990): 149–53.

56. Handler, "Dependent People," 1083–1111; Fraser, "Women, Welfare, and the Politics of Need Interpretation," 156–58.

57. Parsons, "Empowerment."

58. Handler, "Dependent People."

59. A study by Laurence Gary et al. concludes that the nurturing of social and racial solidarity deters drug use in some African American communities. See their essay, "Some Determinants of Attitudes toward Substance Use in an Urban Ethnic Community," *Psychological Reports* 54 (1984), cited in James Jennings, "Blacks, Politics, and the Human Service Crisis," in *Blacks, Politics, and Economic Development*, ed. James Jennings (London: Verso, 1992).

CHAPTER V
REFLECTIONS ON FAMILIES IN THE AGE OF MURPHY BROWN

Thanks to David Alexander, Ruth Colker, Christine DiStefano, Stephen Macedo, Martha Minow, Deborah Rhode, and Molly Shanley for comments on an earlier version of this essay. Thanks to Carrie Smarto for research assistance.

1. Quotations from Quayle's speech are from *Time*, June 1, 1992, 29–30.

2. Carol Gilligan first opposed the norm of justice to more particularist feminist moral concerns, which she called care: *In a Different Voice* (Cambridge: Harvard University Press, 1982). Many feminist theorists followed her in assuming that justice is a value of public bureaucratic life inappropriate to more relationally oriented contexts of action. But in recent years there have been important challenges to this opposition between justice and care. See Susan Okin, *Justice, Gender and the Family* (New York: Basic Books, 1989); Joan Tronto, *Moral Boundaries: A Political Argument for an Ethics of Care* (New York: Routledge, 1993), esp. 77–92; Tronto, "Gender, Care and Justice in Feminist Political Theory," working papers of the Anna Maria Van Shuurman Centrum of the University of Utrecht, March 15, 1991; Marilyn Friedman, "Beyond Care: The De-Moralization of Gender," in Virginia Held, ed., *Justice and Care: Essential Readings in Feminist Ethics* (Boulder: Westview Press, 1995); Sara Ruddick, "Justice in Families," address to American Philosophical Association, December 1992.

3. See *Justice and the Politics of Difference*, chap. 1.

4. James Sterba, *How to Make People Justice* (Totowa, NJ: Rowman and Littlefield, 1991), chap. 5.

5. Okin, *Justice, Gender and the Family*, 114.

6. Selma Sevenhuijsen, "Justice, Moral Reasoning and the Politics of Child Custody," in Elizabeth Meehan and Selma Sevenhuijsen, eds., *Equality, Politics and Gender* (London: Sage), 88–103.

7. See Iris Young, "The Supreme Court and Abortion," *Dissent* (Fall 1992).

8. See Will Kymlicka, "Rethinking the Family," *Philosophy and Public Affairs* 20, 1 (1991): 77–97.

9. See Susan Okin, "Sexual Orientation and Gender: Dichotomizing Difference," presented at the "Democracy and Difference" conference sponsored by the Conference for the Study of Political Thought, April 1993.

10. Adrienne Rich, *Of Woman Born* (New York: W. W. Norton, 1977).

11. Adrienne Rich, "Compulsory Heterosexuality and Lesbian Existence," in Ann Snitow, Christine Stansell, and Sharon Thompson, eds., *Powers of Desire* (New York: Monthly Review Press, 1983), 177–205.

12. See Carole Pateman, *The Sexual Contract* (Palo Alto: Stanford University Press, 1988).

13. Ruth Colker, "Marriage," *Yale Journal of Law and Feminism* 3, 2 (Spring 1991): 321–26.

14. As I will discuss later, courts do not often think they need to give a reason for restricting marriage to heterosexual couples. Occasionally they do, however; in *Singer v. Hara*, the court said that the purpose of marriage is procreation, and this justifies requiring two people of different sexes.

15. *Chambers v. Omaha Girls Club*, 834 F. 2nd 697 (8th cir. 1987).

16. There has been much writing about the function of The Family in promoting consumption in advanced capitalist society. For one interesting recent discussion, see Linda Singer, *Erotic Welfare* (New York: Routledge, 1992), 78–79.

17. See Martha Minow, "Redefining Families: Who's In and Who's Out?" *University of Colorado Law Review* 62, 2 (1991): 269–85.

18. See Richard Mohr, "Policy, Ritual, Purity: Mandatory AIDS Testing," in *Gays/Justice* (New York: Columbia University Press, 1988).

19. G. Sidney Buchanan, "Same-Sex Marriage: The Linchpin Issue," *University of Dayton Law Review* 10 (1985); Hannah Schwarzchild, "Same-Sex Marriage and Constitutional Privacy: Moral Threat and Legal Anomaly," *Berkeley Women's Law Journal* 4 (1988–89): 94–127; Martha Minow, "Free Exercise of Families," *University of Illinois Law Review* 4 (1991): 940.

20. W. J. Wilson, *The Truly Disadvantaged* (Chicago: University of Chicago Press, 1986).

21. William Galston, *Liberal Purposes* (New York: Cambridge University Press, 1991), 284–89; I develop arguments criticizing Galston's position in my essay "Mothers, Citizenship and Independence: A Critique of Pure Family Values" (see chapter VI in this volume).

22. See Terry Arendell, *Mothers and Divorce: Legal, Economic and Social Dilemmas* (Berkeley: University of California Press, 1986); cited in Jan E. Dizard and Howard Gadlin, *The Minimal Family* (Amherst: University of Massachusetts Press, 1990), 143–44.

23. See William A. Vega, "Hispanic Families in the 1980's: A Decade of Research," *Journal of Marriage and Family*, Nov. 1990.

24. See Minow, "Free Exercise of Families," 925–48; Minow argues that legal reasoning about the liberty to live in family forms as one chooses ought to be thought of as analogous to free exercise of religion.

25. Thanks to Drew Leder for the idea that families have "family resemblances."

26. Martha Minow, *Making All the Difference: Inclusions, Exclusion, and American Law* (Ithaca: Cornell University Press, 1990), 268–83.

27. See Carole Pateman, "The Shame of the Marriage Contract," in Judith H. Stiehm, ed., *Women's Views of The Political World of Men* (Dobbs Ferry, NY: Transnational Publishers, 1984.

28. Compare Martha Alberston Fineman, "The Sexual Family," in *The Neutered Mother, the Sexual Family and Other Twentieth Century Tragedies* (New York: Routledge, 1995), 145–75. Fineman argues that family law should be separated from sex. She differs from me, however, in concluding that this means the abolition of regulation of adult relationships except through contract. She would retain family law only in the form of protections for children and their caretakers. I argue that protections may be needed for adults who share lives whether or not they have a sexual relationship.

29. See Foucault, *History of Sexuality* (New York: Vintage, 1982). "In a society such as ours, where the family is the most active site of sexuality, and where it is doubtless the exigence of the latter which maintain and prolong its existence, incest—for different reasons altogether and in a completely different way—occupies a central place; it is constantly being solicited and refused; it is an object of obsession and attraction, a dreadful secret and an indispensable pivot. It is manifested as a thing that is strictly forbidden in the family insofar as the latter functions as a deployment of alliance; but it is also a thing that is continuously demanded in order for the family to be a hotbed of constant sexual incitement" (p. 109).

30. See Mary L. Shanley, "Fathers' Rights, Mothers' Wrongs?: Reflections on Unwed Fathers' Rights, Patriarchy, and Sex Equality," in Patrice DiQuinzio and Iris Marion Young, eds., *Feminist Ethics and Social Policy* (Bloomington: Indiana University Press, 1997).

31. See Nancy D. Polikoff, "This Child Does Have Two Mothers: Redefining Parenthood to Meet the Needs of Children in Lesbian-Mother and Other Non-contractual Families," *Georgetown Law Journal* 78 (February 1990): 459–575.

32. See Adrienne Asch and Michelle Fine, "Shared Dreams: A Left Perspective on Disability Rights and Reproductive Rights," in Marlene Gerber Fried, ed., *From Abortion to Reproductive Freedom: Transforming a Movement* (Boston: South End Press, 1990), 233–40.

33. See Delores Hayden, *Redesigning the American Dream* (New York: W. W. Norton, 1984), 137–38.

Chapter VI
Mothers, Citizenship, and Independence

I am grateful to David Alexander, Ronald Beiner, Lisa Brush, Gerald Dworkin, Steven Elkin, Robert Goodin, Carole Pateman, and Kenneth Winston for helpful comments on earlier versions of this paper.

1. William Galston, *Liberal Purposes* (Cambridge: Cambridge University Press, 1991), chaps. 1–7.

2. U.S. Bureau of the Census, *Statistical Abstract of the United States, 1993–94* (Austin, Tex.: The Reference Press), 101–2.

3. Judith S. Wallerstein and Sandra Blakeslee, *Second Chances: Men, Women and Children a Decade after Divorce* (New York: Ticknor & Fields, 1989).

4. Andrew Cherlin and Frank Furstenburg, "Divorce Doesn't Always Hurt the Kids," *Washington Post* (March 19, 1989), C3.

5. See Rosemary Dunlop and Alisa Burns, "The Sleeper Effect—Myth or Reality? Findings from a Ten-Year Study of the Effects of Parental Divorce at Adolescence" (paper presented at the Fourth Australian Family Research Conference, Manly, NSW, February 1993).

6. P. R. Amato and B. Keith, "Parental Divorce and the Well-Being of Children: A Meta-analysis," *Psychological Bulletin* 110 (1991): 26–46.

7. Dunlop and Burns, "The Sleeper Effect"; Andrew Cherlin also finds that the adverse effects observed in children are often prior to divorce and can be attributed to a hostile family environment; Cherlin, "Longitudinal Studies of Effects of Divorce on Children in Great Britain and the United States," *Science* (June 7, 1991): 1386–89.

8. Dunlop and Burns suggest that one reason that they find lower levels of emotional distress in their studies of children of divorce than do some American studies may be that Australian divorce procedures rely on family court counseling and mediation much more than do those in the United States, which relies on a highly charged adversarial system of divorce settlement.

9. *Statistical Abstract*, 61. These statistics may obscure the fact that unmarried parents may nevertheless be coparenting with other adults in the household. Lesbian parents, for example, usually appear as single mothers in statistics, even when they live in long-term partnerships with another woman.

10. *Statistical Abstract*, 64.

11. Ibid, 77–78.

12. Christopher Jencks, *Rethinking Social Policy: Race, Poverty and the Underclass* (New York: Harper Perennial, 1992), 198; Herbert L. Smith and Phillips Cutright, "Thinking about Change in Illegitimacy Ratios: United States, 1963–1983," *Demography* 25 (1988): 235–47.

13. *Statistical Abstract*, 78.

14. Larry Bumpass, "Children and Marital Disruption: A Replication and Update," *Demography* 21 (February 1984): 71–82.

15. See, e.g., Amitai Etzioni, *The Spirit of Community* (New York: Crown, 1993), chap. 2.

16. Nan Marie Astone and Sara McLanahan, "Family Structure and High School Completion: The Role of Parental Practices," Institute for Research on Poverty discussion paper no. 905–9 (Madison, Wis., 1989).

17. Stephanie Coontz, *The Way We Never Were* (New York: Basic Books, 1992), 224.

18. Sharyne Merritt and Linda Steiner, *And Baby Makes Two: Motherhood without Marriage* (New York: Franklin Watts, 1984), 160.

19. Sara McLanahan, "The Consequences of Single Parenthood for Subsequent Generations," *Focus* (University of Wisconsin, Institute for Research on Poverty) 11 (1988): 16–24.

20. Diana Pearce, "Welfare Is Not *for* Women: Why the War on Poverty Cannot Conquer the Feminization of Poverty," in *Women, the State, and Welfare,* ed. Linda Gordon (Madison: University of Wisconsin Press, 1990), 265–79.

21. Laurence E. Lynn, Jr., "Ending Welfare Reform As We Know It," *American Prospect* (Fall 1993): 88.

22. Pearce, "Welfare is Not *for* Women," 265–79.

23. *Statistical Abstract,* 131.

24. Pearce, "Welfare is Not *for* Women."

25. Jencks, *Rethinking Social Policy,* 235.

26. Teresa L. Amot, "Black Women and AFDC: Making Entitlement Out of Necessity," in Gordon, ed.

27. Jencks, *Rethinking Social Policy,* 149.

28. *Statistical Abstract,* 133.

29. Susan Okin, *Justice, Gender and the Family* (New York: Basic Books, 1989).

30. For an account of the role of "republican motherhood" in American history and its continued effects on reinforcing the inequality of women, see Rogers M. Smith, "'One United People': Second Class Female Citizenship and the American Quest for Community," *Yale Journal of Law and the Humanities* 1 (1989): 229–93.

31. On the masculinity of independence as a citizen virtue, see Carole Pateman, "The Patriarchal Welfare State," in *The Disorder of Women* (Cambridge, Polity, 1989); see also Anna Yeatman, "Beyond Natural Right: The Conditions for Universal Citizenship," *Social Concept* 4 (1988): 3–32.

32. Jeremy Waldron well summarizes this rationale for independence as a virtue of early modern citizenship in "Social Citizen and the Defense of Welfare Provision," in *Liberal Rights* (Cambridge: Cambridge University Press, 1993); see also Susan James, "The Good-Enough Citizen: Female Citizenship and Independence," in *Beyond Equality and Difference: Citizenship, Feminist Politics and Female Subjectivity,* ed. Gisela Bock and Susan James (London: Routledge, 1992).

33. On the paradoxes of women's incorporation into the modern polity and their implications for women's contemporary standing, see Carole Pateman, "Equality, Difference, Subordination: The Politics of Motherhood and Women's Citizenship," in Bock and James, eds., 17–29.

34. See Eva Feder Kittay, "Equality, Rawls, and the Dependency Critique," in *Equality and the Inclusion of Women* (New York: Routledge, 1995).

35. For an important account of the changes in the meaning of dependence and the way the term is increasingly confined to single mothers, see Nancy Fraser and Linda Gordon, "A Genealogy of *Dependency:* Tracing a Keyword of the U.S. Welfare State," *Signs: A Journal of Women in Culture and Society* 19 (1994): 1–29.

36. For an important account of a concept of autonomy along these lines, see Jennifer Nedelsky, "Reconceiving Autonomy," *Yale Journal of Law and Feminism* 1 (1989): 7–35.

37. In the already cited article, Jeremy Waldron gives an important normative argument for this idea of social citizenship originated by Marshall. See also Barry Hindess, "Multiculturalism and Citizenship," in *Multicultural Citizens: The Philosophy and Politics of Identity,* ed. Chandran Kukathas (Canberra: Center for Independent Studies, 1993), 31–46.

38. Deborah A. Stone, "Caring Work in a Liberal Polity," *Journal of Health Politics, Policy and Law* 16 (1991): 547–52.

39. See Harry Boyte, *Community Is Possible* (New York: Harper & Row, 1984).

40. See Frederick W. Bozett, ed., *Gay and Lesbian Parents* (New York: Praeger, 1987).

41. Lynn, "Ending Welfare Reform."

42. A number of writers have pointed out that a consistent commitment encouraging all able-bodied people to make meaningful social contributions entails expanding welfare supports to the working poor, rather than reducing welfare supports. That is, because so many people's wages are too little to give them a decent life, justice requires that they be dependent on public support. See Sar A. Levitan, Frank Gall, and Isaac Shapir, *Working but Poor*, rev. ed. (Baltimore, Johns Hopkins University Press, 1993); Lynn, "Ending Welfare Reform."

43. Delores Hayden, *Redesigning the American Dream* (New York: Norton, 1984), 137–38; Gerda R. Wekerle, "Responding to Diversity: Housing Development by and for Women," in *Shelter, Women, and Development: First and Third World Perspectives*, ed. Hemalata C. Dandekar (Ann Arbor: George Wahr, 1991), 178–86.

CHAPTER VII
HOUSE AND HOME

I am grateful to David Alexander, Robert Beauregard, Edward Casey, Delores Hayden, Deorothea Olkowski, and Geraldine Pratt for helpful comments on earlier versions of this paper. I also benefitted from a discussion of the paper at the University of Pittsburgh women's writing group, including Jean Carr, Nancy Glazener, Paula Kane, Margaret Marshall, and Marianne Novy.

1. Martin Heidegger, "Building, Dwelling, Thinking," in *Poetry, Language, Thought*, trans. Albert Hofstadter (New York: Harper and Row, 1971). Hereafter cited as BDT.

2. Compare Edward Casey, *Getting Back into Place: Toward a Renewed Understanding of the Place-World* (Bloomington: Indiana University Press, 1993), 112. Casey also notes (pp. 176–77) that Heidegger slides into identifying dwelling with construction even though he begins with a wider scope for building.

3. Hannah Arendt also theorized building as a fundamental aspect of human meaning. She distinguishes between labor, activity useful for production and consumption of the means of living, and work, the construction of artifacts that transcend mere life because they are made to be permanent. Thus for Arendt the moment of founding is the primordial moment of action. Through the construction of edifices people create a built environment, a civilization, by means of which they emerge as thinking and speaking subjects. See Hannah Arendt, *The Human Condition* (Chicago: University of Chicago Press, 1958).

4. Aliye Pekin Celik, "Women's Participation in the Production of Shelter," and Victoria Basolo and Michelle Moraln, "Women and the Production of Housing: An Overview," both in Hemalata C. Dandekar, *Shelter, Women and Development: First and Third World Perspectives* (Ann Arbor: George Wahr Publishing Co., 1993).

5. Caroline O. N. Moser, "Women, Human Settlements, and Housing: A Conceptual Framework for Analysis and Policy-Making," in Caroline O. N. Moser and Linda Peake, eds., *Women, Human Settlements, and Housing* (London: Tavistock Publications, 1987); Irene Tinker, "Beyond Economics: Sheltering the Whole Woman," in Blumberg, Rakowski, Tinker and Maneton, eds., *Engendering Wealth and Well-Being* (Boulder: Westview Press, 1995), 261–84.

6. Luce Irigaray, *Ethics of Sexual Difference* (Ithaca: Cornell University Press, 1992), 101. Hereafter cited as ESD.

7. Once of the classic statements of this idea is Herbert Marcuse's *One Dimensional Man* (Boston: Beacon Press, 1964); see also Stuart Ewen, *Captains of Consciousness* (New York: McGraw-Hill, 1976).

8. See James S. Duncan, "From Container of Women to Status Symbol: The Impact of Social Structure on the Meaning of the House," in James S. Duncan, ed., *Housing and Identity: Cross-Cultural Perspectives* (New York: Holmes and Meier Publishers, 1982).

9. Anita Larsson, "The Importance of Housing in the Lives of Women: The Case of Botswana," in Dandekar, *Shelter, Women, and Development*, 106–15.

10. See Jurgen Habermas, *Legitimation Crisis* (Boston: Beacon Press, 1975).

11. See Sophie Watson, *Accommodating Inequality: Gender and Housing* (Sydney: Allen and Unwin, 1988).

12. Delores Hayden compares the suburban desire for the detached single-family home as a nostalgia for the cottage in the woods; see *Redesigning the American Dream* (New York: W. W. Norton, 1983). Carole Despres discusses how the design of homes in contemporary Quebec suburbs nostalgically aims to evoke the traditional Quebequois cottage. Despres, "De la maison bourgeoisie a la maison moderne. Univer domestique, esthetique et sensibilite feminine," *Recherches Feministes* 2, 1 (1989): 3–18.

13. Simone de Beauvoir, *The Second Sex*, trans. H. M. Parshley (New York: Random House, 1952), 451.

14. D. J. Van Lennep, "The Hotel Room," in Joseph J. Kockelmans, ed., *Phenomenological Psychology: The Dutch School* (Dordrecht: Martinus Nijhoff, 1987), 209–15.

15. Ibid, 211.

16. Casey, *Getting Back into Place*, 120.

17. Arendt, *The Human Condition*.

18. See Sara Ruddick, "Preservative Love," in *Maternal Thinking: Toward a Politics of Peace* (New York: Ballantine Books, 1989), 65–81; Joan Tronto, *Moral Boundaries* (New York: Routledge, 1992). Both theorists focus on the preserving and protecting actions of caring persons, but both also talk about the caring for things that supports this activity. In this essay I focus on preserving meanings through things partly because this has been a less noticed aspect of domestic work than material and emotional caring for people. The two are deeply intertwined, of course.

19. On the distinction between nostalgia and memory, see Gayle Greene, "Feminist Fiction and the Uses of Memory," *Signs* 16, 2 (Winter 1991), 290–321.

20. See Keya Ganguly, "Migrant Identities: Personal Memory and the Construction of Selfhood," *Cultural Studies* 6, 1 (January 1992): 27–49; Susan Thom-

ason, "Suburbs of Opportunity: The Power of Home for Migrant Women," Proceedings of the Postmodern City Conference, Sydney University, 1993.

21. See Delores Hayden, *The Power of Place* (Cambridge: MIT Press, 1995).

22. Governments all over the world, in both developed and developing countries, have been cutting social services and allowing prices for basic foodstuffs to rise. The result is usually more domestic work for women. See Haleh Afshar and Carolyne Dennis, *Women and Adjustment Politices in the Third World* (New York: St. Martin's Press, 1993).

23. Biddy Martin and Chandra Talpade Mohanty, "Feminist Politics: What's Home Got to Do With It?" in Teresa de Lauretis, ed., *Feminist Studies/Cultural Studies* (Bloomington: Indiana University Press, 1986), 191–212.

24. Teresa de Lauretis, "Eccentric Subjects: Feminist Theory and Historical Consciousness," *Feminist Studies* 16, 1 (Spring 1990): 115–50.

25. Bonnie Honig, "Difference, Dilemmas, and the Politics of Home," *Social Research* 61, 3 (Fall 1994): 563–97.

26. See Benice Johnson Reagon, "Coalition Politics: Turning the Century," in Barbara Smith, ed., *Home Girls: A Black Feminist Anthology* (Kitchen Table: Women of Color Press, 1983), 356–69. Reagon criticizes the attempt to seek the comforts of home in politics, but as I read her she does not reject the values of home.

27. Martin and Mohanty, "Feminist Politics," 196.

28. Edward Said, *Culture and Imperalism* (New York: Vintage Books, 1993), 87.

29. Martin and Mohanty, "Feminist Politics," 209.

30. De Lauretis, "Eccentric Subjects," 138.

31. Honig, "Difference," 585.

32. bell hooks, "Homeplace: A Site of Resistance," in *Yearning: Race, Gender and Cultural Politics* (Boston: South End Press, 1990), 42.

33. Ibid, 43.

34. Benedict Anderson, *Imagined Communities: Reflections on the Origin and Spread of Nationalism* (London: New Left Books, 1983).

35. Compare Jeremy Waldron, "Homelessness and the Issue of Freedom," in *Liberal Rights: Collected Papers 1981–1991* (Cambridge: Cambridge University Press, 1993), 309–38.

36. Seyla Benhabib affirms this individuating function of home and privacy in her discussion of the need for feminists to retain a certain meaning to a distinction between public and private. See Benhabib, *The Reluctant Modernism of Hannah Arendt* (London: Sage, 1996), 213.

37. For a feminist defense of privacy as the right to inviolate personality, see Jean L. Cohen, "Democracy, Difference and the Right of Privacy," in Seyla Benhabib, ed., *Democracy and Difference: Contesting the Boundaries of the Political* (Princeton: Princeton University Press, 1996).

38. Anita Allen, *Uneasy Access* (Totowa, NJ: Rowman and Allenheld, 1988).

INDEX

abortion: *Planned Parenthood v. Casey* decision on, 100; reproductive freedom and, 130

acquaintance rape, 109

actions: of delinquents, 81; empowerment of collective, 91–92; group united by, 23; linked to practico-inert objects, 25; milieu of, 25; serialized within the milieu, 25; sexual division of labor constraining, 30; social relations as product of, 23–24; taken by groups, 34. *See also* communicative actions

adoption, 110

African American women: living in single-parent homes, 104, 117; moral respect for Anita Hill as, 43–44, 52; political dimension of homeplace for, 159–60; poverty of single parent, 118; racism against single mothers, 78; unwed mother rates among, 117. *See also* race; women

Alcoholics Anonymous, 88

Allen, Anita, 163

American Medical Association, 81

Americans with Disabilities Act of 1990, 105, 112

antigay referendum (Colorado), 96

Arendt, Hannah, 39, 40, 41, 57, 58, 68, 69, 152

arguments: of democratic practice, 63–64; force of the better, 61–62, 63; function of moral, 171n.8; interspersed with other communication, 65; political, 47–49; truth revealed vs. persuasive, 69. *See also* dialogue

asymmetrical reciprocity: in communicative actions, 49–52; ethical relation of, 53; gift-giving and, 54–56; as moral interaction alternative, 39; moral respect and, 39, 49–50; of mother/daughter relationship, 47; sources of, 51–52

Austen, Jane, 158

autonomy, 124, 125–26, 127. *See also* independence

Baier, Annette, 82

"Bandita" philosopher, 22

Barber, Benjamin, 71

battering relationships, 122–23

Beauvoir, Simone de, 10, 134, 135, 147–49, 152, 155

Benhabib, Seyla, 7, 38, 39–41, 45–46, 49, 57

Bergen, Candice, 96

Black Hills, 73

Blakeslee, Sandra, 116

Bohman, James, 71

Bordo, Susan, 20

Brown, Murphy (TV character), 95

building: dual aspect of, 152; female exclusion from, 137–38; male personal identity and, 135, 136. *See also* houses

Butler, Judith, 14, 15, 19, 33

Caraway, Nancie, 21

carceral system, 81

Casey, Edward, 150

Casey v. Planned Parenthood, 100

chicken boycott, 34–35

child care, 132

child-custody disputes, 99–100

child removal, 76–77

children: claims of/obligations to, 107; dependence of, 125; disadvantages of single parent, 117–19; divorce and, 111, 116–17, 181n.8; families promoting well being of, 106; family law protection of, 110–11; impact of family conflict on, 116–17; independence nurtured in, 122; marriage as cure for poor, 119–20; promoting good citizenship of, 115–16; right to safety by, 161–62; sexual abuse of, 109; of single parents by race, 117; state subsidies to poor, 119; of two-parent families, 118, 120. *See also* families; parents

Chodorow, Nancy, 32

Christian confessional discourse, 87

citizenship: contributions to society by, 127–29; denied to women, 121; independence as virtue of, 123–27; male centeredness of, 123; promoted for children, 115–16; state equal recognition of, 132–33; state's interest in good, 120–21. *See also* state

About the Author

IRIS MARION YOUNG is Professor of Public and International Affairs at the University of Pittsburgh. Her previous books include *Justice and the Politics of Difference* (Princeton) and *Throwing Like a Girl and Other Essays in Feminist Philosophy and Social Theory.*